FULFILLING SOCIAL AND ECONOMIC RIGHTS

FULFILLING SOCIAL AND ECONOMIC RIGHTS

SAKIKO FUKUDA-PARR,
TERRA LAWSON-REMER, AND
SUSAN RANDOLPH

OXFORD
UNIVERSITY PRESS

OXFORD
UNIVERSITY PRESS

Oxford University Press is a department of the University of
Oxford. It furthers the University's objective of excellence in research,
scholarship, and education by publishing worldwide.

Oxford   New York
Auckland   Cape Town   Dar es Salaam   Hong Kong   Karachi
Kuala Lumpur   Madrid   Melbourne   Mexico City   Nairobi
New Delhi   Shanghai   Taipei   Toronto

With offices in
Argentina   Austria   Brazil   Chile   Czech Republic   France   Greece
Guatemala   Hungary   Italy   Japan   Poland   Portugal   Singapore
South Korea   Switzerland   Thailand   Turkey   Ukraine   Vietnam

Oxford is a registered trademark of Oxford University Press
in the UK and certain other countries.

Published in the United States of America by
Oxford University Press
198 Madison Avenue, New York, NY 10016

Library of Congress Cataloging-in-Publication Data
Fukuda–Parr, Sakiko, 1950–
Fulfilling social and economic rights / Sakiko Fukuda-Parr, Terra Lawson-Remer,
and Susan Randolph.
pages cm
Includes bibliographical references and index.
ISBN 978–0–19–973550–1 (hardcover : alk. paper) — ISBN 978–0–19–973551–8 (pbk. : alk. paper)
1. Human rights.   2. Human security.   3. Public welfare.   4. Social indicators.   5. Economic
indicators.   I. Lawson-Remer, Terra.   II. Randolph, Susan.   III. Title.
JC571.F776 2015
323—dc23
2014024465

1 3 5 7 9 8 6 4 2
Printed in the United States of America
on acid-free paper

CONTENTS

LIST OF FIGURES

LIST OF TABLES

LIST OF BOXES

ACKNOWLEDGMENTS

THIS BOOK WOULD NOT BE possible without the support and encouragement we received from many individuals and institutions. The financial
support of the National Science Foundation (grant number 1061457),
the Human Rights Institute at the University of Connecticut, and The
New School facilitated the research and development of the book. Josh
De Wind and Lauren Shields helped develop our research into a data
set and an initiative housed at the Social Science Research Council. The
skillful editorial reviews by Mary Lynn Hanley and Rachael Wyant were
enormously helpful in finalizing the manuscript. Finally, we are grateful
to Angela Chnapko, our Oxford University Press editor, for her patience
and guidance throughout the process of bringing this book to fruition.

Our initial explorations benefited greatly from consultations with
Claes Johanssen and David Stewart. The Canadian International
Development Agency funded a workshop in 2008 to discuss our first
proposals for an Index of Economic and Social Rights with experts in
the field. We are grateful to Amy Baker and Noah Schiff, who made
this possible, and the participants at this workshop—Fernando Carrera
Castro, David Cingranelli, Eitan Felner, Emilie Filmer-Wilson, Ricardo
Fuentes, Lyn Freeman, Elizabeth Gibbons, Heather Grady, Shareen
Hertel, Lanse Minkler, Lauchlan Munro, John Packer, David Richards,
John Stewart, and Alicia Yamin—who offered tactful critiques and

shrewd insights that refined the methodology and encouraged our efforts to continue this work.

We were privileged to have been invited by Li Bennich-Björkman of the Johan Skytte Foundation to present our manuscript at a Book Workshop at the University of Uppsala in Sweden. The in-depth scrutiny and discerning comments made over three days by the participants—Edward Anderson, Nehal Bhuta, David Hulme, Anirudh Krishna, Siddiqur Osmani, Charlotta Friedner Parrat, Pedro Pontual, Fredrik Sjöberg, Viviana Stechina, and Suruchi Thapar-Björkert—on an early draft of the book challenged us to reconceptualize it. The skillful planning and coordination of this event by Therese Leijon and the collegiality of the participants made the conference a pure joy.

We owe much to our other collaborators—Shareen Hertel, Michelle Prairie, and John Stewart—for various analyses published elsewhere that this book draws on. We benefited enormously from the dedicated and talented work of students—Madeleine Baer, Salil Benegal, Louise Moreira Daniels, David Greenberg, Joshua Greenstein, Patrick Guyer, Elizabeth Kalteski, Abid Khan, Michée Lachaud, Sosena Lemma, Lhens Vilson, and Alexandria Eisenbarth—who spent long hours providing capable research assistance and sometimes coauthoring papers.

We owe a great debt to the intellectual community of research and practice engaged in human rights, human development, and measurement. The origins of this book lie in the renewed efforts since the early 2000s to develop methodologies for the measurement of human rights. Individually and collectively we attended many workshops and meetings on human rights indicators and participated in projects. Once we advanced our research, we presented our papers to many audiences and received valuable feedback. Throughout, we discussed many issues with colleagues in informal conversations. We learned a great deal from all these engagements. In many cases the controversies that these debates raised inspired us to pursue our project as it became clear that there was a need to develop new methodologies, create a database, and resolve questions about the progressive realization of social and economic rights. The individuals, institutions, and projects we worked with are too numerous to list comprehensively, but we would like to mention a few who influenced our thinking in special ways. The Economic and Social Rights Research Group at the University of Connecticut's Human Rights

Institute has been a particularly stimulating community. The *Human Development Report 2000*, which Sakiko Fukuda-Parr coauthored, especially the work of Kate Raworth on indicators and measurement, was an important point of departure for this book. Others involved in this publication helped shape the emergence of this book, particularly Philip Alston, Christian Barry, Haishan Fu, Sir Richard Jolly, and Danilo Turk. The collaboration with Malcolm Langford in leading the Metrics for Human Rights and Development Network and the series of workshops have been a fruitful venue for following new advances in the field. Through all these processes, several individuals have been particularly frequent interlocutors from whom we have learned a great deal: Matthew Bishop, Audrey Chapman, Dalton Conley, Mac Darrow, Kevin Davis, Olivier de Schutter, Bill Easterly, Nicolas Fasel, Dani Kaufmann, Rajeev Malhotra, Sally Engle Merry, Lanse Minkler, David Richards, Meg Satterthwaite, and Polly Vizard.

To all of those named as well as those whom we may have omitted, and to those who have helped fund the research backing this book, we will be forever grateful. Of course, the opinions, findings, conclusions, and recommendations expressed in this book remain our own and do not necessarily reflect the views of our contributors.

Finally, we shout out our enduring thanks to our families and friends, who so gracefully tolerated our persistent and at times obsessive preoccupation with this book. This book would not have come about without your consistent support, faith, encouragement, and love.

FULFILLING SOCIAL AND ECONOMIC RIGHTS

I

Introduction

Today, when we talk of human rights we understand that this discussion should not be limited to the traditional civil and political rights. The international world has gradually come to realize the critical importance of social and economic rights in building true democracies which meet the basic needs of all people. The realization of these needs is both an essential element of a genuine democracy as well as essential for the maintenance of democracy. . . . In formulating our Constitution, we learned from the experiences of people in other countries who have struggled with similar problems. In this way and in other ways, our Constitution demonstrates the growing globalization of the struggle for human rights.

—Nelson Mandela, foreword to S. Leckie, *National Perspectives on Housing Rights* (2003)

Assessing the Progress of Countries by the Real Freedoms People Enjoy

What is the yardstick by which the progress of countries and people ought to be measured and judged? The standard metric is a measure of economic production or consumption—per capita income, as variously defined by gross domestic product (GDP), gross national product, or gross national income. Many of us commonly speak of countries' well-being in such shorthand, assuming, perhaps unconsciously, that higher per capita economic production and consumption is indeed what is valued by individuals. Yet few would disagree with Charles Dickens that Ebenezer Scrooge was misguided to seek fulfillment in his store of wealth at the expense of human compassion and values.[1]

Economists use per capita income growth as a good substitute or a "proxy" measure for human progress, assuming that higher per capita income increases human well-being. But this is not always the case. Average income does not reflect how income is distributed. More fundamentally, higher income does not always translate into improvements in many important aspects of human lives.[2] Countries have experienced growth that has been "jobless," generating profits but neither productivity increases nor employment opportunities for workers; "ruthless," dislocating people from homes and livelihoods and widening inequalities; "futureless," stepping beyond planetary boundaries and meting out environmental destruction; and "rootless," obliterating cultural identities and heritage (U.N. Development Programme [UNDP] 1996).

The conflation of material production with human well-being and the dramatic oversimplification of the relationship between economic growth and its social consequences have long been challenged. As long ago as the fourth century BC, Aristotle wrote: "The life of money-making is one undertaken under compulsion, and wealth is not the good we are seeking; for it is merely useful and for the sake of something else" (350 BC, 5).

What is that something else? What ultimately matters to people's well-being? Amartya Sen and Martha Nussbaum, two contemporary worldly philosophers, argue that what matters to people is the real freedoms they enjoy to lead a fulfilling life with dignity.[3] Sen elaborated a theory of what this meant, articulating freedom as "capabilities": the range of choices that individuals have to do the things they value and be whom they want to be.[4] He (1992, 1999) proposed that the evaluation and comparison of individual well-being and of social arrangements should focus on an assessment of capabilities. Moreover, he (1999) argued that the expansion of capabilities that effectively expand freedoms is the purpose of "development" and the priority objective of public action. Nussbaum (2011a) further argues that some essential capabilities (such as being able to go to school and to access clean drinking water) are entitlements—core elements of a just society and fundamental political and social priorities that ought to be guaranteed in every national constitution. Failures to secure these essential capabilities are human rights abuses (Nussbaum 2011a). Taking this abstract concept forward, what are the concrete freedoms that our economic, social, and political institutions of governance are obligated to provide? Nussbaum (2000) has her list of ten essential capabilities. Sen (1999) points out the importance of "instrumental freedoms" in five areas: social opportunities, economic facilities, transparency guarantees, protective security, and political liberties. But he (2003a) desists from offering a list, saying that it is not up to him to decide but for societies to draw up their own lists through a process of democratic consultation. Each of us might draw up a somewhat different list, but there are certain freedoms that would likely show up on all of our lists and which also show up on Nussbaum's list. These are the freedoms that would be essential to all people, regardless of their cultural traditions, religion, gender, age, or life situation.

In 1948 the U.N. General Assembly adopted such a list, reflecting the consensus of a global community recommitted to promoting fundamental human rights in the wake of the horror of the Holocaust and the decimation of World War II. Drawn up by representatives from countries of the East, West, North, and South after much debate and consultation (Glendon 2001),[5] the Universal Declaration of Human Rights (UDHR) articulates a list of essential rights that provide substantive meaning to the abstract notion of human freedom. The UDHR has since been augmented by many more specific international human rights treaties and instruments, giving greater content and meaning to these human rights principles. Surely the rights articulated in the UDHR offer an important yardstick for measuring human progress—if by *progress* we mean not simply rising production and consumption but improving human well-being and the real freedoms that people enjoy.

Social and Economic Rights—A Universal Political Project

The UDHR, in its thirty articles, lists fundamental and universal economic, social, cultural, civil, and political rights. Subsequent treaties and legal instruments outline specific norms that have achieved international political consensus, not merely lists that are made by one "expert" or one country. They reflect consensus standards that apply universally in all countries, guaranteeing the equal rights of individuals. They elaborate those essential freedoms that should be guaranteed in the constitution of each and every country and stand as the priority objective of national and international economic, social, and political arrangements. Surely these common commitments constitute one of the most significant achievements of the international community during the twentieth century.

Along with civil and political rights, the UDHR (United Nations 1948) spells out six substantive social and economic rights:

1. the right to food (Article 25): the knowledge, freedom, and means to procure sufficient nourishing food;
2. the right to health (Article 25): the freedom and means to access healthcare and other determinants of health so one may enjoy a long and healthy life;
3. the right to education (Article 26): the freedom to acquire quality and relevant education and training throughout one's life, supporting creativity and human flourishing, notably free and compulsory primary education;
4. the right to housing (Article 25): the freedom and ability to secure housing that protects one from the elements and disease;
5. the right to work (Articles 23–24): the freedom and ability to secure productive work that is safe and provides income sufficient to support a family; and
6. the right to social security (Articles 22–23, 25): the freedom from threats of insecurity in the enjoyment of these social and economic rights due to circumstances such as sickness, disability, old age, unemployment, or loss of livelihood for reasons beyond one's control.

These rights have been subsequently elaborated in international law, starting with the International Covenant on Economic, Social and Cultural Rights (ICESCR) (United Nations 1966b), signed by 161 states at the time of this writing. The series of General Comments by the Committee on Economic, Social and Cultural Rights and other legal instruments have further elaborated on the substantive content of these rights and the nature of corresponding state obligations for their realization. The norms are reflected in the related treaties for children—the Convention on the Rights of the Child—and women—the Convention on the Elimination of All Forms of Discrimination against Women.

These social and economic rights are freedoms that may be taken for granted by many but are frequently and systematically denied to much of humanity. Consider Fatimata Konte, a thirty-six-year-old market woman in Kroo Bay, an informal settlement in Freetown, Sierra Leone. She described her life in this way: "We women in Sierra Leone suffer too much. From the day a child is born, a child must work. Every day I must go to the market; it's all I can do to survive. I work hard in the market so we can eat. I work for my daughter so she can go to school. She is in class four. She wants to learn. I want her to be somebody." Fatimata was pregnant with her eighth child, and her biggest fear was "that this child will die too" (Malkani and Vitali 2010), for she had already lost five.

Fatimata's situation is not uncommon in her country, where one in twelve children die before their fifth birthday and where women face a one-in-eight lifetime risk of succumbing to death from complications of pregnancy or childbirth (UNICEF 2013A).[6] Medical services are sparse, a situation compounded by the lack of other basic infrastructure, such as adequate water and sanitation systems, and vulnerability to the recurrent floods and monsoons that beset coast settlements of West Africa.

Despite the unprecedented wealth and technological breakthroughs that were achieved in the twentieth century on a global scale, social and economic rights are far from being realized. In 2012, 6.6 million children under five died from preventable diseases (United Nations 2013). About 1.2 billion people, or 22 percent of the world population, lived on less than $1.25 per day in 2010, while one in four children were stunted and 7 percent were obese, both as a result of malnutrition, and some fifty-seven million children were out of school. Beyond these statistics, in countries around the world and in myriad forms, abuses of social and economic rights occur daily—from dangerous work on construction sites in New York City to inadequate schooling in rural South Africa to elevated risks of cancer due to the dumping of hazardous wastes in Buenos Aires and beyond. The economic poverty of households and the state is the conventional explanation for these situations, but that is not the only reason. These situations also arise from public policy priorities that neglect essential infrastructure such as clean water supply facilities and critical public goods such as the regulation of working conditions. They also arise from discrimination that denies economic and social opportunities and a voice to poor and marginalized people. Often it is the structures of power that lead to the lack of voice; discrimination on the basis of gender, ethnicity, race, and other identities; and unequal treatment under the law.

Social and economic rights standards are norms that protect human beings from "basic threats"[7] to security and subsistence (Shue 1980, 13). As Nelson Mandela's reflections quoted at the opening of this chapter remind us, social and economic rights are more relevant today than ever before and are gaining increasing attention (Hertel 2006; Minkler 2013). Globalization and the liberalization of markets have created enormous wealth and opportunities but have simultaneously brought threats to security and subsistence for many. Investments to build dams create energy to power growing economies but also dislocate local communities, upending livelihoods and cultural moorings (Lawson-Remer 2012). Trade reduces prices and expands consumer choice, creating new job opportunities for some but also displacing others. Financial capital flows expand access to capital for many poorer countries but also create giant waves of volatility that can cause havoc in financial systems and usher in economic recessions. In today's context, the major function of human rights is to "tame the negative forces and tendencies of the current global economic system" (Salomon 2007, p.1). As one civil society activist remarks: "Economic, social and cultural rights are the only means of self-defense for millions of impoverished and marginalized individuals and groups all over the world. These rights are playing an increasing role in the way that grassroots organizations in many parts of the world see their struggles" (Kunnemann 1995, 332).

In adopting the UDHR, states not only articulated human rights norms as a "common standard of achievement for all peoples and all nations" but also pledged to "promote respect for these rights and freedoms and by progressive measures, national and international, to secure their universal and effective recognition and observance" (United Nations 1948, Preamble). According to international human rights law, states are obligated to take all measures to foster the full realization of rights. Formal legal guarantees are by no means sufficient and can often mask grave shortcomings in rights fulfillment. The design of appropriate economic and social policies is essential for the progressive realization of social and economic rights. The granting of human rights thus compels states to put in place the necessary social arrangements not only to respect and protect but also to fulfill rights. Human rights norms provide principles and standards that can guide the formulation of economic policies with due regard to their human consequences and can promote decision-making procedures that are fair, giving as much voice to the powerless and the potential losers as to the powerful winners of the marketplace.

A Framework for Social Evaluation

Going back to our starting question: How should the progress of countries and peoples be judged? What if, instead of judging countries by per capita income and its growth, we turn the question around and judge the success of nations according to how well they translate their resources into expanded freedoms: the freedom for people to be and do the things they value and to pursue meaningful lives with dignity? And if we use international human rights as the standards that define these freedoms, surely we can evaluate the success and failings of states and the progress of humanity. Might we not then be able to hold states accountable for the commitments made to realize human rights, based on evidence of how much they have achieved and how much they fall short of their obligations? Might we perhaps learn whether there is scope to direct existing available resources to improving human lives? And to the extent that there is scope, might we not then be able to identify the kinds of economic institutions, policies, and practices that better enable us to translate economic resources into human flourishing? And last but not least, might we not be able to assess whether we are succeeding in advancing freedom from fear and freedom from want, implementing one of the most important political projects of the international community?

This book responds to this challenge, using international human rights as the standard to evaluate the success and failings of states and the progress of humanity. To do so requires the specification of a quantitative measure capable of tracking progress and regress, identifying strong and weak performance, and exploring policy-relevant questions. Such a measure must be rigorously rooted in international human rights norms and command wide acceptance as an unbiased tool that is not driven by economic or political interest groups. It needs to (1) provide a summary measure of social and economic rights—not a plethora of diverse indicators; (2) incorporate the correlate obligations of duty bearers—not only the enjoyment of rights by rights holders; (3) reflect the relative standards of fulfillment subject to resource constraints—not a universal one-size-fits-all level of achievement; and (4) use objective data and a methodology that is both transparent and accessible to a wide range of users, including civil society groups with a mission to hold their governments to account.

A Summary Quantitative Measure

For the purposes of our project, we need a summary measure of performance that is capable of showing trends over time and disparities across subnational population groups. To obtain a complete picture of a human rights situation being assessed, the summary measure would need to be used in conjunction with many other quantitative and qualitative indicators. But without the aggregated measure, it would be difficult to obtain an overall picture of trends. It would be difficult to identify good performance and poor, as well as the most glaring shortfalls, which can draw public attention to the urgent problems requiring policy attention, thereby motivating advocacy and reform.

In any framework of social evaluation, a wide range of data is required to capture all the dimensions of a situation one might consider. In theory, tracking progress in human rights realization could make use of a wide range of indicators on each feature of the rights and obligations relevant to a human right. But this may not be the most practical or desirable strategy to use in developing effective metrics for our purpose. A plethora of indicators would be difficult to condense into a coherent picture and might even deflect attention from the overall trends and major issues. A simple, summary index—such as GDP or the Human Development Index (HDI)—is more effective in revealing the essential trends. This was a major factor that motivated the creation of the HDI in spite of the multiplicity of human development indicators that were readily available. Amartya Sen recalls how he was persuaded to help Mahbub ul Haq develop the HDI in 1990: "As I listened to Mahbub, I could not help hearing an echo of T. S. Eliot's poem *Burnt Norton*,

'Human kind / Cannot bear much reality'" (2003c, x). The challenge is not amassing as much information as possible but emphasizing the critical issues relevant to the objective at hand. A measurement tool needs to be both selective in the variables included and aggregated to the level appropriate for its analytical use.

Correlate Obligations of Duty Bearers

Even if we need an aggregate measure of a country's status and progress in fulfilling its social and economic rights obligations, why would we need an entirely new indicator? Why wouldn't socioeconomic data such as child mortality and literacy suffice as human rights measures? In fact, it has long been assumed that standard data of this kind are adequate to measure the extent of human rights realization (Claude and Jabine 1986).[8] This view continues to be held among some human rights measurement scholars (see Landman and Carvalho 2010, 113), and socioeconomic outcome data are increasingly promoted and used in human rights advocacy (Felner 2009b). According to the U.N. Office of the High Commissioner for Human Rights, such indicators "could meet (at least implicitly) all the definitional requirements of a human rights indicator," defined as "specific information on the state or condition of an object, event, activity or outcome that can be related to human rights norms and standards; that addresses and reflects human rights principles and concerns; and that can be used to assess and monitor the promotion and implementation of human rights" (2012, 16). But this is a fundamentally misleading view. The normative framework of human rights differs substantively from other normative frameworks for evaluating social progress, requiring a distinct set of measurement tools that capture the distinctive aspects of the human rights framework.

Socioeconomic outcome indicators, such as those used in the HDI, focus on the well-being of individuals—their enjoyment of a right. This is only one side of human rights realization and does not take into account the obligations of societies to respect, protect, and fulfill these rights. The essence of human rights is that they are entitlements that people have a right to claim and states and others in society have a duty to secure. While capabilities and rights are closely related (Fukuda-Parr 2011; Nussbaum 2011a; Vizard, Fukuda-Parr, and Elson 2011) and both are primarily concerned with freedom and dignity, they differ sharply in one aspect: Rights incur correlate obligations, while capabilities do not (Sen 2004; UNDP 2000). In short, the fundamental conceptual difference between human development progress and human rights fulfillment is that the latter entails not only the enjoyment of a right by individuals but also a correlate obligation of duty bearers (Sen 2004). The advance of human rights must therefore be evaluated not only by reference to the level of rights enjoyment by rights holders but also by the level of the duty bearers' compliance with their obligations. This is the essential difference between the metrics of human rights and those of capability expansion or human development (Fukuda-Parr 2011). Thus the value added of a specific human rights measure among the panoply of available socioeconomic outcome data is an assessment of state performance.

Consider again Fatimata's situation. She is a victim not just of economic downturns and the low GDP per capita of her country but also of the neglect of her human rights as social and political priorities by her government and the international community. Human rights are fundamentally about protecting people from threats to their human dignity and freedom (Shue 1980). Fatimata struggles for herself and her family to be adequately nourished, avoid premature death, be educated, have productive and decent work, and secure housing that provides a home—all of which are essential to a life of dignity that she has a right to expect and demand. They are not merely human aspirations but entitlements. As they are human rights obligations, the government is compelled to consider them as urgent policy priorities among many and in the face of numerous competing claims for resources, incentives, and regulations.

Setting Relative Standards—Progressive Realization of Maximum Available Resources

How do we evaluate the performance of Sierra Leone and its government in complying with their human rights obligations? As we will elaborate in chapters 2 and 3, one issue that has remained unresolved in measurement efforts is how to capture the concept of progressive realization. A central feature of social and economic rights norms is that the level of obligation is relative and takes account of the diverse situations of countries, which are obligated to achieve full realization "progressively, to the maximum of available resources." As stated in Article 2.1 of the ICESCR: "Each State Party to the present Covenant undertakes to take steps, individually and through international assistance and co-operation, especially economic and technical, to the maximum of its available resources, with a view to achieving progressively the full realization of the rights recognized in the present Covenant" (United Nations 1966b). A unique challenge to measuring performance in fulfilling social and economic rights is therefore the need to set relative standards for countries' obligations that differ according to the level of resources available (see, for example, Chapman 1996; Rosga and Satterthwaite 2009).

In short, given resource constraints, states are not obligated to immediately ensure the full realization of all guaranteed social and economic rights; rather, over time they must progressively realize these rights by devoting the maximum available resources to their fulfillment. Countries around the world face hugely different levels of deprivation and capacity. Inherent in the idea of progressive realization is that a government's ability to fulfill rights commitments depends on the level of resources (financial and other) available in the country. Consequently, the performance of states with regard to progressively realizing social and economic rights cannot be judged solely on outcomes—the enjoyment of rights by people. For example, the United States and Sierra Leone cannot be compared on the basis of their respective levels of maternal mortality considering the hugely different levels of capacity in these two countries.

With a per capita income of $580 per year in 2012, Sierra Leone is among the dozen most resource-poor countries in the world (UNICEF 2013a). Many other constraints of administrative capacity, environmental health, historical legacy, and a multitude of other factors also weigh on the pace of progress that can be made in Sierra Leone and the many developing countries with similar constraints and situations. Accordingly, Sierra Leone's 2012 child mortality rate of 182 per 1,000 cannot be compared with the eight per 1,000 in the United States (UNICEF 2013b) to conclude that Sierra Leone is performing much worse in fulfilling social and economic rights obligations. Indeed, the government took the extraordinary step for a resource-poor country of introducing free, universal health care for pregnant women and children under five and their mothers. This will make a difference. For one thing, women like Fatimata will not have to worry about getting into debt should their pregnancies become complicated and require extra medical care. Should we then consider that Sierra Leone is a good performer because such a proactive policy was adopted? Yet we also find that government expenditure on health is a paltry 1 percent of GDP, half of what is allocated to the military, implying that health receives less priority than defense (O'Donoghue 2010). We need a measure that can go beyond the ad hoc assessment of a single government policy to fully assess a society's performance. Rigorous assessment requires a consideration of what is feasible within the limitations of resource constraints and whether progress is being made.

Objectivity and Transparency—To Avoid the Pitfalls of Political Abuse

Human rights indicators are tools that are intended to expose violations of and monitor compliance with legal commitments. They are intended to build accountability but can have powerful political effects and be used strategically in international politics to discredit states or to erroneously claim a clean record. The potential for political misuse and abuse has been an important source of opposition from human rights advocates to quantitative country performance measures (Carr Center for Human Rights 2005; Raworth 2001; UNDP 2000). An appropriate human rights measure must effectively empower advocates, and the design of the measurement tool needs to take account of the political dynamics of human rights monitoring.

In this regard, some methodological choices are critical to ensuring that the indicators are unbiased, acceptable to all stakeholders, and accessible to human rights advocates with limited technical and financial resources. First, regarding the data source, objective data from survey or administrative sources generally command wider acceptance than subjective data that are specially constructed. Second, regarding transparency, data derived using a published methodology that can be scrutinized, challenged, and replicated are more credible than data derived in a nontransparent manner. Third, regarding methodological accessibility, measures using a complex methodology requiring a high level of expertise in statistical methods are less accessible to under-resourced groups including governments of small low-income countries and local civil society groups.

In this light, we need a measure that departs from the approach in measuring civil and political rights, which has historically relied on *creating data* by converting subjective qualitative information into numeric data—or "qualitative ratings" (Raworth 2001). Many of the most widely used quantitative measures of political and civil rights, such as the Freedom House Index and Transparency International's Corruption Perception Index, rely on data based on the subjective opinion of "experts." Others, such as the Cingranelli and Richards Index and the Political Terror Scale, create numeric scores from a content analysis of country situation reporting with international coverage, notably from the U.S. State Department and Amnesty International. The methodology is published in varying degrees of detail but would not be easy to replicate without resort to significant resources. One reason why civil and political rights need to resort to creating quantitative data is the inherent difficulty of counting civil and political rights. This is one of the major obstacles to human rights measurement and a source of controversy about quantifying human rights (Barsh 1993).

Unlike civil and political rights, social and economic rights can draw on a wealth of socioeconomic statistics to build measurement tools and do not necessarily need to resort to creating new data. National and international statistical offices have long collected data through surveys and administrative reporting that span decades. The U.N. Statistical Committee and U.N. statistical agencies have developed standards of definitions and methods of collection to harmonize international socio-economic data series. These data series not only are based on proven methodologies but have been legitimated through a process of technical and governmental review.

Of course, the use of objective data and a transparent, replicable methodology does not eliminate political bias. Following the long-standing warnings about the limitations of human rights measurement (see, for example, Barsh 1993), a new debate has emerged that challenges the objectivity of quantitative data. This debate draws on recent research in the sociology of knowledge on indicators, audit, and standardization that problematizes indicators used in governance.[9] Inherent in quantification is the transformation of a concept's meaning, which involves simplification, decontextualization, and reification (Porter 1995; Power 1997). This has profound implications for the use of statistical indicators in human rights evaluations (or "audit" processes), as in any other field (Merry 2009; Power 1997).

Behind the apparent objectivity of statistical data are processes of their selection and application that involve subjective decisions and the potential for political manipulation and disguising of important issues. Their selection involves a series of judgments and choices about how a right is defined, what features are emphasized, and which of the available statistical indicators are chosen, in the hands of technocratic "experts" (Davis, Kingsbury, and Merry 2012; Merry 2009; Rosga and Satterthwaite 2009). These processes are inherently political, in the hands of those so-called experts such as the Office of the High Commissioner for Human Rights and its working groups of human rights practitioners who developed the human rights indicators to be used by the Committee on Economic, Social and Cultural Rights (Rosga and Satterthwaite 2009) or the violence against women indicators to be used by the Committee on the Elimination of Discrimination against Women (Merry and Coutin 2014). In their application they could detract attention from important issues that "cannot be counted," thus undermining and distorting accountability processes; Rosga and Satterthwaite (2009) argue that this can effectively close democratic debate on issues that are captured in the selected indicators.

These insights do not imply that quantitative indicators have no place in human rights assessment but, rather, that they should be used alongside other kinds of assessments with a careful critical lens that recognizes both their power and their limitations. The sources and methodologies need scrutiny, and most important, they should be used contextually in combination with qualitative information. Quantitative indicators carry both "promise and peril" (Merry 2009). Thus, warning against the peril and their unquestioning use, Rosga and Satterthwaite conclude that they hold the promise to open up "opportunities to use the language of science and objectivity as a powerful tool to hold governments to account" (2009, 258).

The Social and Economic Rights Fulfillment Index

In the absence of an appropriate indicator in the current battery of available measurement tools, we construct the Social and Economic Rights Fulfillment (SERF) Index—a summary measure of social and economic rights performance based on international norms. It uses international administrative and survey data that incorporate both rights holders' and duty bearers' perspectives, are amenable to revealing broad trends in progress and regress over time, and are comparable across countries. The SERF Index measures the performance of countries on the fulfillment of their substantive social and economic rights obligations: the right to adequate food, the right to housing, the right to education, the right to social security, the right to health, and the right to decent work. The index defines the rights of individuals and the obligations of states based on international human rights law.

The SERF Index can be disaggregated by right as well as by subnational population groups to shed light on many different aspects of rights fulfillment. The resultant data set, covering a majority of the world's countries, can be used to assess country performance and to diagnose the drivers and consequences of good performance. It can thus help inform policy formulation for the realization of social and economic rights.

The index addresses the two essential and previously unresolved issues in the measurement of social and economic rights: (1) how to simultaneously incorporate the perspectives of both the duty bearers and the rights holders and (2) how to set relative standards for progressive realization to the maximum of available resources. Our approach is to assess social and economic rights performance by comparing the level of rights enjoyment achieved against what the country could feasibly achieve given the resources available, based on historical data. We develop a methodology, the Achievement Possibilities Frontier, for this purpose. This approach operationalizes the progressive realization principle and allows apples-to-apples comparisons across countries.

Mindful of the pitfalls of abuse and bias in human rights measurement, we consciously designed the index to facilitate wide use, especially by local civil society groups in developing countries. The methodology does not require a high level of statistical expertise to replicate and is independently verifiable. It uses objective administrative and survey data collected by official statistical agencies and harmonized internationally to permit international comparison.

Our overarching motivation in developing the SERF Index is to devise a quantitative yardstick against which to judge countries' performance and progress in providing the social and economic rights essential to human dignity and that can facilitate identification of the kinds of economic institutions, policies, and practices that better enable us to translate economic resources into human flourishing. The SERF Index does not attempt to assess the extent to which countries ensure the *procedural rights* of nondiscrimination, participation, and accountability, and these challenges constitute an important agenda for future research. Nor does it judge country performance with regard to civil, political, or cultural rights. In these regards, especially, the SERF Index complements other human rights assessment approaches and in so doing provides a more comprehensive means of revealing both the potential to expand the concrete freedoms that our economic, social, and political institutions of governance are obligated to provide and the means to realize that potential.

Overview of the Book

In the following chapters we provide a detailed explanation of the SERF Index: its conceptual framework (chapter 2), the methodology for measuring progressive realization and aggregation (chapter 3), and the selection of indicators and data sources (chapter 4). These chapters explain how our approach is guided by a close reading of international human rights law, including the UDHR, the ICESCR, relevant General Comments, and other texts. They explain indicator choices and walk readers through the methodology of calculation step by step so that the index can be replicated.

We then present the insights revealed by the index. In chapter 5 we discuss global trends. There is evidence of steady improvement in rights fulfillment in the world as a whole, overall and for each of the six rights. But there is no room for complacency. Human rights are far from being realized, and state performance varies enormously, with many countries showing huge deficits and even retrogression. When we disaggregate national results to groups within countries—by region, race, and ethnicity in Brazil, India, and the United States—we obtain a richer picture of extreme disparities in state performance. In chapter 6 we examine the characteristics of countries that tend to perform well and of those that perform poorly. We find some surprising and counterintuitive relationships between rights fulfillment, on the one hand, and democratic governance, civil and political rights, social spending, economic growth, gender equality, and legal commitments, on the other. In chapter 7 we examine several potential criticisms that could challenge the index methodology, and we find the approach robust. Additionally, this chapter explores the interesting questions of trade-offs, policy choices, historical legacies, and discrimination.

In the concluding chapter, chapter 8, we reflect on what we learn from the SERF Index. We reflect on whether it provides a rigorous empirical assessment of government performance in fulfilling social and economic rights so as to hold states to account. We consider what we can learn from it about the scope for directing resources and redesigning policies to accelerate the pace of progress in expanding human freedoms. In the process, we also consider the insights it contributes to theorizing about social and economic rights.

Concluding Remarks

The frustration with traditional measures of countries' progress, and the embrace of alternatives to GDP, has accelerated in recent years. In 2008 the French presidency commissioned a report from leading social scientists to explore the limitations of current economic and social measures and to propose some possible alternatives. The major recommendations of the 2009 *Report by the Commission on the Measurement of Economic Performance and Social Progress* are instructive, as they represent a paradigm shift in the mainstream conventional wisdom: the commission concluded that, for starters, better measures of economic performance in a complex economy are required, specifically approaches that take into account the household perspective and distribution and inequality. More fundamentally, the commission endorsed the need to measure multidimensional aspects of well-being: material living standards (income, consumption, and wealth), health, education, personal activities including work, political voice and governance, social connections and relationships, sustainability and the conditions of the environment (present and future), and insecurity of an economic as well as a physical nature. They further argued that quality-of-life indicators in all dimensions should assess inequalities in a comprehensive way (Stiglitz, Sen, and Fitoussi 2010).

But what dimensions of quality of life should be examined? Missing from the commission's recommendations is an explicit normative framework for selecting the important outcomes to measure human progress. This is a political question about valuable ends and priorities. Unlike other economic and social metrics of societies' performance, human rights, as reflected in international human rights law, are an irreducible, nonnegotiable normative framework for assessing human well-being. Adopted by countries through binding international treaties, human rights reflect an explicit consensus regarding global norms. By using international human rights as the standard that defines our shared values, we can more appropriately evaluate the successes and failings of states and the progress of humanity.

2

Measuring Social and Economic Rights
The SERF Index Approach

IN CHAPTER 1, WE INTRODUCED THE SERF Index, explained its purpose and provided a brief overview of the concept.* This chapter elaborates further on the SERF concept as an approach to measuring social and economic rights, while the following chapters (3 and 4) explain in detail the construction of the index and the methodology of calculation. In other words, this chapter conceptualizes "what" the index measures, while chapter 1 explains "why" and "for what" it was created, and chapters 3 and 4 explain "how" it is constructed.

To recap from chapter 1, we created the SERF Index to measure the performance of states in fulfilling social and economic rights. Our goal was to develop a data set using a rigorous measurement tool that is conceptually rooted in international human rights norms, uses objective and empirically verifiable data, and applies a methodology that is accessible to a wide range of stakeholders. State performance in realizing human rights depends on the enjoyment of rights by people in a country (the rights holders) and the extent to which the state (the duty bearer) is complying with its obligations. These obligations are not only to respect and protect rights but also to take proactive measures to fulfill rights, so as to ensure the progressive realization of rights to the maximum of available resources. The SERF Index introduces an innovative methodology—the Achievement Possibilities Frontier—that sets relative standards for evaluating state performance, or benchmarks for evaluation, in order to capture the principle of "progressive realization to the maximum of available resources." These core elements of the SERF Index make possible a rigorous quantitative assessment of overall state performance in social and economic rights fulfillment.

This chapter grounds the obligations of fulfillment and progressive realization in the normative framework of international human rights law and shows how the SERF Index differs from—and complements—other tools and methodological approaches in the evolving field of human rights measurement. The chapter begins by elaborating the principles and standards regarding the nature of state obligations for social and economic rights, particularly with respect to the obligations of fulfillment and progressive realization. We then articulate the implications of this normative framework for the design of measurement tools and locate the index in the context of evolving approaches to measuring social and economic rights.

International Legal Framework on State Obligations for Social and Economic Rights

As noted in chapter 1, six substantive social and economic rights were included in the Universal Declaration of Human Rights. The International Covenant on Economic, Social and Cultural Rights was adopted by the U.N. General Assembly in 1966 and entered into force in 1976 (United Nations 1987a). It sets forth the nature of these rights and the corresponding obligations of state parties. In addition to the six substantive rights discussed at length in chapter 1, every person has three procedural rights: the right to nondiscrimination; the right to accountability and remedy; and the right to participation in the making of policies, plans, laws, and other measures that affect one's substantive rights. Implicit in all of these procedural rights is a right to information. The nature of these substantive and procedural rights drives the selection of indicators in the SERF Index and is therefore further elaborated in chapter 4. The nature of states' obligations frames the overall construction of the index and is elaborated in this chapter.

State obligations for social and economic rights were set out in the ICESCR in general terms and have been further elaborated in a series of documents since. *The Limburg Principles on the Implementation of the International Covenant on Economic, Social and Cultural Rights* enunciated in 1986 (United Nations 1987b) guided early interpretation of states' obligations.[1] Starting in 1989, the Committee on Economic, Social and Cultural Rights (CESCR), the ICESCR's monitoring body set up in 1984, has issued a series of General Comments to clarify the nature of state obligations. These include *General Comment 3: The Nature of States Parties' Obligations* (U.N. CESCR 1990), *General Comment 9: The Domestic Application of the Covenant* (U.N. CESCR 1998), and several General Comments issued on each of the specific substantive rights.[2] In addition, further clarifications are articulated in *The Maastricht Guidelines on Violations of Economic, Social and Cultural Rights* (United Nations 2000), developed by a committee of independent jurists in 1997 and recognized by the United Nations in 2000.[3] These instruments spell out three core elements of the normative framework regarding the nature of state obligations: (1) the duties to respect, protect, and fulfill; (2) the obligations of result and conduct; and (3) the obligations of progressive realization to the maximum of available resources.

Duties to Respect, Protect, and Fulfill

States meet their obligation to *respect* by abstaining from interfering with people's enjoyment of their social, economic, and cultural rights. They meet their obligation to protect by ensuring that third parties—be they other individuals, other entities such as corporations, other states, or international organizations—refrain from interfering with people's enjoyment of their social, economic, and cultural rights. Finally, states have an obligation to fulfill rights by taking proactive measures. These include providing the necessary goods and services for the realization of rights but also facilitating access to these goods and services such as by legislative, administrative, budgetary, or judicial measures.

Of these, the duty to fulfill is a positive duty, requiring proactive action, and is essential for advancing the realization of rights, not just maintaining a status quo. The extent to which governments take the duty to fulfill seriously, and give priority to those policies that accelerate the realization of rights, is essential to ensure the enjoyment of rights by people. The obligation to fulfill is particularly important where people do not enjoy rights because of systemic causes—for example, they are not in school because the school is too far away and inaccessible, they are undernourished because food prices are too high relative to their wages, or they suffer from birth defects due to toxic poisoning from pollutants. These situations affect a large number of people and arise from the failures to fulfill. They occur not only in poor countries but in rich countries as well. The importance of the obligation to fulfill will be further elaborated later in this chapter in the discussion of the obligation of progressive realization.

Obligations of Result and Conduct

Each of the three kinds of duties—to respect, protect, and fulfill—entails obligations of conduct and obligations of result. According to the *Maastricht Guidelines*, "The obligation of conduct requires action reasonably calculated to realize the enjoyment of a particular right . . . [while] the obligation of result requires States to achieve specific targets to satisfy a detailed substantive standard" (United Nations 2000, para. 7).

The obligations of result and conduct are linked, because we should expect that a state more fully meeting its obligation of conduct will increase the extent to which people in the country enjoy a particular right and, thus, the extent to which its obligation of result is met—although this relationship is not guaranteed, as we see in chapter 5. But the two obligations are not substitutable. For example, a state may make a concerted effort to reduce child death from preventable causes and accord high priority to this objective in its development plans. Its conduct in complying with the obligations to respect, protect, and fulfill rights might be exemplary. Yet, as the case of Fatimata in Sierra Leone (chapter 1) illustrates, child survival outcomes may be mediocre for a host of reasons, including the magnitude of problems faced, obstacles such as malaria that may be out of the state's immediate control, and the means, both financial and technical, that are available from both domestic and international sources. Thus outcome measures, on their own, are not adequate for judging state performance. Later sections of this chapter will explore the implications of relying on outcome data to monitor state performance and to "name and shame" governments for violations.

Obligations of Progressive Realization

A central principle defining the duties of states regarding social and economic rights is the obligation of progressive realization, a principle that is reflected in several legal instruments, as shown in Box 2.1. According to ICESCR, states are required to progressively ensure that all of their citizens and residents enjoy all of their social, economic, and cultural rights in their fullest expression. Article 2.1 requires states to "*take steps . . . to the maximum of its available resources*, with a view *to achieving progressively* the full realization of the rights recognized in the present Covenant by all appropriate means" (United Nations 1966b, Art. 2, para. 1; emphasis ours). After much debate in the General Assembly over the differences in the implementation of civil and political rights versus economic, social, and cultural rights, it was acknowledged and included in the ICESCR that the implementation of social and economic rights requires not only resources but also the time and capacity to develop sufficient programs for their realization—a point we elaborated in chapter 1. Thus the language of implementation became the obligation to progressively realize social and economic rights within the specific context of each state. This framing also concedes that developing countries' ability to fully realize such rights differs but insists that their shortage of resources does not exempt them from taking action.

Box 2.1. Progressive Realization of Social and Economic Rights in International Treaties

---

International law articulates the obligations for the implementation of economic, social, and cultural rights according to the principle of "progressive realization." In the words of the ICESCR: "2. Each State Party to the present Covenant *undertakes to take steps*, individually and through international assistance and co-operation, especially economic and technical, *to the maximum of its available resources*, with a view *to achieving progressively* the full realization of the rights recognized in the present Covenant by all appropriate means, including particularly the adoption of legislative measures" (emphasis added) (United Nations 1966b, Part 2, Article 2, para. 1). The obligation of progressive realization derives from a long-standing principle in international human rights, first inspired by Article 22 of the Universal Declaration of Human Rights, which states: "Everyone, as a member of society, has the right to social security and is entitled to realization, through national effort and international co-operation and in accordance with the organization and resources of each State, of the economic, social and cultural rights indispensable for his dignity and the free development of his personality" (United Nations 1948, Art. 22). Article 28 of the UDHR stipulates the right of everyone to live in an international world where all of the rights outlined in the document "can be fully realized." In the context of post–World War II, drafters of the declaration recognized the distinctly different starting points of every country but saw the rights as a measurement for nation-states to constantly aspire to, hence the inclusion in the Preamble that states should, "by progressive measures, national and international," work toward these universal standards (Glendon 2001).

Subsequent to the adoption of the ICESCR, the concept has been articulated in numerous documents. The following are some of the principal sources (emphases ours):

Limburg Principles on the Implementation of the International Covenant on Economic, Social and Cultural Rights (United Nations 1987b)

Paragraphs 21, 23, and 24: "to achieve progressively the full realization of the rights"

21. The obligation "*to achieve progressively* the full realization of the rights" requires States Parties to move as expeditiously as possible towards the realization of the rights. Under no circumstances shall this be interpreted as implying for States the right to deter indefinitely efforts to ensure full realization. On the contrary, all States Parties have the obligation to begin immediately to take steps to fulfill their obligations under the Covenant.

23. The obligation of *progressive* achievement exists independently of the increase in resources; it *requires effective use of resources available.*

24. *Progressive implementation* can be effected not only by increasing resources, but also by the development of societal resources necessary for the realization by everyone of the rights recognized in the Covenant.

General Comment 3 on Economic, Social, and Cultural Rights: Nature of State Party Obligations (U.N. CESCR 1990)

Paragraphs 1, 2, and 9

1. Article 2 is of particular importance to a full understanding of the Covenant and must be seen as having a dynamic relationship with all of the other provisions of the Covenant. . . . In particular, while the Covenant *provides for progressive realization* and acknowledges the constraints due to the limits of available resources, it also imposes various obligations which are of immediate effect. Of these. . . is the "undertaking to guarantee" that relevant rights "will be exercised without discrimination."

2. The other is the undertaking in article 2 (1) "to take steps," which in itself, is not qualified or limited by other considerations. . . . Thus while the full realization of the relevant rights may be achieved progressively, steps towards that goal must be taken within a reasonably short time after the Covenant's entry into force for the States concerned. Such steps should be deliberate, concrete and targeted as clearly as possible towards meeting the obligations recognized in the Covenant.

9. The principal obligation of result reflected in article 2 (1) is to take steps "with a view to achieving progressively the full realization of the rights recognized" in the Covenant. The term *progressive realization* is often used to describe the intent of this phrase. The concept of progressive realization constitutes a recognition of the fact that full realization of all economic, social and cultural rights will generally not be able to be achieved in a short period of time. In this sense the obligation differs significantly from that contained in article 2 of the International Covenant on Civil and Political Rights which embodies an immediate obligation to respect and ensure all of the relevant rights. Nevertheless, the fact that realization over time, or in other words progressively, is foreseen under the Covenant should not be misinterpreted as depriving the obligation of all meaningful content. It is on the one hand a necessary flexibility device, reflecting the realities of the real world and the difficulties involved for any country in ensuring full realization of economic, social and cultural rights. On the other hand, the phrase must be read in the light of the overall objective, indeed the raison d'être, of the Covenant which is to establish clear obligations for States Parties in respect of the full realization of the rights in question. It thus imposes an obligation to move as expeditiously and effectively as possible towards that goal. Moreover, any deliberately retrogressive measures in that regard would require the most careful consideration and would need to be fully justified by reference to the totality of the rights provided for in the Covenant and in the context of the full use of the maximum available resources.

Convention on the Rights of the Child (1989, Article 4)

The Convention on the Rights of the Child differs in state obligation and requires that states (Part 1, Article 4) undertake measures *to the maximum extent of their available resources*, without explicit mention of progressive realization.

Committee on the Rights of the Child, General Comments
(2003, Part 1, Paragraphs 7–8)

Similar to the ICESCR, this notes that Article 4 is intended to obligate states to show the progressive realization of rights despite its lack of direct mention: "Even where the available resources are demonstrably inadequate, the obligation remains for a State party to strive to ensure the widest possible enjoyment of the relevant rights under the prevailing circumstances" (2003, Part 1, para. 8).

Maastricht Guidelines on Violations of Economic, Social and Cultural Rights (U.N. CESCR 2000)

Part 2, Paragraph 8: Margin of Discretion

As in the case of civil and political rights, States enjoy a margin of discretion in selecting the means for implementing their respective obligations. . . . The fact that the full realization of most economic, social and cultural rights can only be *achieved progressively*, which in fact also applies to most civil and political rights, does not alter the nature of the legal obligation of States which requires that certain steps be taken immediately and others as soon as possible. Therefore, the burden is on the State to demonstrate that it is making *measurable progress* toward the full realization of the rights in question. The State cannot use the "progressive realization" provisions in article 2 of the Covenant as a pretext for non-compliance.

Part 2, Paragraph 10: Availability of Resources

In many cases, compliance with such obligations may be undertaken by most States with relative ease, and without significant resource implications. In other cases, however, full realization of the rights may depend upon the availability of adequate financial and material resources. Nonetheless. . . resource scarcity does not relieve States of certain minimum obligations in respect of the implementation of economic, social and cultural rights.

Part 2, Paragraph 14, Section f: Violations through Acts of Commission

Violations of economic, social and cultural rights can occur through the direct action of States or other entities insufficiently regulated by States. Examples of such violations include:

> The calculated obstruction of, or halt to, the *progressive realization* of a right protected by the Covenant, unless the State is acting within a limitation permitted by the Covenant or it does so due to a lack of available resources or force majeure.

Convention on the Rights of Persons with Disabilities
(2006, Article 4 General Obligations, Paragraph 2)

With regard to economic, social and cultural rights, each State Party undertakes to take measures to the maximum of its available resources and, where needed, within the framework of international cooperation, with a view to achieving *progressively* the full realization of these rights, without prejudice to those obligations contained in the present Convention that are immediately applicable according to international law.

The principle of progressive realization has its origins in the UDHR and is further elaborated in numerous legal instruments and notably in *The Limburg Principles* (United Nations 1987b), *General Comment 3* (U.N. CESCR 1990), and the *Maastricht Guidelines* (United Nations 2000). It is also developed in the specific contexts of the Convention on the Rights of the Child and the Convention on the Rights of Persons with Disabilities (see Box 2.1). This is a complex principle and can be unpacked into three elements: progressive implementation, maximum resources, and taking steps.

Progressive Implementation over Time

Although the intent of the obligation of progressive realization is to recognize that full enjoyment of rights will take time due to resource constraints faced by some countries, and to provide state parties with flexibility in timing to achieve full realization of rights, it is not an escape hatch for state parties to postpone meeting their obligations or a pretext for noncompliance. Rather, it imposes on states "an obligation to move as expeditiously and effectively as possible towards the goal [of full realization]." They must take "deliberate, concrete, and targeted" steps toward the full realization of all social, economic, and cultural rights (U.N. CESCR 1990, para. 2). In other words, states are required to take positive action to fulfill rights, not merely to respect or protect rights.

In addition, states are obligated to take certain specific steps immediately. States have a core obligation to fulfill the minimum essential level of each social and economic right, with immediate effect (U.N. CESCR 1990). States must also take immediate action to guarantee equal protection and nondiscrimination in the fulfillment of rights. It is important to note that the SERF Index has been constructed to ensure that it can be disaggregated by relevant population groups to track disparities and to highlight possible evidence of discrimination.

Taking Steps

States are given flexibility with regard to the means used to realize the covenant rights, but they are required to employ all means—legislative, administrative, judicial, economic, social, and educational—appropriate to the right concerned and the country's economic, political, and social organization. It is important to note the wide range of measures and policy tools to which these means refer. *General Comment 3* makes this clear, stating, "Adoption of legislative measures, as specifically foreseen by the Covenant, is by no means exhaustive of the obligations of State parties. Rather, the phrase 'by all appropriate means' must be given its full and natural meaning" (U.N. CESCR 1990, para. 4). It further notes that what would constitute "appropriate" means cannot be prescribed.

The realization of social and economic rights requires a variety of actions by diverse actors, not by the state alone. On the other hand, what is called for is that the state elaborate specific policy frameworks and plans for realization. For example, *General Comment 15*, on water, calls for an "integrated strategy" (U.N. CESCR 2003). In other words, the state must actively put in place the social arrangements that create an enabling environment for the realization of rights. While recent advocacy for social and economic rights has focused on state provisioning, it should be noted that this is only one of the measures to fulfill rights; direct provision may in some cases be necessary for rights fulfillment but in many other instances will be inappropriate and insufficient to comply with the obligations of fulfillment.

Resources

The phrase "to the maximum of its available resources" refers to financial and other resources available within a country (U.N. CESCR 1990, para. 9) as well as those external resources available from international cooperation (U.N. CESCR 1990, para. 13). It assumes that achieving full enjoyment of social and economic rights is conditioned by the availability of resources. It also assumes that full enjoyment of rights is a high priority in the allocation of these resources and gives attention to the vulnerable in times of economic crises (U.N. CESCR 1990, 12).

Some have interpreted *resources* as resources at the disposal of the government. However, according to Alston and Quinn (1987), this was not the intention of the covenant. *Resources* means total national resources, expressed by one delegate during the drafting process as referring to "the real resources of the country and not to budgetary appropriations" (Alston and Quinn 1987, 178).

The Demand for Quantitative Indicators of Social and Economic Rights

The normative framework outlined here has important implications for assessing performance, which require new approaches to monitoring that differ from the methods that have long been used to monitor civil and political rights. Debates about these implications and the development of methodological approaches and tools for measurement began in the late 1980s along with an overall revival of interest in social and economic rights. Until then, little attention had been paid to social and economic rights in general in the context of the Cold War, during which the Western powers championed civil and political rights. When the CESCR was set up in 1985 and began in earnest to monitor state compliance with ICESCR, it found the existing approach being used in civil and political rights inadequate for its purpose (Rosga and Satterthwaite 2009). The committee sought new approaches and methods, particularly quantitative tools, generating a new wave of debates and literature on social and economic rights monitoring and measurement.[4] This work has followed a distinct path, separate from the methodological developments for monitoring civil and political rights, though the two paths are increasingly in conversation.

Progressive Realization versus the Violations Approach

Characterized as the "violations approach" (U.N. Office of the High Commissioner for Human Rights [OHCHR] 2012, 23), the practice in monitoring civil and political rights established since the 1950s has focused on identifying specific events or cases involving state failures to respect rights. The data used are qualitative case information. The information base focuses on obligations of outcomes without distinguishing them from conduct and on obligations to respect and protect without attending to the obligations to fulfill. In contrast, the normative framework of ICESCR requires information on the different elements of state obligations articulated—the three types of duties, the distinction between obligations of result and conduct, and the principle of progressive realization.

The normative framework of the International Covenant on Civil and Political Rights (ICCPR) does not articulate the obligations in the detail elaborated in the ICESCR. In the words of ICCPR, states undertake "to respect and to ensure to all individuals . . . the rights recognized in the present Covenant" (United Nations 1966a, Article 2.1), without qualifications about taking steps, progressive implementation, or resource availability. The obligation is to respect and ensure rather than to "take steps." These contrasts in the wording of the ICCPR and the ICESCR do not imply that the two sets of rights carry different types of obligations but, rather, that the nature of state obligations has been more fully developed for ICESCR through the General Comments and the *Maastricht Guidelines* than for ICCPR. While the wording of state obligations under ICESCR and ICCPR differs, the consensus among human rights theorists is that the principles apply equally and the "concepts, tools and analytical frameworks developed in one realm have migrated across regimes to apply in the other" (Rosga and Satterthwaite 2009, 265).[5]

The Demand for Measurement Tools

A major element of the progressive realization approach is to evaluate progress and regress over time according to the magnitude of enjoyment of rights among the population and in relation to the resources available. However, events and case-based information cannot be aggregated and therefore compared across time within or across countries. Each case is unique, so aggregating cases would be adding apples and oranges (Raworth 2001). Qualitative evidence of violations reveals the depth and severity of particular people's suffering but does not indicate the magnitude of state failures or how systematic the violations are. Qualitative, case-based information provides rich contextualized evidence necessary for the analysis of processes that lead to human rights violations or to their realization, the nature of those violations, and what actions and policies enable them. However, it is of limited value for the ongoing and comparative assessment of the human rights situation and processes that require aggregation and comparison. Documenting specific cases contributes little to assessing patterns of state behavior shown by the pervasiveness of violations, targeting of specific population groups, and trends in improvement or deterioration. Quantitative data overcome these limitations: they can be aggregated and disaggregated and compared over time and across population groups. They make possible a more systematic and rigorous analysis of the magnitude, scope, trends, and patterns amenable to more objective interpretation and assessment.

As the OHCHR points out, "There is a need for suitable information, for example in the form of statistics, indicators or even indices, in order to undertake a situation analysis, inform public policy, monitor progress and measure performance and overall outcomes" (2012, 1). It is not surprising, then, that U.N. human rights treaty bodies and special rapporteurs have led the demand for the development and use of quantitative measurement tools to monitor progress in pursuit of their mandates to monitor states' compliance and identify priority global issues.[6]

In its first General Comment, the CESCR (1989, paras. 6–7) suggested that states set benchmarks of progress and include both quantitative and qualitative data in their monitoring systems and status reports. Danilo Turk, the first special rapporteur on economic, social, and cultural rights, championed the development of human rights indicators and measurement as a centerpiece of his work throughout his tenure from 1986 to 1992, noting in his first report, "Indeed, without the availability of a measurement device based on some form of statistical data, there is little chance of obtaining an overall picture which shows the extent to which these rights are realized" (1990, para. 7). His proposal to convene a meeting to discuss indicators for social and economic rights propelled wide-ranging debates among human rights scholars, officials, and activists starting in the early 1990s.

The use of indicators has been an integral part of the CESCR's evolving approach to monitoring ICESCR implementation (Rosga and Satterthwaite 2009). In the 2000 General Comment on health (U.N. CESCR 2000), and repeated in General Comments on water (U.N. CESCR 2003), gender equality (U.N. CESCR 2009), work (U.N. CESCR 2005), intellectual property, and social security, states are called upon to deploy indicators to set benchmarks or targets and monitor progressive achievement in the context of sectoral development strategies (U.N. CESCR 2000).

The Committee on the Elimination of Discrimination against Women has consistently promoted greater use of quantitative data, stating in its *General Recommendation 9* that "statistical information is absolutely necessary in order to understand the real situation of women in each of the State parties to the Convention" (1989, 1). The committee has also consistently promoted the development of new data sets on emerging issues including violence against women (1992), political participation (1997), and time use (1991).

By the mid-2000s, the demand for quantitative measures had gathered momentum, and in 2005, the intercommittee of treaty bodies, which includes chairs of all ten human rights treaty bodies, requested that the OHCHR study the use of quantitative measures. This led to a series of consultations and submissions proposing a conceptual framework for the use of indicators and a set of "illustrative indicators" for assessing human rights, including civil, political, economic, social, and cultural rights (U.N. OHCHR 2006, 2008b), and resulted in the 2012 publication *Human Rights Indicators: A Guide to Measurement and Implementation* (U.N. OHCHR 2012). Outside of the United Nations, many other bodies, such as the Inter-American Commission, the Organization of American States,[7] the U.K. Equality and Human Rights Commission,[8] and civil society organizations such as the Center for Economic and Social Rights (CESR), have promoted the use of quantitative indicators (Felner 2009b).

Measurement Approaches for Social and Economic Rights

In response to the new demand by CESCR, the 1990s saw a proliferation of debates among scholars and practitioners on measurement for monitoring state compliance with human rights obligations. While the initial demand was for quantitative tools in general, the debates soon became framed as a search for "indicators." By the 2000s, a range of proposals emerged on frameworks for selecting indicators. While a comprehensive review and listing of proposed indicator frameworks is beyond the scope of this book, we highlight the methodological trends that have emerged in developing indicators to locate the SERF Index in the context of these developments.

The 2012 OHCHR publication represents the culmination of a twenty-year process within the U.N. human rights system that builds on conceptual work by the Secretariat and the pioneering work of special rapporteurs on education (Tomasevski 2006) and health (Hunt

2005). Several other proposals have been advanced by civil society groups such as the Centre on Housing Rights and Evictions (2009) on water, the Right to Education Project (2013) on education, and the Food First Information and Action Network and CESCR member Eibe Riedel on the right to food and water (Riedel 2006),[9] as well as by Special Rapporteur Paul Hunt and collaborators on the right to health (Backman et al. 2008).[10] The NGO CESR championed the use of socio-economic outcome data (Felner 2009a). It developed a methodological procedure for assessing human rights performance that used quantitative data in the context of a broader qualitative analysis (CESR 2012).

This body of proposals constitutes a major step in developing measurement tools for monitoring social and economic rights. Yet the methodological approach it has pursued—the categorical approach of breaking down the normative framework into fragmented aspects of rights and obligations and offering numerous indicators focused on narrowly defined attribute, as elaborated further below—has left gaps in the critical elements and tools required to make an overall assessment of state performance that incorporates progress and regress, the magnitude of the problem, and evaluation of performance according to the principle of progressive realization by setting relative standards to take account of resource constraints. As explained in chapter 1, the SERF Index was developed in response to the urgent need for a measure that could fill this gap. The SERF Index is an overall summary measure, aggregated to and across each of the six core substantive rights. To locate the SERF Index in the evolution of human rights measurement approaches, we present a summary mapping of major streams of work (Table 2.1). It includes two streams of efforts that focus on civil and political rights and a third stream, motivated by the CESCR, for social and economic rights monitoring. In the pages that follow, we discuss how the SERF Index differs from and complements this third stream of work, which began in the late 1990s.

The "Categorical Approach"

Initial efforts in the early 1990s revealed that responding to the call to identify social and economic rights indicators was not straightforward. The conclusion of many proliferating workshops (for example,

TABLE 2.1 Mapping Human Rights Measurement Approaches

	"First-Generation" Approach, 1970s–Present—Composite Indices[a]	"Second-Generation" Approach, 1990s–Present—Statistical Analysis to Reveal Violations[b]	"Third-Generation" Quantitative Data, 2000s–Present—"Indicators"[c]	SERF Index
Conceptual approach	Violations	Violations	Violations and progressive realization	Progressive realization to the maximum of available resources
Determinants of human rights performance—information input	Outcomes (rights holder enjoyment violations)	Outcome (rights holder enjoyment violations)	Structure, process, and outcomes (duty bearer conduct and rights holder enjoyment levels)	Outcomes against benchmarked obligations (duty bearer conduct and rights holder enjoyment levels)
Focus—substantive right	Civil and political rights, especially physical integrity	Civil and political rights, especially physical integrity	Social and economic rights	Social and economic rights
Focus—obligations	Respect and protect	Respect and protect	Respect, protect, fulfill	Fulfill

Scope—level of aggregation by population	National	Event	National, disaggregation in some cases	National, subnational groups
Scope—level of aggregation by right	Composite by substantive right	Varies	Detailed aspects of rights and obligations to respect and protect ("categorical approach")	Six core substantive rights and composite for six rights (summary approach)
Data source	"Qualitative ratings"—quantitative scores based on qualitative reports	Case-specific evidence	State policies, socioeconomic survey data	Socioeconomic survey and administrative data
Use	Advocacy, research	Advocacy, research, truth commissions	Committee on Economic, Social and Cultural Rights and other U.N. monitoring	Committee on Economic, Social and Cultural Rights monitoring, advocacy, research

[a] E.g., Political Terror Scale, Freedom House, Cingranelli–Richards Index, etc.

[b] E.g., P. Ball; Human Rights Information and Documentation Systems, International, tools; etc.

[c] E.g., Office of the High Commissioner for Human Rights guidelines, IBSA, etc.

United Nations 1993) and studies (for example, Chapman 1996; Green 2001; Robertson 1994) was that agreement on indicators could not be achieved without first clarifying concepts regarding what aspects of rights and obligations were to be measured and what normative standards remained ambiguous (Rosga and Satterthwaite 2009; Welling 2009). Consequently, it became standard procedure to develop indicators by first conceptualizing the different "attributes" of rights and obligations (U.N. OHCHR 2012, 30). Working on indicators for the right to health, Hunt (2005) developed a framework for identifying three types of indicators that reflected different categories of rights and obligations: outcome, process, and structure, roughly corresponding to the obligations of outcome and conduct. Others focused on the categories of rights relevant to substantive rights, such as accessibility, affordability, and quality for the right to water (Centre on Housing Rights and Evictions 2009) and availability, accessibility, affordability, and adaptability for the right to education (Right to Education Project 2013). Work on OHCHR indicators proceeded by identifying features of rights; efforts to develop indicators soon adopted a procedure to first conceptualize different "features" of substantive rights and obligations.

This process—aptly called by Welling the "categorical approach, or a systematic breakdown of the E[conomic] and S[ocial] R[ights] framework" (2009, 950)—inevitably results in a proliferation of indicators, each with a narrow scope. Thus, the Right to Education Project proposes more than two hundred indicators. The OHCHR framework breaks down each right into dozens of subcomponents, each of which is identified with dozens of indicators. For example, the right to health is broken down into five component rights—sexual and reproductive health; child mortality and healthcare; the natural and occupational environment; the prevention, treatment, and control of diseases; and accessibility to health facilities and essential medicines. Each of these five component rights is in turn broken down into three dimensions: structural, process, and outcome. Indicators are then proposed for each of these dimensions. Thus, for example, for just one of these component rights, sexual and reproductive health, the index proposes a total of eighteen indicators (U.N. OHCHR 2012, 90, Table 3). While such indicator sets are important in the analysis of specific situations, they do not provide an overall picture of state compliance with social and economic rights.

As explained in chapter 1, it can be overwhelming to have too much information.

While making a conceptual advance in terms of clarifying the multiple aspects of each social and economic right, this fragmentation leaves human rights assessments with an overwhelming plethora of indicators—potentially the entire gamut of existing socioeconomic statistics for outcome indicators as well as a number of process and structural indicators—from which to choose. This is unworkable at the most basic level as a metric for aggregate comparison across time and countries. Eibe Riedel, a long-term member of the CESCR, thus commented at a workshop of Human Rights Information and Documentation Systems, International (HURIDOCS)—a network on human rights measurement—that the use of indicators in the CESCR "has been sporadic, haphazard and unsystematic at best. . . and probably the most besetting problem in relation to the use of indicators. . . is their sheer quantity. . . [as] indicators can swell up to formidable size and committee members get bogged down in the wealth of figures required and asked for, and have little time left for proper analysis" (HURIDOCS 2009, 25).

Indeed, it is precisely the apparently massive range of data requirements that has frustrated the development of quantitative methods to monitor social and economic rights. Chapman argued that while measurement is essential for monitoring progressive realization, "it necessitates the development of a multiplicity of performance standards for each right in relationship to the varied social, developmental, and resource context of specific countries" (1996, 31). She therefore concluded that it would not be feasible to meet the onerous data requirements and suggested that CESCR should abandon monitoring progressive realization in favor of a violations approach, as is used for civil and political rights.

Progressive Realization

Recalling the three aspects of the principle of progressive realization—implementation over time, taking steps, and resources—the indicator frameworks proposed to date evaluate progressive implementation over time by tracking the selected socioeconomic outcome indicators and taking steps by "structural" and "process indicators" that include a variety of policy positions such as constitutional commitments and the adoption of plans. None addresses the underlying issue of resource constraints and the need to set relative standards for achievement considering different starting points and state resource capacity. Some address the issue of resources, but only in a very limited way, such as an obligation to allocate public finances to human rights priorities through budget analyses (CESR 2012). The limitation of these indicators is that it is difficult to compare them across countries and time in order to evaluate the progress, regress, and magnitude of realization.

Most of the proposals advance indicator sets that are relevant for assessing state performance, but the key limitation is that they do not offer a rigorous benchmark, that is, criteria for evaluating the scores. How do we evaluate whether reducing infant mortality by 10 percent was adequate? How do we know if having a health plan is a significant step in fulfilling rights? Rather than set benchmarks based on an econometric basis, OHCHR (2012) and the Food First Information and Action Network and Riedel propose a consultative process for coming to agreement on appropriate benchmarks (Riedel 2006). But that, too, leaves the problem of how the stakeholders should evaluate what is adequate progress.

The SERF Index aims to fill this gap. Over the years, a number of other scholars had addressed the issue of benchmarks, and the need to relate human rights enjoyment with resource constraints, and made some proposals for methodological approaches (Cingranelli and Richards 2007; Duvall and Shamir 1980; Foweraker and Landman 1997; Landman, Kernohan, and Gohdes 2012; Richards and Clay 2010). Chapter 3 explains how the SERF methodology differs from these approaches. These proposals were not taken up by initiatives to develop measurement tools and data sets. The OHCHR guidelines did not take up the issue of benchmarking. This is not surprising since the CESCR guidelines on the use of indicators for assessing state performance ask states to select indicators and set their own benchmarks (U.N. OHCHR 2012, 25).

Data Sources and Types

While the initial search for "indicators" was for quantitative data, the indicator projects have evolved to include nonnumeric qualitative data. For example, the OHCHR (2012, 89) guide includes well-established socioeconomic statistical series, such as the prevalence of underweight children under five, but also qualitative information, such as the time frame and coverage of national policy on nutrition and nutrition adequacy norms, and numeric data that are nationally specific and cannot be compared cross-nationally,[11] such as the proportion of the targeted population covered under public nutritional supplement programs.

Measurement Approaches in Civil and Political Rights

A comparison of these evolving trends in social and economic rights measurement with the longer history of approaches in civil and political rights reveals some interesting contrasts and helps locate the SERF Index in the evolution of human rights measurement overall. While the trend in assessing social and economic rights has been to eschew composite indices, the opposite has been a major goal in the civil and political rights field, dating back to the 1970s, and motivated research by academics and civil society groups.[12] It is important to note that these indices were developed for use in political science research and in policy advocacy, rather than in compliance monitoring by the U.N. human rights system, and that the methodology has been to quantify qualitative case information as discussed in chapter 1.

The second track in civil and political rights metrics has been the use of statistical methods in specific cases and events. Starting in the 1980s, human rights advocates began to innovate statistical applications in estimating the extent and depth of violations, notably of disappearances and arbitrary killings by authoritarian regimes in Guatemala and elsewhere.[13] These methods and data sets focused on obligations to respect and protect rather than the obligations to fulfill rights and are useful for the violations approach but not the progressive realization approach. The new trends in social and economic rights measurement use existing data, in contrast to the methodology in the civil and political rights tradition, to create quantitative data on the basis of ranking qualitative information, as noted in chapter 1.[14]

Concluding Remarks

Alston and Quinn call the standard of *progressive realization to the maximum of available resources* the "linchpin of the whole Covenant"

(1987, 172). It has simultaneously complicated and frustrated efforts to monitor countries' fulfillment of their economic and social rights obligations (Chapman 1996; Robertson 1994). Despite the centrality of the principle of progressive realization, the difficulty in operationalizing the standard has led NGOS and even the CESCR to sidestep the issue (Chapman 2007; Felner 2009b). They have "usually refrained, when monitoring specific countries, from addressing issues of ESC rights that are bound to the requirements of progressive achievement and resource constraints, focusing instead on various immediate obligations related to ESC rights which are not dependent on resource availability. These duties include the *duty to respect. . ., the duty to protect. . .,* as well as the most tangible aspects of the *duty to guarantee the exercise of rights without discrimination*" (Felner 2009b p.2), aspects that can be assessed using a violations approach. There is an urgent need to complement these approaches with measures addressing the extent to which countries are meeting their obligation to fulfill economic and social rights to the maximum extent feasible within the context of the resources available to them and progressively extending the full complement of social and economic rights to all.

Methodological choices for designing a measurement tool depend on the purpose for which the tool is to be used. Our purpose to assess human progress by the standards of the progressive realization of social and economic rights requires an instrument that reflects resource and capacity constraints in achieving levels of rights enjoyment outcomes. However, recent approaches to developing measurement tools for social and economic rights have focused on using outcome indicators to track rights enjoyment, and on subattributes of rights employing data sources that are specific to a country of a subgroup that are not amenable to cross-country comparison. The SERF Index addresses these gaps in creating an aggregated composite index that can track overall progress in social and economic rights fulfillment based on empirically derived relative benchmarks of what is feasible given the country's resources. The next chapter presents the methodologies for setting the relative benchmark (the Achievement Possibilities Frontier methodology) and for aggregation.

3

Constructing the SERF Index

Progressive Realization and Aggregation

IN THIS AND THE NEXT chapter we elaborate on the construction of the SERF Index. While the next chapter explains the selection of indicators, this chapter presents the concept of the Achievement Possibilities Frontier (APF)—an innovative approach that establishes a relative standard by which a country's fulfillment of its social and economic rights obligations can be judged—and describes the methodology for constructing the index. The previous chapter introduced the conceptual framework of the index and explained that, given the obligation of *"progressive realization to the maximum of available resources,"* specifying the relative extent of a state's human rights obligations has posed by far the most serious challenge to assessing social and economic rights fulfillment. The SERF Index methodology responds to this long-standing challenge with APFs, which reveal the best countries can do in terms of social and economic rights outcomes at any given level of resource availability. This approach brings empirical rigor to the previously slippery legal concept enshrined in Article 2.1's principle of progressive realization to the maximum of available resources. Using evidence-based APFs to rigorously benchmark states' economic and social rights obligations, the SERF Index provides an unbiased metric that allows apples-to-apples comparisons of rights fulfillment across countries and across time.

The basic SERF Index methodology comprises four steps. First, we construct APFs for the socioeconomic indicators used to reflect public enjoyment of a given social or economic right. The APF benchmarks, for any resource level, the value of the indicator it is feasible for a country to achieve. Second, we calculate the percentage of obligation fulfilled with regard to each indicator, as revealed by the distance between actual and feasible levels of rights enjoyment. We then aggregate the results for the different aspects of each given social or economic right to construct a single rights fulfillment index for each right. Finally, we aggregate all the rights fulfillment indices into a composite index, which provides a holistic measure of social and economic rights fulfillment. We leave the task of translating the abstract legal norms into parsimonious indicator sets, reflecting enjoyment of the substantive economic and social rights and specifying the precise APFs for each indicator so selected, to the next chapter. Here we elaborate the basic SERF Index methodology. As with all efforts to translate complex ideas into numbers and indicators, the devil is in the details of how this is done. Numbers can obfuscate as well as clarify, since all measurement contains embedded assumptions (Davis et al. 2012; Lawson-Remer 2012). We have sought to ensure that our efforts are of the clarifying kind—the devilish details of the SERF Index methodology are elaborated below.

Benchmarking State Obligations: Achievement Possibilities Frontiers

To measure the extent to which countries are fulfilling their social and economic rights obligations, we must be able to benchmark the level of obligations with regard to each indicator of rights enjoyment for every given level of resource availability. The benchmarks should reflect what is feasible when a country allocates the maximum of its available resources to fulfilling social and economic rights and uses the most effective means to do so.

Building on the long-standing framework of "production possibility frontiers" used in economics, we construct Achievement Possibilities Frontiers by plotting the value of a given socioeconomic indicator against available resources for all countries and then identifying the outer boundary of the plot. Just as a production possibility frontier shows the maximum output of a good possible for any given resource input, the APF reveals how well a country can perform—the level of social and economic rights it can provide—at any given level of resources. In creating the APF we use data from all countries for all years for which data are available over a period of roughly a decade. The selected time is long enough to encompass a range of policy experiences but not so long as to span substantial techno-logical advances in knowledge concerning the means to translate economic resources into improvements in human well-being. We then define an APF curve for each indicator by identifying the observations on the outer edge of the plot and using econometric techniques to fit a curve that best traces this outer envelope. Thus, the following functional relationship is estimated:

$$X_f = f(Y), \qquad (3.1)$$

where X_f refers to the value of the indicator observations on the outer envelope of the scatterplot for the indicator concerned and Y refers to the corresponding value of resource availability.

Figure 3.1 shows a prototype APF. The value of the right enjoyment indicator is plotted on the vertical axis, and the value of available resources

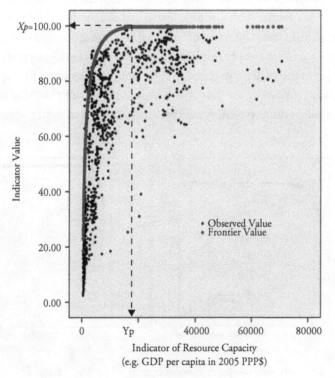

FIGURE 3.1 Prototype Achievement Possibilities Frontier

is on the horizontal axis. Each dot is an observation from a particular country in a particular year that maps the value of the right enjoyment indicator in the country concerned for the year concerned against the value of the country's available resources in the same year. The APF is the solid curved line tracing the outer envelope of the plot. Full enjoyment of a right aspect, for example, the enjoyment of reproductive health as an aspect of the right to health, by all people in a country occurs when the frontier value of the indicator reflecting that right aspect reaches its maximum value (denoted as Xp). The corresponding value of the resource indicator (denoted as Yp) reflects the minimum level of resources required to ensure enjoyment of that right aspect by everyone in the population. For resource levels above Yp where the frontier plateaus, resources are more than sufficient to ensure that everyone enjoys that right aspect.

The shape of the frontier as it rises to its maximum value reflects the rate at which resources can be transformed into rights enjoyment. The shapes of the frontiers differ between indicators since the relationship between resource availability and rights fulfillment is specific and idiosyncratic (see Figure 3.2). Indeed, some frontiers may even fail to reach their maximum over the relevant range of the resource indicator. A frontier that rises more steeply implies greater ease of transforming resources into enjoyment of that particular right aspect. For example, country experience demonstrates that it is possible to ensure that 100 percent of the rural population enjoys access to an improved water source at a

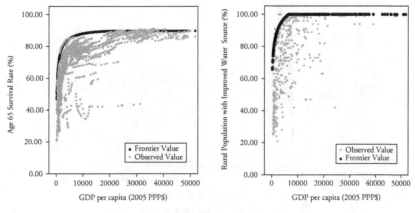

FIGURE 3.2 Ability to Transform Resources into Right Enjoyment Differs across Right Aspects

per capita income level of only $6,450 (2005 purchasing power parity dollars [PPP$]), whereas a per capita income of $26,450 (2005 PPP$) is needed to reach the maximum age sixty-five survival rate of 90 percent. While knowledge of how best to transform resources into rights enjoyment—best practice technology—will certainly change over time, it is unlikely to change rapidly or abruptly, and so the frontier is expected to be essentially stable over the medium term. One can readily verify this presumption in any specific application of the SERF methodology by checking that the observations defining the frontier do not cluster toward the end of the period concerned. In the case of the SERF Index, as the next chapter verifies in Table 4.4, they do not.

The APF approach benchmarks country compliance relative to what is feasible to achieve using best practices given the country's resource base, and this is a key advantage over the residuals approach used widely to assess country compliance with political and civil rights (Duvall and Shamir 1980; Foweraker and Landman 1997; Landman et al. 2012) and country effort to fulfill economic and social rights (Cingranelli and Richards 2007; Kimenyi 2007), which rates countries' fulfillment of rights relative to the average performance across countries rather than best practice performance.

From Achievement Possibilities Frontiers to the SERF Index: Basic Methodology

A country's performance in fulfilling its rights obligations is revealed by the gap between the country's actual performance on each rights indicator and its feasible performance as determined by the evidence-based APFs. A country's performance scores on the indicators of each right aspect are calculated as a percentage reflecting how well a country is doing compared with what is possible; the score is a country's actual value on an indicator as a percentage of the frontier value at that country's resource availability level. In short, the performance score for a particular right aspect (P) for a country is simply the percentage of what could be achieved using best practices, as determined by the APF, given the country's available resources. That is,

$$P = 100(X/X_f),\qquad\qquad (3.2)$$

where X is the observed value of the indicator in the country and year concerned and X_f is the frontier value of the indicator at that country's resource availability level. The APF approach offers the theoretical coherency of judging whether a country is devoting the *maximum of available resources to progressively realize* social and economic rights on the basis of what the best-performing countries with the same resource capacity have *actually* achieved.

Construction of the component right indices is then straightforward. Each right index is computed as the simple average of the indicator performance scores reflecting different aspects of the right.[1] Thus, indicating the different right aspects with the subscript i, the index for right k is defined as

$$R_k = \sum(P_i) / n, \tag{3.3}$$

where the P_i performance indicator scores included in the summation are only those relevant to right k and n is the number of performance indicators relevant to right k.

The SERF Index then aggregates the component right indices. In our calculations in this book we use a simple average of the rights indices to generate the aggregate SERF Index score, but it is also possible, if desired, to weigh more heavily those rights where fulfillment falls shortest. Specifically, the composite SERF Index is defined as follows:

$$\text{SERF} = \left[\sum R_k^{1/\alpha} / m \right]^{\alpha}, \tag{3.4}$$

where m is the number of substantive rights indicators (six in the case where data permit the construction of indicators for all of the substantive rights) and α is a weight that allows one to place greater emphasis on the right where fulfillment falls shortest. Setting $\alpha = 1$ weights each right index equally. The greater the value of α selected, the greater the emphasis placed on those rights where fulfillment falls shortest. More formally, the value assigned to α specifies the degree of substitutability permitted between the rights. Setting $\alpha = 1$ implies perfect substitutability; a decrease of ten percentage points on one

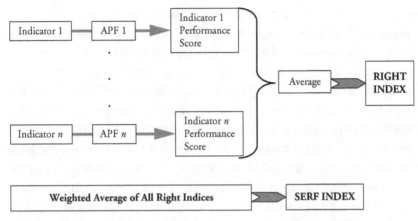

FIGURE 3.3 Construction of the Social and Economic Rights Fulfillment Index

rights index score coupled with an increase of ten percentage points on another leaves the value of the SERF Index unchanged. Setting $\alpha > 1$ implies less-than-perfect substitutability, so that a ten-percentage-point decrease in the score on one right index will not be fully compensated by a ten-percentage-point increase on another, resulting in a decrease in the SERF Index value. As the value of α increases toward infinity, the composite SERF Index score approaches the lowest of the right index scores. Figure 3.3 illustrates the construction of the component right indices and the composite SERF Index.

From Achievement Possibilities Frontiers to the SERF Index: Some Refinements

There are two shortcomings of the basic methodology described above. First, the practical range of some indicators may differ substantially, and this has not been taken into account. Consider two indicators that might be included in constructing a Right to Health Index: one focused on child health, the child survival rate (100 percent – percent child mortality rate); the other focused on adult health, the age sixty-five survival rate (100 percent – percent age sixty-five mortality rate). Observed values of the child survival rate in the 2000 to 2010 period range from 75.9 to 99.8 percent across all countries for which there are data, while the observed values on the age sixty-five survival rate range between 16 and

90 percent.[2] If adjustments are not made, the implication of this dramatic difference in indicator ranges is that the performance indicator score on the age sixty-five survival rate would disproportionately drive country scores on the Right to Health Index. Even if all the scores making up a given right index are weighted equally, the indicator exhibiting the widest range between its observed maximum and minimum values will drive overall performance on the right index concerned. Therefore the indicators reflecting each right aspect must be rescaled to equal zero at the value one observes in a totally failed state with a subsistence per capita income level that devotes no effort to ensuring social and economic rights and to equal 100 percent when the indicator reaches its maximum feasible value.

Second, a country's performance indicator score for a particular right aspect is not sensitive to whether its resource capacity is just barely sufficient to fulfill the right aspect or many times more than is necessary to fulfill it. Consider, for example, the case of two countries with a primary school completion rate of 80 percent, both with resource levels greater than those needed to ensure that 100 percent of children complete primary school. Both countries achieve a performance indicator score of 80 percent on the primary school completion rate even if one has ten times the resource capacity of the other. Conceptually, however, the country with the greater resource capacity warrants a lower rating.

To address the first problem we rescale the performance indicator scores using the following formula, where X is the observed value of the indicator, X_m is the practical minimum value of X, X_f is the frontier value of X, and S is the rescaled indicator performance score:

$$S = 100\,(X - X_m)\,/\,(X_f - X_m) \tag{3.5}$$

While determining the frontier value of X is straightforward, determining the minimum practical value of X, X_m, is not, since the available data do not permit us to observe the lowest value of the indicator that might be observed in any context. One can approximate this value using the minimum value of the indicator observed when constructing the APF. Figure 3.4 illustrates how the rescaling formula works. Note that the X_m value is identified as the lowest observed value of the indicator at *any* level of resource availability.

To rescale the circled X value, the indicator range is rescaled as the proportionate distance between X_m and the value of the frontier at the per capita gross domestic product (GDP) level corresponding to the circled observation. In the example shown, the rescaled indicator value is equal to 70, and accordingly, the rescaled performance indicator score is 70 percent.

Figure 3.4 also illustrates the second problem. For countries with per capita income level at or above Yp, the income level where the APF first reaches its maximum value, the frontier value of X, X_f, equals the value of X at the frontier's peak, Xp—that is, $X_f = Xp$. Consider the observation on the dotted vertical line extending from Yp and the observation surrounded by a square. The P and S scores for both countries are identical, but conceptually, the country whose observation is surrounded by the square should be judged the more deficient of the two with regard to fulfilling the right aspect concerned. To address this problem, we calculate an adjusted performance indicator score, A, that imposes a "penalty" on the country's S score when the country has more than sufficient resources to ensure that everyone in the population enjoys a particular right aspect, yet not everyone does. Thus, the final indicator performance score for a

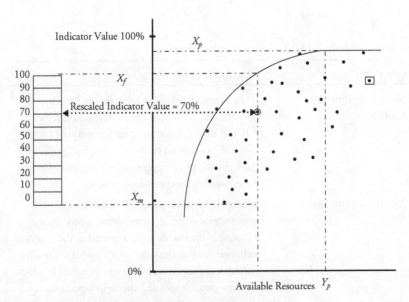

FIGURE 3.4 Rescaling Indicator Values
Source: Randolph, Prairie, and Stewart 2012, Figure 2.

particular aspect of a right, A, incorporating the penalty, depends upon whether the country's income is below or above Yp:

$$A = S \quad \text{if } Y \leq Yp \tag{3.6}$$

or else

$$A = f(S,Y,Yp) \quad \text{if } Y > Yp \tag{3.7}$$

The crux of this approach revolves around how to set the penalty. Table 3.1 sets forth eight criteria that are relevant to evaluating alternative penalty formulas. The following penalty formula meets all of the criteria:

$$A = 100 \left[\left(\frac{S}{100} \right)^{(Y/Y_p)^{\beta}} \right] \tag{3.8}$$

TABLE 3.1 Desirable Criteria in a Penalty Formula

Criterion	Description
No penalty on 100% fulfillment	If the observed value of the indicator reflects complete fulfillment of the right aspect (100% of Xp), the adjusted performance score equals 100%. This ensures that all countries completely fulfilling the right aspect are not penalized inappropriately for expanding their resource capacity.
Asymptotic equality	When $Y > Yp$ and accordingly the adjusted performance score, A, incorporates a penalty, the adjusted performance score approaches the observed indicator score as the value of the resource capacity indicator approaches Yp (the resource level at which it is first possible to fulfill the right aspect) from above. This ensures that the adjusted performance score does not jump as a country's resource capacity increases from below Yp to above Yp.

(*Continued*)

TABLE 3.1 (Continued)

Criterion	Description
Increasing penalty with resource capacity	As a country's resource capacity increases beyond Yp, so too does the penalty imposed on the indicator score. This criterion is at the heart of ensuring that countries with the capacity to ensure that all their citizens and residents enjoy a particular right aspect but fail to do so are penalized more the greater their resource capacity. It also ensures that two countries with the capacity to fully fulfill a right aspect and the same raw score on the relevant indicator receive different performance scores if their resource capacities differ.
Penalty decreases with rising Yp values	The feasible rate of transformation between resources and the fulfillment of the different rights aspects differs. The penalty imposed should be lower the greater the resource cost of a given increase in the indicator score. Differences in the feasible rate of transformation in the fulfillment of the different rights aspects are related to the Yp values of the different indicators, with higher Yp values reflecting lower feasible rates of transformation.
Penalty declines with increasing achievement	The resource cost of enabling some segments of the population to enjoy a particular right aspect are greater than that cost for other segments of the population. In particular, as the percentage of the population enjoying a particular right aspect increases, the cost of extending the right to additional, harder-to-reach segments of the population increases. The penalty should reflect this reality.
Meaningful range	The adjusted performance scores incorporating the penalty should range from 0 to 100%.
Flexibility	The penalty formula should include a parameter that allows the severity of the penalty imposed to vary. This criterion facilitates sensitivity analysis.
Simplicity	A penalty formula that is easier to understand and calculate is preferred, all else constant. (Of course, this is largely subjective.)

The ratio Y/Yp is the ratio of the country's resource capacity to the minimum resource level at which it is possible to ensure that everyone in the population enjoys a particular right aspect. An income ratio of 2 implies that a country has twice the resources needed to fulfill the right aspect concerned, a ratio of 3 implies that resources are three times the needed amount, and so on.[3] The adjustment parameter β allows one to vary the magnitude of the penalty imposed on countries that are able to fulfill the right aspect concerned but fail to do so. The higher the value of β selected, the greater the penalty imposed. Feedback from experts from numerous forums that explored the effects of selecting alternative values of β guided our decision to set $\beta = 0.5$ in the construction of the SERF Index. Figure 3.5 plots the impact of the penalty on the adjusted performance indicator score. A country with a rescaled performance indicator score (S score) of 95 percent sees its adjusted performance indicator score fall to 85 percent as its resource capacity rises to ten times the minimum needed to fulfill the right aspect concerned. As is readily apparent, the lower the S score, the higher the penalty imposed for any value of β selected. If the S score is 60 percent instead of 95 percent, a

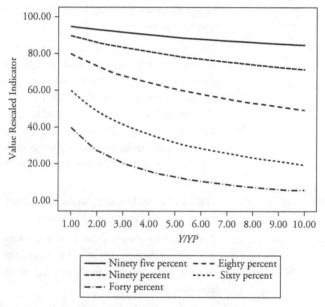

FIGURE 3.5 Impact of Penalty on Indicator Performance Scores
Source: Fukuda-Parr, Lawson-Remer, and Randolph 2011b, Figure 2.

40 percent penalty instead of a 10 percent penalty is imposed as resource capacity rises to ten times the amount needed to fulfill the right.

Upon incorporating both refinements, the revised formula for a given rights index is

$$R_k = \Sigma A_i / n, \tag{3.9}$$

where R_k is the index for right k, A_i is the adjusted performance indicator score for right aspect i, and n is the number of adjusted performance indicators relevant to right k.

Constructing the Achievement Possibilities Frontiers

Here we detail two key issues involved in the construction of the APFs for the SERF Index: the specification of an indicator of resource availability and the estimation of the frontiers.

Maximum Available Resources

State capacity for fulfilling social and economic rights depends on a number of factors. Countries that have higher incomes, more efficient institutions, and more extensive human resources (education, administrative and technical skills, etc.) internally, and more financial and other support at their disposal from the international community, have a greater capacity to fulfill social and economic rights (Boix 2001; Brown and Hunter 2004; Kaufmann and Kraay 2002; Kaufmann, Kraay, and Mastruzzi 2005). At the same time, a state's capacity to fulfill social and economic rights depends on its policy choices. In particular, country growth rates, which determine resource availability, are determined in part by a wide range of social and economic policies, from energy to transport to trade and investment (Acemoglu, Johnson, and Robinson 2001, 2002; Burnside and Dollar 2000, 2004; Stiglitz 2004). Likewise, government revenues depend not only on a country's total productive capacity but also on its policy choices in terms of taxation. A state does not have a lower level of social and economic rights obligations because it chooses to collect less government revenue; failing to collect the revenue necessary to pursue policies promoting social and economic rights fulfillment itself reflects a failure of the state to meet its human rights obligations. Similarly, the talent a state is able to attract into government service depends on choices regarding financial and other forms of compensation, while the available pool of talent depends on previous choices regarding human capital investments.

These multiple determinants of state capacity reinforce the importance of a parsimonious selection of an indicator for resource availability. Indeed, the simplest and most straightforward measure of a country's economic wealth is per capita GDP. A country's per capita GDP reflects the per-person domestic resources a state can potentially tap and hence the resources potentially available to fulfill each person's social and economic rights. GDP per capita is therefore specified as the indicator of state resource capacity for the SERF Index. To ensure comparability in purchasing power across countries and over time, GDP per capita is measured in constant (2005) purchasing power parity dollars.[4]

We recognize that per capita GDP at any given time is not a fully exogenous measure of resource availability, since a low per capita GDP can result from poor macroeconomic policy choices by a state. For example, in the case of Zimbabwe, low per capita GDP reflects a failure to undertake measures to protect and grow its productive capacity so as to generate sufficient financial resources to better fulfill social and economic rights. One solution to this endogeneity problem would be to use a country's predicted rather than actual per capita GDP, making the measure of resource availability the per capita GDP a country with given characteristics would be able to enjoy were it to follow sound economic policies. This approach is explored in greater detail in chapter 7, but the SERF Index findings are virtually the same under this alternative approach.

While the International Covenant on Economic, Social and Cultural Rights (ICESCR) and *General Comment 3* of the Committee on Economic, Social and Cultural Rights (CESCR) (1990) emphasize that the phrase "to the maximum of available resources" includes resources made available through international assistance including financial and technical assistance, several factors guide the decision to exclude bilateral and multilateral aid from the tally of available resources. First, while the policies of foreign governments and international institutions clearly influence aid flows, the resources at a country's disposal from the international community are in part a reflection of the country's policy choices. For example, a country may need to align its political stance with a donor's political and strategic interests to attract substantial bilateral aid. Second, data on the dollar value of foreign aid and particularly technical assistance have serious limitations.[5] Third, much of official development assistance and foreign aid is tied, reducing its value to recipient countries by anywhere from 10 to 40 percent (McKay and Aryeetey 2004; Organisation for Economic Co-operation and Development and Development Assistance Committee 2004).

Conceptually, it is less clear whether or not to include other resource flows in the assessment of "maximum available resources." Countries are also free to contract loans from official and private sources and attract other forms of financial flows. Should these financial flows be included when tallying maximum available resources? Or just a portion of them, perhaps those that are publicly guaranteed? Loans in particular generate future obligations for repayment—a drain on resources. This raises the question of whether to subtract per capita debt-repayment obligations from per capita GDP when calculating available resources. However, to do so implies that debt repayment takes priority over meeting social and economic rights obligations; the General Comments of the CESCR the treaty monitoring body of the ICESCR indicate that it does not. Each of these issues deserves consideration. Although we do not take into account the value of net foreign resource flows (both debt and aid) in the basic construction of the SERF Index, the methodology could readily be adapted to do so. In chapter 7 we empirically examine the impact of accounting for the effect of aid flows on the SERF Index.

Frontier Estimation

As will be recalled, the first step in constructing the frontier is to plot the actual value of the indicator against available resources for all countries for all years for which data are available over a significant time period.[6] In constructing the SERF Index we guard against three potential sources of measurement error.

First, if a country is engaged in a civil war or other major conflict, we consider the data suspect, both due to growth collapses during a major conflict and in light of the physical and financial challenges posed to data collection during ongoing conflict. We therefore identified countries that were engaged in major conflicts (Uppsala Conflict Data Program/Peace Research Institute Oslo [UCDP/PRIO] 2008) and eliminated these observations from the frontier estimation exercise.[7]

Second, in the wake of the 1990s post-Soviet breakup, per capita income plummeted in many of the countries transitioning from a command to a market economic system. Yet much of the schooling and healthcare physical infrastructure (schools, health clinics, hospitals, etc.), as well as critical human capital (trained teachers, doctors, and other healthcare professionals), developed prior to the transition remained robust. The fact that per capita GDP deteriorated to a much greater extent than the physical and human capital infrastructure that supports social and economic rights fulfillment enabled these transitional economies to fulfill social and economic rights to a greater extent relative to their per capita GDP than otherwise would be feasible, providing an unrealistic snapshot of the possibility of rights fulfillment with low levels of economic resources. Therefore, for purposes of the frontier specification, we assign these post-Communist transition countries their per capita GDP level at the onset of the transition until whenever their per capita GDP level rebounded to the pretransition level. Third, to guard against setting an unreasonably high standard that relies on particularly favorable characteristics or circumstances in one country, we require that the frontier be defined based on observations over time from a minimum of four countries.

In estimating the frontiers, we first use visual inspection to identify the observations on the outer edge of the plot. We then use econometric methods to specify the frontier. Multiple functional forms are considered and estimated—linear, logarithmic, inverse, quadratic, power, growth, and exponential. To identify the best fit relationship, we make use of both statistical measures of goodness of fit (R-square etc.) and visual inspection of the shape of the estimated frontiers. Functional forms (such as quadratic functions) that track the upward-sloping portion of the frontier are often combined with linear relationships fitting the plateau portion of the frontier. We then use the best fit relationship to specify the frontier value for every per capita GDP level.[8]

For example, consider the age sixty-five survival rate as a possible indicator of one aspect of the right to health. The left-hand panel of Figure 3.2 shows the scatterplot of the age sixty-five survival rate against per capita GDP (2005 PPP\$) for all countries and all years for which data are available between 1990 and 2006. Letting Y stand for per capita GDP measured in 2005 PPP\$ LnY stand for the natural log of Y, and 65S stand for the percentage age sixty-five survival rate, the equation for the best fit relation is

$$65S = 90.820 + 35.481(LnY) - 1.742(LnY^2) \text{ for } Y < \$26,450 \quad (3.10)$$

The frontier plateaus at a percentage age sixty-five survival rate of 89.85 percent (the Xp value) at a per capita income level of \$26,450 (the Yp value), and so the frontier value of the percentage age sixty-five survival rate remains constant at 89.85 percent for per capita income levels greater than or equal to \$26,450. Chapter 7 compares the approach used here with an alternative approach, the estimation of stochastic frontier production functions.

The minimum value of the percentage age sixty-five survival rate observed in any country is 20 percent, and so for a country with an age sixty-five survival rate of 70 percent, its rescaled indicator performance score, S, is calculated as

$$S = (100)\left[(70 - 20)/(X_f - 20)\right] \quad (3.11)$$

Here, if the country's per capita GDP (2005 PPP\$) for the year concerned is less than \$26,450, X_f is then determined by plugging the country's per capita GDP into Equation 3.10 above. If it is greater than \$26,450, X_f is set equal to \$26,450. In this latter case, the penalty formula would need to be applied to determine the country's final adjusted performance indicator score. So, for example, if the country's per capita GDP were \$52,900, and accordingly Y/Y_p equals 2, its final score would be calculated as

$$A = \left[100(70 - 20)/(89.85 - 20)\right]^{\sqrt{2}} \quad (3.12)$$

And the country's adjusted performance indicator score on this aspect of the right to health would equal 62.3.

Concluding Remarks

This chapter details the basic SERF Index methodology. Socioeconomic statistics such as school enrollment and infant mortality rates tell us the extent to which rights-holding individuals enjoy social and economic rights. Per capita income in a country gives us some sense of resource availability. By relating countries' per capita GDP with their performance on socioeconomic statistics that reflect social and economic rights enjoyment, the construction of Achievement Possibilities Frontiers benchmarks each country's level of obligation. The basic SERF Index methodology rigorously assesses states' fulfillment of their social and economic rights obligations by measuring the gap between actual and feasible social and economic rights enjoyment. With an understanding of the basic SERF Index methodology in hand, we now turn to the task of selecting parsimonious indicator sets of rights enjoyment that reflect the substantive social and economic rights guaranteed under international law. Our focus is on applying the methodology to the international context, although several examples are provided to illustrate the selection of indicator sets in other contexts. The SERF Index methodology is flexible and can be adapted to examine social and economic rights fulfillment at the subnational level, to focus on social and economic rights fulfillment for vulnerable population subgroups, as well as to track progress in fulfilling the particular social and economic rights challenges faced by a given nation.

4

Constructing the SERF Index

From Rights Enjoyment to Indicators

WE NOW TURN TO THE task of translating the abstract legal norms into indicator sets that reflect the enjoyment of different substantive social and economic rights and then specifying the Achievement Possibilities Frontiers for each indicator selected.* The chapter proceeds by first elaborating the fundamental social and economic rights guaranteed to all people under international law. We then discuss the criteria governing indicator selection. Our focus next turns to the task of specifying indicators to measure the extent to which each of the substantive social and economic rights is enjoyed. Our discussion is initially directed to the choice of indicators within the international context for constructing the SERF Index. Current data availability necessarily constrains the selection of indicators in any context. We comment on the limitations imposed by current data constraints with the goal of guiding both international data-collection efforts and data selection for national-level analyses facing less onerous data constraints. We gain additional insight into defining indicator sets in the context of different data constraints through an overview of indicator sets defined in the context of two subnational analyses: one of Brazil, where data limitations imposed challenging constraints on indicator selection, and the second of the United States, where data constraints were less serious. The final section applies the methodology developed in the previous chapter to the indicator sets selected for the SERF Index to specify the SERF Index APFs.

Normative Content of the Substantive Social and Economic Rights

As noted in earlier chapters of this volume, the Charter of the United Nations (United Nations 1945), the Universal Declaration of Human Rights (United Nations 1948), and the International Covenant on Economic, Social and Cultural Rights (United Nations 1966b) enumerate broad substantive social and economic rights. Together, these rights are essential to substantive freedoms. The universality of these rights implies that *every* person, regardless of where she or he lives, and regardless of his or her ethnic or socioeconomic status or other characteristics, is entitled to enjoy these rights because these rights are indivisibly linked to the inherent "dignity and worth of the human person" (United Nations 1945, Preamble). The General Comments of the Committee on Economic, Social and Cultural Rights more finely delineate the substantive rights and elaborate the normative content of each of these rights. In all, the General Comments cover seven substantive economic and social rights: the rights to food, physical and mental health, education, housing, work, social security, and water. The Office of the High Commissioner for Human Rights (2012) guidelines on using indicators to monitor human rights collapse these into six substantive economic and social rights: the rights to food, physical and mental health, education, housing, social security, and work. We follow OHCHR's classification of the substantive social and economic rights here, treating the right to water as a key component of the right to housing.[1] Below, we discuss, in turn, the normative content of each of the six substantive rights along with their key attributes as specified in OHCHR's (2012) guidelines.

The Right to Food

The right to food is guaranteed in the UDHR, Art. 25, para. 1 (United Nations 1948); the ICESCR, Art. 11 (United Nations 1966b); and the Convention on the Rights of the Child (CRC), Art. 28 (United Nations 1989).[2] As elaborated in *General Comment 12*, the right to food encompasses "physical and economic access at all times to adequate food or means for its procurement" (U.N. CESCR 1999b, para. 6). The right to food entails more than just access to a diet sufficient for "mental and physical growth, development, and maintenance, and physical activity. . . in accordance with human physiological needs" (U.N. CESCR 1999b, para. 9). Adequacy is defined relative to the "prevailing social, economic, cultural, climatic, ecological and other conditions" (U.N. CESCR 1999b, para. 7) and thus requires that food accord with the non-nutrient-based concerns of consumers. The requirement that access be sustainable links the notion of adequate food with food security—meaning accessibility at all times for both present and future generations. *General Comment 12* further specifies that the right requires not only that adequate food be physically accessible to everyone but also that the cost of food not be so high as to jeopardize the fulfillment of other basic needs (U.N. CESCR 1999b). The core content of the right to adequate food is specified as "the availability of food in a quantity and quality sufficient to satisfy the dietary needs of individuals, free from adverse substances, and acceptable within a given culture; the accessibility of such food in ways that are sustainable and that do not interfere with the enjoyment of other human rights" (U.N. CESCR 1999b, para. 8). OHCHR (2012, 89) identifies four attributes associated with the right to food that indicators should seek to reflect: food nutrition, food availability, food accessibility, and food safety and protection.

The Right to Education

The right to education is not only intrinsically valuable; it is also instrumentally important for realizing political and civil rights as well as other social, economic, and cultural rights. The aims and objectives of the right to education "reflect the fundamental purposes and principles of the United Nations as enshrined in Articles 1 and 2 of its Charter" (U.N. CESCR 1999c, para. 4). The right to education is articulated in the UDHR, Art. 26.2 (United Nations 1948); ICESCR, Arts. 13 and 14 (United Nations 1966b); the Convention on the Elimination of All Forms of Discrimination against Women (CEDAW), Arts. 10 and 14.2.d (United Nations 1979); and the CRC, Art. 29.1 (United Nations 1989). Two of the General Comments from CESCR, *General Comment 11* (1999a) and *General Comment 13* (1999c), elaborate its content.[3]

The right to education as articulated in Article 13 of the ICESCR (United Nations 1966b) encompasses a right to five different levels or types of education: primary education (Article 13.2.a), secondary education (Article 13.2.b), technical and vocational education (Article 13.2.b), higher education (Article 13.2.c), and fundamental education (Article 13.2.d). *General Comment 13* elaborates four aspects of the right to education that apply to each of the five types of education: availability, accessibility, acceptability, and adaptability (U.N. CESCR 1999c). Availability entails ensuring a sufficient number of educational institutions of each type. Accessibility requires that everyone, including especially vulnerable individuals and groups, can (1) access the educational institutions either in person or using technologies such as the Internet (physical accessibility) and (2) afford to attend them (economic accessibility). There are differences in the nature of accessibility guaranteed across the five educational levels. The right to education requires that primary education be compulsory and free of charge, while secondary, technical/vocational, and fundamental education must be generally available to all. The right of access to higher education is of course dependent on a student's apparent capacity or ability; given ability, the right guarantees equal access to all. Acceptability confers a right to a quality, relevant, and culturally appropriate education, while adaptability entails a right to an education fitting the current needs of the student population and society. Articles 13.2.e and 13.4 of the ICESCR (United Nations 1966b) further underscore the right to a quality education accessible to all. Article 13.2.e confers the right to an adequate fellowship system and decent material conditions of teaching staff, while Article 13.4 confers the right to educational freedom, but with the proviso that educational standards be maintained and extreme disparities of educational opportunities not be induced.

The OHCHR's (2012, 93) guidelines for identifying relevant economic and social rights indicators identify four attributes associated with the right to education that indicators should seek to reflect: universal primary education, accessibility to secondary and higher education, curricula and educational resources, and educational opportunity and freedom.

The Right to Health

The right to health figures prominently in numerous international instruments. Article 25.1 of the UDHR (United Nations 1948), Articles 12.1 and 12.2 of the ICESCR (United Nations 1966b), Article 5.e.iv of the

International Convention on the Elimination of All Forms of Racial Discrimination (ICERD) (United Nations 1965), Article 11.1.f and Article 12 of CEDAW (United Nations 1979), and Article 24 of the CRC (United Nations 1989) all address the right to health. The right to health guarantees every person the "highest attainable standard of physical and mental health" (United Nations 1966b, Art. 12.1). *General Comment 14* of the CESCR (2000) further elaborates its content with reference to all of the above international legal instruments. While the right to health does not guarantee good health, it guarantees more than simply the right to healthcare. It encompasses a right to the "underlying determinants of health, such as food and nutrition, housing, access to safe and potable water and adequate sanitation, safe and healthy working conditions and a healthy environment" (U.N. CESCR 2000, para. 4), and thus the other social, economic, and cultural rights are integral to it. It extends to the freedom to control one's health and body and "takes into account such socially related concerns as violence and armed conflict" (U.N. CESCR 2000, para. 10).

The right to health implies entitlement to timely and appropriate healthcare and related facilities, goods, and services and protections that foster physical and mental health, including, but not limited to, maternal, child, and reproductive health; workplace and natural environmental health; the prevention, treatment, and control of diseases (including related education); and health rehabilitation. This requires that such facilities, goods, services, and programs be available in sufficient quantity, accessible to everyone both physically and economically, acceptable with regard to both medical ethics and cultural norms, and of good quality (scientifically and medically appropriate).

The OHCHR (2012, 90) guidelines identify five attributes associated with the right to health: prevention, treatment, and control of diseases; accessibility to health facilities and essential medicines; natural and occupational environment; sexual and reproductive health; and child mortality and healthcare.

The Right to Housing

Article 11.1 of the ICESCR (United Nations 1966b) provides the most comprehensive articulation of the right to housing, and *General Comment 4* (U.N. CESCR 1992), its most extensive elaboration, although other international instruments address different elements of the right, notably the UDHR, Art. 25.1 (United Nations 1948); ICERD, Art. 5.e.iii (United Nations 1965); CEDAW, Art. 14.2 (United Nations 1979); and CRC, Art. 27.3 (United Nations 1989).[4]

The right to housing entitles every person to adequate housing, defined in *General Comment 4* as housing that is (1) habitable, in that it provides adequate protection from the elements and disease vectors and is physically safe; (2) accessible to those services, materials, facilities, and infrastructure "essential for health, security, comfort and nutrition. . . [including] sustainable access to natural and common resources, safe drinking water, energy for cooking, heating and lighting, sanitation and washing facilities, means of food storage, refuse disposal, site drainage, and emergency services" (U.N. CESCR 1992, para. 8); and (3) culturally appropriate. Further, the right to housing entitles every person to afford-able housing with legal security of tenure. *General Comment 4* links affordability to other social and economic rights by defining afford-ability as a level that does not threaten or compromise "the attainment and satisfaction of other basic needs" (U.N. CESCR 1992, para. 8). The right to legal security of tenure entails "legal protection against forced eviction, harassment, and other threats" (U.N. CESCR 1992, para. 8), as is further elaborated in the CESCR's *General Comment 7* (1998a).The OHCHR's (2012, 94) guidelines summarize these as the following four attributes: habitability, accessibility to services, affordability, and security of tenure.

The Right to Decent Work

The right to work is treated extensively in the ICESCR (United Nations 1966b) with three articles: Articles 6, 7, and 8 devoted to it. It is additionally proclaimed in the Declaration on Social Progress and Development (United Nations 1969). The centrality of the right to work is further recognized in *General Comment 18* of the CESCR (2005, para. 1) as essential to human dignity and for the realization of other social, economic, and cultural rights, as well as political and civil rights. The objectives of the right to work speak to the "fundamental purposes and principles of the United Nations. . . [and are] also reflected in the Universal Declaration of Human Rights" (U.N. CESCR 2005, para.

3). Given its broad reach, various other U.N. international covenants also elaborate different aspects of the right to work. The right to work features prominently in Article 11.1.a. of CEDAW (United Nations 1979); Article 32 of CRC (United Nations 1989); and Articles 11, 25, 26, 40, 52, and 54 of the International Convention on the Protection of the Rights of All Migrant Workers and Members of Their Families (United Nations 1990). It is likewise specifically recognized in a number of regional instruments.[5]

The normative content of the right to work has several dimensions. First, the right guarantees access to freely chosen, independent (self-employment) or dependent (wage or salaried labor) work and protection against being "unfairly deprived of employment" (U.N. CESCR 2005, para. 6). Second, it includes a right to "decent" work, which entails working conditions that are safe and respect workers' physical and mental integrity, as well as a rate of remuneration that is sufficient to support the worker and his or her family. *General Comment 18* specifies four distinct elements of the right to work: availability, accessibility, acceptability, and quality (U.N. CESCR 2005). The availability dimension requires that there be a sufficient number of decent jobs to enable all those who want to work the opportunity to do so. Accessibility has both a physical and an informational dimension. Everyone, including people with disabilities, has a right to work that is physically accessible. The informational dimension confers a right to the necessary information to locate decent work opportunities and obtain decent work. Acceptability and quality include the right to decent work as defined above, as well as a right to form unions. *General Comment 18* links formal-sector employment with decent work and informal-sector employment with a lack of worker protections (safety, security, adequate remuneration) and thus links the right to acceptable and quality work with a right to formal-sector employment for all those who desire it.

The OHCHR (2012, 95) guidelines summarize the normative content of the right to work as work displaying four attributes: access to decent and productive work; just and safe working conditions; protection from forced labor and unemployment; and training, skill upgrading, and professional development.

The Right to Social Security

The right to social security as a tenant of international law dates back at least to the United Nations' formative years. The 1944 Declaration of Philadelphia, establishing the aims and objectives of the Charter of the International Labour Organization (ILO), confers a right to social security in Part III.f (ILO 1944). The right to social security is recognized in Articles 22 and 25.1 of the UDHR (United Nations 1948) and is incorporated into international treaty law under multiple international conventions, most prominently Art. 9 of the ICESCR (United Nations 1966b) but notably Art. 5.e.iv of ICERD (United Nations 1965), Arts. 11.1 and 14.2 of CEDAW (United Nations 1979), and Art. 26 of CRC (United Nations 1989), as well as regional human rights treaties.[6]

The right to social security as elaborated in *General Comment 19* includes "the right not to be subject to arbitrary and unreasonable restrictions of existing social security coverage, whether obtained publicly or privately, as well as the right to equal enjoyment of adequate protection from social risks and contingencies" (U.N. CESCR 2008 para. 9). More particularly, it entitles everyone to social security, including social insurance to secure people's well-being in the event they suffer "(a) lack of work related income caused by sickness, disability, maternity, employment injury, unemployment, old age, or death of a family member; (b) unaffordable access to health care; [or] (c) insufficient family support, particularly for children and adult dependents" (U.N. CESCR 2008, para. 2).

Essential elements of the right to social security as elaborated in *General Comment 19* include its availability, adequacy, and accessibility. Availability implies the existence of a system or systems capable of providing universal coverage. Adequacy requires that benefits be sufficient to enable everyone to realize "an adequate standard of living and adequate access to health care" (U.N. CESCR 2008, para. 22) consistent with human dignity. Accessibility has five aspects: coverage (all must be able to access coverage), eligibility ("qualifying for benefits must be reasonable, proportionate and transparent" [U.N. CESCR 2008, para. 24]), affordability (any direct or indirect contributions required must be stipulated up front and not so high as to compromise attainment of other economic and social rights), participation and information about the system (the right to participate in the administration of the system and to "seek, receive and impart information" [U.N. CESCR 2008, para. 26]), and physical access (to information, to make contributions, and to access benefits). *General Comment 19* also specifies that the right to social security encompasses nine types of coverage—healthcare, sickness, old age, unemployment, employment injury, family and child support, maternity, disability, and survivors and orphans—so as to cover the principle social risks and contingencies.

The OHCHR (2012, 96) guidelines summarize the normative content of the right to social security as the existence of a social security system that provides income security for workers; affordable access to healthcare; family, child, and dependent-adult support; and targeted social assistance schemes.

Criteria Governing Indicator Selection

Having outlined the substantive social and economic rights guaranteed under international law, we now turn to the task of translating the abstract legal norms into indicator sets reflecting the fulfillment of these different substantive social and economic rights. Indicator selection first involves establishing criteria for this task in order to determine the types of indicators that are appropriate. Only then can we identify relevant indicators for the rights to be measured. We focus the discussion on the choice of indicators as applied to the international context. However, the discussion of criteria that govern the choice of indicators at the international level applies with few adaptations to other contexts, as is subsequently explored in applications to Brazil and the United States at the subnational level.

Beyond the crucial issue of concept validity—that is, how well an indicator reflects what one seeks to measure—additional prerequisites for the consideration of any indicator are that it be reliable, based on objective information, and publicly accessible. Reliability in the statistical sense, as it is used here, means that the value of the indicator is consistent in repeated measurements. Objective information is information one can directly observe and verify (e.g., number of children enrolled in primary school), in contrast to subjective information, which relies on people's perceptions. Transparency requires that the means of generating the data be accessible to the public in sufficient detail so that the data could in principle be re-created by anyone desiring to do so. A central raison d'être for the SERF Index is to empower citizens and advocates to hold their governments accountable to meet their social and economic rights obligations. Because the index is based on publicly available data and a transparent methodology, social and economic rights fulfillment scores are demystified and made more accessible.

In addition, the indicators must be intertemporally comparable and, in the context of an international index, internationally comparable. This is not only essential to tracking country progress and enabling analyses exploring issues related to the causes and consequences of social and economic rights fulfillment as discussed previously; it is crucial to the strategy we employ to assess the feasible level of social and economic rights fulfillment at any given resource level, as elaborated in chapter 3.

The above criteria prioritize confining the choice of indicators to publicly available, quantitative, socioeconomic, and other administrative statistics. These sorts of indicators are derived from statistical surveys and administrative records and generally compiled by national statistical institutions or international organizations using a standardized methodology. As noted in chapter 2, although data reporting can be manipulated for political and other purposes, and while quantitative data inherently contain and mask embedded assumptions, the standards typical of national statistical institutes provide at least a measure of assurance of impartiality and objectivity in data collection, processing, and reporting. For the SERF Index, we have further restricted our indicator choice to data sets made available by authoritative, international institutions with a goal of disseminating high-quality, comparable data, such as the World Bank's World Development Indicators, the International Labour Organization's Key Indicators of the Labour Market, the U.N. Statistics Division's Millennium Development Goals Indicators, and the World Health Organization (WHO) Statistical Information System.[7] Indicator choice for studies focused on a single country or at the subnational level in many cases will enjoy greater latitude, in that these studies will be able to draw on high-quality data available through authoritative national, academic, and private institutions that are comparable both intertemporally and across subnational units. Such studies can also utilize more contextually rich data and, should official data be contested, alternative data sources that are judged to be more reliable.

For the SERF Index, we have also restricted our choice of indicators to those that are (at least in some countries), or potentially can be, disaggregated across subgroups in the population. This enables the computation of the SERF Index by population subgroup in order to allow assessment of the extent to which a state meets its obligation of nondiscrimination. The utility of the index is greater if it can be updated with reasonable frequency; thus we exclude from consideration any indicators that are not updated. Additionally, to ensure that the index reflects the current status of rights enjoyment, we prioritize flow indicators over stock indicators. Stock indicators such as the literacy rate reflect past government policies, whereas flow indicators such as school enrollment and completion rates better reflect current policies.

Beyond these general screens, a number of other factors guide our selection of indicators. The task of selecting indicator sets for resource availability and each of the substantive social and economic rights involves translating the relevant legal texts into a limited number of attributes or aspects and then choosing appropriate indicators of those attributes. Beyond the central concern of concept validity, three issues are paramount in this regard.

First, a detail-oriented interpretation of the legal instruments and selection of corresponding attributes and indicators would yield an unmanageable number of indicators. The critical challenge is to select a limited number of indicators that are most relevant to fulfilling a given right. Constraints of data availability, of course, shape this process. Most indicators differentiate better along a particular segment of the income distribution. For example, access to potable water is universal among high-income Organisation for Economic Co-operation and Development(OECD) countries but poses a significant challenge in low-income countries. As noted by the OHCHR, it is not always possible to define "universal" indicators that are relevant to all countries, and accordingly, "there is a need to strike a balance between universally relevant indicators and contextually specific indicators" (2012, 44). For this reason, and the related fact that the indicator sets with wide coverage in high-income OECD countries differ from those with wide coverage in developing countries, we choose to develop a core SERF

Index for non-OECD low- and middle-income countries and a separate supplemental SERF Index for high-income OECD countries. In the case of both country groups, in the event several relevant indicators of a given right aspect are available, greater priority is given to the indicator that provides better differentiation across countries on the extent to which that right aspect is enjoyed. More detail as to the difference in the selection of core versus high-income OECD indicators is provided throughout this chapter.

Second, some indicators are "bellwether indicators," in that that they are relevant to multiple aspects of economic and social rights fulfillment. For example, access to potable water is an underlying determinant of health and nutrition, as well as being related to the right to housing. Where appropriate, such bellwether indicators receive preference. This criterion also keeps the number of indicators used to construct the SERF Index manageable.

Finally, human rights are concerned with the rights of all people and thus the well-being of everyone. As such, indicators that reflect the proportion of the population that enjoys a given level of well-being are preferred to those reflecting "average" well-being.

Rights Enjoyment Indicator Sets for the SERF Index

The selection of indicators for the SERF Index is practically constrained by current data availability. Maintaining broad country coverage proves to be an issue when selecting indicator sets reflecting each substantive right, and trade-offs must be made between country coverage and other concerns. Further, unfortunately, international socioeconomic data that are currently available and that also meet the relevant criteria fail to cover all the attributes we desire to incorporate into the SERF Index. With these caveats in mind, below we discuss the indicators selected to measure the enjoyment of each right in constructing the SERF Index. Table 4.1 lists the indicator sets, while the appendix provides the primary data source and definition of each indicator. The discussion closes with an overview of the limitations imposed by current data constraints, with the goal of guiding both international data-collection efforts and data selection for state-level analyses facing less onerous data constraints.

TABLE 4.1 Social and Economic Rights Fulfillment Index Indicator Sets

Indicator Set	Country Group	Main Index	Historical Series	Indicator
Available Resources	Both	√	√	Gross Domestic Product Per Capita (2005 PPP$)
Right to Food	Core	√	√	Malnutrition Prevalence—Height for Age (% children under 5) (→ % not stunted)
	High-income OECD	√	√	Low-Birth-Weight Babies (→ % not low birth weight)
Right to Education	Core	√	√	Primary School Completion Rate
	Both	√		Gross Combined School Enrollment Rate
	Both		√	Gross Secondary School Enrollment Rate
	High-income OECD	√		Average of Average Math and Science Programme for International Student Assessment Scores
Right to Health	Core	√	√	Contraceptive Prevalence Rate (% women 15–49)
	Both	√		Survival to Age 65 (% cohort)
	Both		√	Life Expectancy at Birth
	Both	√	√	Child Mortality Rate (→ % under 5 survival rate)

(Continued)

TABLE 4.1 (Continued)

Indicator Set	Country Group	Main Index	Historical Series	Indicator
Right to Housing	Core	√	√	Improved Sanitation (% population with access)
	Core	√		Rural Improved Water (% rural population with access)
	Core		√	Improved Water (% population with access)
Right to Work	Core	√	√	Poverty Head Count (<$2.00 per day 2005 PPP$) (→ % population not poor)
	High-income OECD	√	√	Long-Term (>12 months) Unemployment Rate (% of unemployed) (→ % unemployed not long-term unemployed)
	High-income OECD	√	√	Relative Poverty Rate (% population with < 50% of median income) (→ % not relatively poor)

Note: OECD = Organisation for Economic Co-operation and Development.

The Right to Food Indicators

As mentioned, the OHCHR (2012) identifies four attributes associated with the right to food that indicators should seek to reflect: food nutritive value, food availability, food accessibility, and food safety and protection. If nutritious food is available, accessible, and safe, then nutritional status will improve, and in fact, OHCHR (2012) specifies malnutrition rates as relevant outcome indicators for the right to food that reflect all four attributes.

A single indicator, the child (under five) stunting rate, is selected to signify the denial of the right to food for the core SERF Index. Children are most vulnerable to malnutrition, and households deferentially protect children's nutrition.[8] The child stunting (low height for age) rate is more sensitive to both chronic caloric insufficiency and a diet chronically lacking in adequate protein and micronutrients and is less likely to be influenced by temporary illness than other indicators of child undernutrition.

In high-income OECD countries, malnutrition takes the form of food insecurity and the consumption of high-calorie foods of poor nutritional quality (in part as a consequence of food insecurity, since these foods are cheaper) and often manifests in obesity. However, obesity is also caused by a host of factors other than food insecurity and accordingly is not an appropriate indicator. Data on food insecurity are increasingly available for high-income OECD countries but are not yet harmonized across countries, nor are they generally available from publicly accessible databases. In their stead, we select the percentage of infants with low birth weight for high-income countries. Poor maternal nutrition is an important cause of prematurity and low birth weight (Kramer 1987; WHO 2006). Low birth weight is also linked to poor maternal and child health (WHO 2013), so this indicator simultaneously reflects the enjoyment of the right to health.

The Right to Education Indicators

The OHCHR (2012) identifies four attributes associated with the right to education that indicators should seek to reflect: universal primary education, accessibility to secondary and higher education, curricula and educational resources, and educational opportunity and freedom. The first two attributes associated with the right to education identified by OHCHR (2012)—universal primary education and accessibility to secondary and higher education—are dimensions of access; the third—curricula and educational resources—reflects quality. The last attribute—educational opportunity and freedom—incorporates elements of both access and quality. Thus, assessment of the enjoyment of the right to education should include indicators of both access and quality.

For developing countries, although access to primary education is improving, primary completion rates depend on ensuring culturally appropriate options and, in many cases, sufficient family income supplements to make up for the forgone production and earnings of a child. The primary school completion rate monitors whether a country's children realize their core right to education and is among those indicators specified by OHCHR (2012) for monitoring enjoyment of the right to education. The primary school completion rate is selected in preference to either the gross or net primary school enrollment rate given its focus on the extent to which children actually complete primary school.

In high-income OECD countries, and indeed increasingly in low- and middle-income countries, a primary education does not secure the level of knowledge necessary to effectively participate in society. The gross combined school enrollment rate is selected to capture access to all levels of formal education for both developing and high-income OECD countries.[9] Internationally harmonized quantitative indicators of educational opportunity and freedom with reasonable coverage are not available, but these attributes are certain to go hand in hand with enrollment rates.

School attendance is not sufficient to ensure acquisition of the requisite skills needed to function and flourish in adult life. Unless schools are adequately funded and adopt an appropriate curriculum, the knowledge gained will be woefully inadequate. Similarly, unless teachers are adequately trained and present at work, student achievement will be lower. The Programme for International Student Assessment (PISA) administers tests that measure the knowledge and skills needed in adult life. The average of a country's combined mean math and mean science scores is selected to measure educational quality for high-income OECD countries. Although an increasing number of low- and middle-income countries participate in this program, coverage among them is still insufficient to include an indicator of educational quality in the education index for core countries.[10]

The Right to Health Indicators

While fulfillment of the right to health does not guarantee any single person a long and healthy life, at the level of the population as a whole, lower mortality rates and longer life expectancy go hand in hand with greater enjoyment of the right to health. The age sixty-five survival rate provides a broad assessment of the extent to which the full range of attributes associated with the right to health are enjoyed, and it is particularly sensitive to three of the attributes identified by OHCHR (2012) as associated with the right to health: prevention, treatment, and control of diseases; accessibility to health facilities and essential medicines; and natural and occupational environment. Further, it is relevant to high- and low-income countries alike and enjoys broad country coverage. The age sixty-five survival rate is selected over life expectancy at birth, the indicator highlighted by OHCHR (2012), because it more directly reveals the proportion of the population that can enjoy a long and healthy life. Life expectancy is an average; a country may enjoy a high life expectancy rate despite the fact that a substantial number of subgroups in the population fail to enjoy a long and healthy life.

Sexual and reproductive health and child mortality and healthcare are two attributes identified by OHCHR (2012) as key, and mental health is also an intrinsic focus of the right to health. While no adequate indicator for mental health is available at this time, there are several relevant indicators of child mortality and healthcare as well as of sexual and reproductive health from which to choose. The child (under five) mortality rate is selected over the infant mortality rate so as to better capture the effects of children's sustained access to primary medical services and health-promoting policies. Child mortality also reflects environmental risks, such as poor water and air quality, two key elements of the underlying determinants of health. This "bellwether" indicator is relevant to high-income OECD countries and developing countries alike and is nearly universally reported.

Although it is rare to die in childbirth in high-income OECD countries, obstetric complications remain a major source of mortality among women of childbearing age in developing countries. The maternal mortality rate would seem an appropriate indicator of sexual and reproductive health for developing countries, and in fact it is one of the indicators specified by OHCHR (2012). However, Yamin and Maine explain that "maternal mortality rates and ratios do not provide an effective way of tracking a country's progress with respect to reducing the incidence of maternal deaths over time. Indeed, rates are likely to be the most incomplete and inaccurate in countries with the most limited access to reproductive health care, precisely those countries where maternal mortality poses the greatest health problem" (1999, 567). Data on their preferred indicator, the percentage of women with access to comprehensive obstetric care centers, are not yet available for a sufficient number of countries to include in the SERF Index at this time. The contraceptive use rate is indicative of the empowerment of women, with implications for the health of the entire family. The contraceptive prevalence rate is selected as the indicator for access to reproductive healthcare for core countries in light of its better differentiation among middle-income and especially upper-middle-income countries than other alternatives and the importance of contraceptive use, and condoms in particular, in stemming the spread of HIV/AIDS and other sexually transmitted diseases.

The Right to Housing Indicators

Although OHCHR (2012) identifies four attributes associated with the right to housing that indicators should seek to reflect—habitability, accessibility to services, affordability, and security of tenure—data constraints confine measurement of the enjoyment of the right to housing to indicators of services accessibility. Among the housing services, materials, facilities, and infrastructure central to decent housing, access to clean water and sanitation facilities are the most essential and continue to pose a challenge for low- and middle-income countries. Access to potable water and sanitation facilities are also underlying determinants of health and are inextricably related to the right to food. The centrality of access to water for human dignity resulted in the CESCR (2003) identifying access to clean water as a right in itself.

The percentage of the rural population that enjoys access to an improved water source provides better variation among middle-income countries than does the percentage of the total population with such access and is included in the right to housing indicator set of the core SERF Index. The percentage of the total population with access to improved sanitation varies significantly even across upper-middle-income countries and is accordingly selected as the second indicator for the enjoyment of the right to housing for the core SERF Index.

Access to clean water and sanitation are effectively universal in high-income OECD countries. While homelessness, insecure tenure, and lack of affordable housing continue to be problems in high-income OECD countries, there does not yet exist an appropriate indicator for the right to housing with sufficient, comparable country coverage, leading us to omit this right from our index for high-income OECD countries for now.

The Right to Decent Work Indicators

Access to productive work and work conditions that are consistent with human dignity and safety are central aspects of the right to work. Data on the employment-to-population ratio (e.g., ILO's Key Indicators of the Labour Market, Indicator 2) are widely available and reasonably comparable. At first glance, this indicator would appear to be an appropriate indicator of access to employment, and indeed the OHCHR (2012) indicator guide includes it as such. However, employment ratios tend to be higher when schooling opportunities are more limited, social security or other forms of social insurance are rare or nonexistent, and acute poverty requires that even children work. In short, access to work is not the same as access to productive work, particularly in developing countries.

Therefore, due to data constraints, for the core SERF Index the percentage of the population that is living on less than $2.00 per day (measured in 2005 PPP$) is used as a proxy for lack of access to productive work. This is the income level the World Bank currently specifies as necessary to avoid poverty (Ravallion, Chen, and Sangraula 2008). Those living on less than $2.00 a day either do not have access to employment or do not have access to productive employment sufficient to ensure their family a decent standard of living. To the extent that transfer payments from government or private social security programs enable households to escape poverty, this indicator captures a key element of the right to social security while simultaneously obfuscating deprivation of the right to employment.

Unemployment rates are included among the outcome indicators for the right to work in OHCHR's (2012) guide. The percentage of the unemployed who are long-term unemployed is used to measure the absence of sufficient access to employment and skill-upgrading opportunities in the SERF Index for high-income OECD countries. By defining the long-term unemployment rate relative to the unemployed population rather than the labor force, variations induced by macroeconomic cycles are minimized, and the focus is directly placed on the general exclusion of some people from employment. For high-income OECD countries, the lack of decent work is assessed using the percentage of the population with income less than 50 percent of the median income. This relative poverty indicator tracks workers denied work with sufficient pay to support themselves and their families; comparable data on this indicator are available from the Luxembourg Income Study (2009). As was the case for the $2.00/day poverty line used to assess access to decent employment for core countries, to the extent that social security programs as opposed to employment enable individuals to enjoy incomes in excess of 50 percent of the median income, this indicator misclassifies people as enjoying the right to decent employment while simultaneously capturing an aspect of the right to social security.

OHCHR (2012) identifies two additional attributes: protection from forced labor and unemployment, and skill upgrading and professional development. All but a handful of countries outlaw forced and slave labor, and as a result, data on forced and slave labor consist primarily of counts of violations, or estimates based on such counts, and hence are incomparable across countries. Although data from some countries are available on opportunities for professional development and upgrading skills, these are not yet harmonized internationally, and country coverage is limited. The exploitation of opportunities for professional development and skills upgrading enhances labor productivity and increases employability, and so to an important degree, these attributes are captured in data on labor productivity and unemployment.

The Right to Social Security Indicators

The OHCHR's (2012) guide identifies four attributes associated with the right to social security that indicators should seek to reflect: income security for workers; affordable access to healthcare; family, child, and adult-dependent support; targeted social assistance schemes. Currently, there exist no internationally comparable data sources that focus directly on social security coverage (percentage of population covered) overall or by type of social risk, precluding the inclusion of this dimension in the SERF Index at this time. However, as noted above, the absolute poverty rate used in the construction of the core SERF Index and the relative poverty rate used in the construction of the SERF Index for high-income OECD countries do indirectly capture access to social security, in that those falling below the poverty level lack access to an adequate social safety net.

Limitations of Rights Enjoyment Indicators

Data constraints continue to circumscribe our ability to incorporate key aspects of the six social and economic rights into the SERF Index. A direct indicator of food security encompassing the psychological dimensions (worry, social exclusion), as well as the quality and quantity dimensions, is needed, especially for high-income OECD countries. Although such indicators are available for individual countries, the development of a food security scale that is common across countries and separates out the different dimensions of hunger for children and adults has proved challenging but remains an important goal (Deitchler et al. 2011).

Two issues are of particular importance when it comes to accurately measuring enjoyment of the right to schooling. As noted previously, an adequate assessment of the extent to which children enjoy the right to schooling requires an indicator of the quality dimension. In this regard, continued expansion of the number of countries participating in international testing programs is a priority. The primary completion rate and school enrollment rates, coupled with indicators of learning outcomes, measure access to fundamental education for children but ignore adult access to fundamental education. The standard currently used to assess literacy—the ability to "read and write a short, simple statement on their everyday life" (U.N. Educational, Scientific and Cultural Organization Institute for Statistics 2014)—is too low to ensure that adults enjoy fundamental education. Moving forward, the SERF Index needs an indicator with a literacy and numeracy standard that adequately reflects adults' access to the skills they need to fully function and flourish in today's society.

Two priorities stand out with regard to measuring enjoyment of the right to health as well. Expanding country coverage on the percentage of women with access—physical and financial—to basic and comprehensive obstetric care centers is essential to monitoring access to reproductive healthcare and is a key element of the joint U.N. guidelines for monitoring maternal health. A similar effort needs to be launched to collect data on access to mental healthcare. Enjoyment of mental health is a key aspect of the right to health, yet, as noted previously, internationally comparable data on access to mental healthcare are sorely lacking.

The percentage of the population that is homeless or living in temporary or unsafe structures captures three aspects of the right to housing: habitability, affordability, and security of tenure. Unfortunately, data on the percentage of the population that is homeless or living in slums, temporary shelters, or unsafe structures remain sparse even in high-income OECD countries, and definitions vary in those countries that do collect such data. Nor are direct indicators of the affordability of housing, such as the percentage of the population spending more than 30 percent of their income on housing, widely available. The absence of harmonized indicators on the enjoyment of the right to housing relevant to high-income countries poses a serious challenge to monitoring high-income countries' progress in meeting their commitments under the ICESCR. The collection of harmonized data on these aspects of the enjoyment of the right to housing warrants high priority. Further, while the percentages of the population with access to an improved water source and improved sanitation are good proxies for access to clean drinking water and adequate sanitation, they are not ideal. As discussed by Bartram (2008), access to an improved water source as currently measured does not ensure access to potable water. Further, "the benchmark for sanitation is use at home, whereas for water it is an improved communal source—a protected well or spring, for example [within one kilometer of dwelling]. Applying benchmarks that require both drinking water and sanitation at home would better represent what is needed to protect health and secure social benefits" (Bartram 2008, 283).

The ILO's Key Indicators of the Labour Market (KILM) program spearheads current efforts to refine concepts, measurement approaches, and related data sets to monitor the right to work. The KILM data set includes several indicators that are relevant to monitoring access to work, the productivity of labor, and the quality of work (ILO 2014). Of particular relevance are KILM3 and KILM12. The ILO's vulnerable employment rate (KILM3) addresses key dimensions of work quality, the security of work, and benefit provision. The ILO's time-related unemployment indicator (KILM12) provides information on underemployment and job instability, which are other aspects of concern. Country coverage is as yet limited for these indicators, and comparability poses problems. However, these problems will surely decrease in the future, enabling a richer assessment of the right to work.

While absolute and relative poverty indicators capture important aspects of the right to social security, disentangling enjoyment of the right to productive work from the right to social security requires the launching of an effort to systematically collect comparable data on access to social security.

Finally, efforts to collect data disaggregated by population subgroups within a country—race and ethnicity, income class, geographic location, age, disability status, and so on—need to be intensified so as to assess inequality in rights enjoyment across population subgroups.

Adaptations of Rights Enjoyment Indicators

The APFs derived for the SERF Index can be used to assess compliance at the subnational level as has been done in India with regard to the right to food (Hertel and Randolph, 2015). Below we describe how the SERF Index was adapted to enable an examination of historical trends in social and economic rights performance as well as for subnational analyses of Brazil and the United States, exploiting richer data available at the subnational level.

Historical Trends

Several of the indicators selected for the core and high-income OECD SERF Index discussed above are not available across multiple decades for a substantial number of countries. Accordingly, we adapt the indicator sets as required when examining historical trends in social and economic rights enjoyment. In particular,

- with regard to measuring the enjoyment of the right to education, the gross secondary school enrollment rate is substituted for the combined school enrollment rate for both core and high-income OECD countries and—in the case of high-income OECD countries, we omit the educational quality indicators, since PISA scores are not available prior to the 2000s;
- with regard to the right to health, life expectancy at birth is substituted for the age sixty-five survival rate; and
- with regard to measuring the right to housing, the percentage of the population with access to an improved water source is substituted for the percentage of the rural population with access.

See also Table 4.1 for a summary of the differences between the SERF Index and its historical variant.

Selecting Indicator Sets for Country-Specific SERF Indices

Although data constraints preclude taking into account all of the substantive social and economic rights in the construction of the core and high-income OECD SERF Index, these limitations can often be overcome at the national level. Frequently richer national data sources not only enable the construction of a national SERF Index that is better targeted to relevant social and economic rights concerns for the country but also enable disaggregation by geographic region and population subgroup. The construction of a national SERF Index provides a tool for advocates to map the particular social and economic rights dimensions that are in greatest need of attention, to spotlight circumstances where the principle of nondiscrimination is being violated, and to interrogate the effectiveness of the implementation of different policy regimes in varying subnational units. Studies have constructed national SERF indices for both Brazil (see Fukuda-Parr et al. 2010) and the United States (see Randolph et al. 2012). Both studies exploit national data sources that map differences in social and economic rights fulfillment across subnational units; the U.S. SERF Index additionally maps differences in social and economic rights fulfillment by sex and racial/ethnic group. Here we highlight how we adapted the indicator sets in each case.

Brazilian SERF Index

The Brazilian SERF Index adapts the indicator sets both to better reflect the Brazilian context, and to exploit the richer data available at the sub-national level for Brazil relevant to some rights and to overcome data constraints relevant to others. First, federal- and state-level governments share responsibility for meeting social and economic rights obligations. To reflect this shared responsibility, state-level available resources are measured using the average of federal per capita GDP and the state's per capita GDP level (measured in constant year 2000 reals). Second, we estimate APFs using state-level historical data from Brazil. Third, we adapt and expand the indicators used to assess rights enjoyment:

- For the right to education, rather than using the primary school completion rate and the gross combined school enrollment rate, we use the net enrollment rate of seven- to fourteen-year-olds.
- We substitute the percentage maternal survival rate, considered reliable data for Brazil, for the contraceptive prevalence rate in constructing the Right to Health Index. Additionally, we substitute life expectancy for the age sixty-five survival rate.
- Maternal nutrition strongly influences child nutritional status, and accordingly, given the availability of relevant data in Brazil, we substitute the percentage of normal-birth-weight (>2,500 grams) newborns for the percentage of children who are not stunted in constructing the Right to Food Index.
- Comparable state-level data on housing quality are available in Brazil, enabling the inclusion of an indicator of housing quality in the construction of the Right to Housing Index, specifically, the percentage of the population living in housing constructed out of durable materials.
- We substitute Brazil's national poverty line for the World Bank's $2.00 (2005 PPP$) per day poverty line to better reflect the income required for a decent standard of living in Brazil. In addition, we include an indicator reflecting access to secure

work with benefits in the Right to Work Index, specifically, the percentage of the population that is not working in vulnerable employment situations.

Table 4.2 compares the indicators used in the construction of the Brazilian SERF Index with those used in the construction of the core SERF Index.

TABLE 4.2 Comparison of Indicators Used in the Brazilian Social and Economic Rights Fulfillment (SERF) Index with Those Used in the Core Country SERF Index

Right and Attribute	Brazilian SERF Index Indicator	Core Country SERF Index Indicator
Right to Food		
Access and quality	% Newborns >2,500 Grams	% Under 5 Not Stunted
Right to Education		
Access	Net Enrollment rate 7- to 14-Year Olds	Primary Completion Rate
		Combined School Enrollment Rate
Right to Health		
Broad population focus	Life Expectancy at Birth	Age 65 Survival Rate
Child focus	Under 5 Survival Rate	Under 5 Survival Rate
Reproductive health	Maternal Mortality Rate	Contraceptive Use Rate
Right to Decent Work		
Access and quality: productive work	% Not Poor (national poverty line)	% Not Poor ($2.00/day poverty line)
Quality: security and benefits	% Not in Vulnerable Employment	None
Right to Decent Housing		
Essential infrastructure	% Population with Access to Improved Water	% Rural Population with Access to Improved Water
	% Population with Access to Improved Sanitation	% Population with Access to Improved Sanitation
Durable housing	% Population Living in Durable Structures	None

U.S. SERF Index

The greater richness of data harmonized across states in the United States enabled the construction of a more comprehensive U.S. SERF Index incorporating all six of the substantive social and economic rights. Table 4.3 compares the indicators used to construct the U.S. SERF Index with those used to construct the supplementary SERF Index for high-income OECD countries. Several differences merit highlighting. First, the U.S. index incorporates the right to

TABLE 4.3 Comparison of the Indicators Used in the U.S. Social and Economic Rights Fulfillment (SERF) Index with Those Used in the Supplementary SERF Index for High-Income Organisation for Economic Co-operation and Development (OECD) Countries

Right and Attribute	U.S. SERF Index Indicator	Supplementary High-Income OECD Country SERF Index Indicator
Right to Food		
Access and quality	% Food Secure, assessed by the U.S. Department of Agriculture's Food Security Scale	% Normal-Birth-Weight Babies
Right to Education		
Access	Net Secondary School Enrollment Rate	Gross Combined School Enrollment Rate
Quality	Summed 4th Grade Reading and Math and 8th Grade Reading and Math National Assessment of Educational Performance Scores	Average Math and Science Programme for International Student Assessment Scores
Right to Health		
Broad population focus	Life Expectancy at Birth	Age 65 Survival Rate
Child focus	% Child Survival Rate	% Child Survival Rate
Reproductive health	% Normal-Birth-Weight Babies	None

(Continued)

TABLE 4.3 (Continued)

Right and Attribute	U.S. SERF Index Indicator	Supplementary High-Income OECD Country SERF Index Indicator
Right to Decent Work		
Access	% of Youth (20–24) Not Unemployed	% of Labor Force Not Long-Term Unemployed
Quality: decent wage	% Population with >50% Median Income	% Population with >50% Median Income
Quality: security and benefits	100% – Involuntary Part-Time Employment Rate	None
Right to Decent Housing		
Access	% Students in School Who Are Not Homeless	None
Affordability	% Renters Spending Less than 30% Income on Housing	None
Right to Social Security		
Access	% Population with Health Insurance	None
Sufficiency	% Population with Income Above the Absolute Poverty Line (national poverty line)	None

housing and the right to social security. The right to housing indicators include an indicator of access (the percentage of students in school who are not homeless) and an indicator of the affordability of housing (the percentage of renters spending less than 30 percent of their income on housing). The right to social security indicators include an indicator of access (the percentage of the population with health insurance) and an indicator of sufficiency (the percentage of the population that is not absolutely poor based on national standards). Second, to assess the right to food, the U.S. SERF Index uses a more direct indicator than the high-income OECD SERF Index.

Specifically, it uses the U.S. Department of Agriculture (USDA) food security indicator rather than the percentage of normal-birth-weight babies.[11] Third, with regard to the right to education, it uses the net rather than gross secondary school enrollment rate and uses achievement scores on the U.S. National Assessment of Educational Performance test instead of scores on PISA, since National Assessment of Educational Performance scores are available by sex and ethnic group by state. Finally, when assessing decent work, it includes an indicator of the security of work and access to benefits and substitutes an indicator of the youth unemployment rate for the long-term unemployment rate.

International SERF Index Frontier Estimates

Table 4.4 shows the countries defining the APF for each indicator used to construct the international SERF Index, as well as the lowest value observed over the 1990 to 2006 period. Table 4.5 specifies the equations defining the APF for each indicator along with the maximum value of the indicator, Xp, and the income level at which the indicator first reaches its maximum value, Yp. PISA only began in 2000. Excluding this indicator, as can be seen from Table 4.4, nearly half of the observations used to define the frontiers were observed over the 1990 to 2000 period, with not an insubstantial number corresponding to the 1990 to 1995 period, indicating that the frontiers are stable over the medium term. As can also be seen from Table 4.4, the minimum value of the indicators varies widely, from 0 percent (for the percentage of the rural population with access to an improved water source) to 72 percent (for the percentage of the population with greater than 50 percent of the median income) to 310 (for the average math and science PISA score). This underscores the importance of rescaling the basic performance indicators (P); had they not been rescaled, those indicators with the widest practical range would have disproportionately driven the rights indices.

The enjoyment of several of the rights—in particular, education, health, and housing—depends on the provision of goods and services that have a large public goods character, such as public schools, health clinics and services, and water and sanitation infrastructure. As a result, the values of the indicators dependent on these public goods and

TABLE 4.4 International Social and Economic Rights Fulfillment Index Indicators, Frontier Observations, and Minimum Values

Right and Index Version	Indicator	Country and Year for Observations Defining the Frontier[a]	Minimum Value[b]
Right to Food			
Core countries	% Not Stunted	Togo 2006; The Gambia 2000; Senegal 2005; Jordan 1997; Dominican Republic 2000; Macedonia, FYR 2004	36% (Burundi in 2000)
High-income OECD countries	% Not Low Birth Weight	**Sweden 2004**; Iceland 1992; Korea, Rep. 2000; Finland 1992	40% (Lao PDR in 1991, 1994)
Right to Education			
Core countries	Primary School Completion Rate (max. = 100%)	Congo, Dem. Rep. 1992, 1994; Burundi 1993; Malawi 2002; Myanmar 2005; China 1990	0% (10% Mali in 1990)
Both versions	Gross Combined School Enrollment Rate	Zimbabwe 1999–2001; Malawi 1999–2002; Timor-Leste 2001–2002; Kiribati 2000; Guyana 2005; Micronesia, Fed. Sts. 2007; Bolivia 2002–2004; Tonga 2003; Cuba 2005–2007; Ukraine 2008; Brazil 2000; Argentina 2002; Kazakhstan 2005–2006; Libya 2002–2003; Slovenia 2003; New Zealand 1999, 2000–2003; Korea, Rep. 2004	0% (14% Afghanistan in 2001)
High-income OECD countries	Average of Country Average Math and Science Programme for International Student Assessment Scores	Indonesia 2003, 2006; Jordan 2006; Thailand 2000; Latvia 2000, 2003; Poland 2003; Korea, Rep. 2000, 2003; Japan 2000; Finland 2006	310 (Peru in 2000 = 312.5 → 310)

(*Continued*)

Right and Index Version	Indicator	Country and Year for Observations Defining the Frontier[a]	Minimum Value[b]
Right to Health			
Core countries	Contraceptive Prevalence Rate (% women 15–49)	Zimbabwe 1994, 1999; Vietnam 1997, 2000, 2002, 2005, 2006; Paraguay 2008; Thailand 2000; Bulgaria 1995; Ukraine 2002; Uruguay 1997; United Kingdom 1993, 2001, 2002; Hong Kong SAR, China 1992	0% (Guinea in 1993 = 1%)
Both versions	% Child Survival Rate	Vietnam 1990, 1995, 2000, 2005, 2006; China 1990; Syrian Arab Republic 2005, 2006; Ethiopia 2005, 2006; Burundi 1995; Thailand 2005, 2006; Croatia 2006	68% (Niger in 1990)
Both versions	Survival to Age 65 (% cohort)	Liberia 2003–2008; Togo 2006–2008; Nepal 2007–2008; Vietnam 1998–2008; Kiribati 2006; Cuba 1998–2007; Albania 2001–2003, 2005–2008; Costa Rica 2007–2008; Malta 2003–2007; Cyprus 2000, 2004, 2006–2008; Israel 2005–2006, 2008; Japan 2004, 2008; Iceland 2004, 2006–2008	20% (Zimbabwe in 2003 = 20.73% → 20%)
Right to Housing			
Core countries	% Rural Access to Improved Water (% Rural Population)	Bangladesh 1990, 1995; Belarus 1990, 1995, 2000; Burundi 1990, 1995; Comoros 1990, 1995, 2000, 2006; Mauritius 1990, 1995; Nepal 1990, 2000; Thailand 1990; Tonga 1990, 1995, 2006; Uruguay 1990, 1995; Zimbabwe 1990, 1995, 2000; Egypt 1995, 2000, 2006; Lebanon 1995, 2000; Maldives 1995; The Gambia 2006; Malawi 2006; Micronesia, Fed. Sts. 2006; São Tome and Principe 2006; Vietnam 2006	0% (0% Cambodia and Mozambique in 1990)

(*Continued*)

TABLE 4.4 (Continued)

Right and Index Version	Indicator	Country and Year for Observations Defining the Frontier[a]	Minimum Value[b]
Core countries	% Access to Improved Sanitation	Malawi 2000, 2004; Djibouti 1995, 2000, 2004; Samoa 1990, 1995, 2000; Jordan 1990	0% (3% Ethiopia in 1990)
Right to Work			
Core countries	% Not Absolutely Poor (% Income≥$2.00 per day [2005 PPP$])	Kenya 1997, 2005; Lao PDR 2006; Guyana 1993; Djibouti 1996; Moldova 2007; Albania 1997; Azerbaijan 2005; Bosnia and Herzegovina 2004	0% (1% Guinea in 1991)
High-income OECD countries	% Not Relatively Poor (% Income ≥50% Median Income)	**Finland 1995**; Luxembourg 1994; Czech Republic 1992; Slovakia 1992	72% (Peru in 2004= 72.8→72)
High-income OECD countries	% Unemployed Not Long-Term Unemployed	**Norway 2000**; Korea, Rep. 1991–1993, 1995–2008; Iceland 2008; New Zealand 2008	26% (Slovak Republic in 2006 = 26.9% → 26%)

Note: OECD = Organisation for Economic Co-operation and Development.

[a] The value of the indicator for countries listed in bold is the frontier value specified for high-income OECD countries in the case that the frontier is horizontal and less than 100 percent. It is the country with the fourth-highest score on the indicator. The three other countries listed in the same cell enjoyed higher scores.

[b] The observed percentage minimum values are rounded down to the nearest whole percentage. For example, in case of the Programme for International Student Assessment scores, the observed minimum value for Peru of 312.5 was rounded down to 310. For certain indicators the minimum values are specified as 0 percent in recognition of the likelihood that the enjoyment of these right aspects has depended on public provision and/or policies. The actual observed minimum values over the 1990 to 2006 period are shown in parentheses. In these cases the actual observed minimum observed values are near zero.

Source: Adapted and updated from Tables A.2 and A.3 in Fukuda-Parr, Lawson-Remer, and Randolph 2011b.

services are likely to be zero or close to zero in the subsistence context when governments fail to place any emphasis on ensuring social and economic rights. For several indicators—primary school completion rate, combined school enrollment rate, contraceptive use rate, improved rural sanitation, improved rural water—the minimum value used to rescale the indicators is set at 0 percent since the enjoyment of these right aspects depends on public provision and/or policies. Indeed, the observed minimum values of these indicators over the 1990 to 2006 period are near zero (Table 4.4).

For each indicator, plots of the values of the indicators observed in all countries over the 1990 to 2006 period against their corresponding per capita GDP values along with the estimated APF are shown in Figures 4.1, 4.2, 4.3, and 4.4. Recall that the frontier shapes show the rate at which resources can be transformed into rights enjoyment and

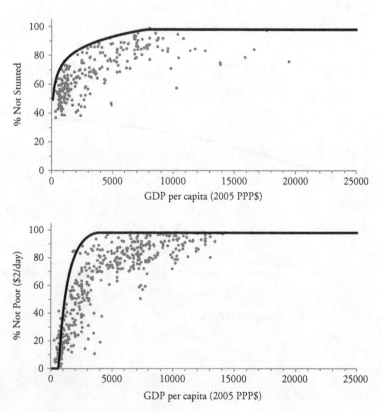

FIGURE 4.1 Right to Food and Right to Work Frontiers—Core Countries

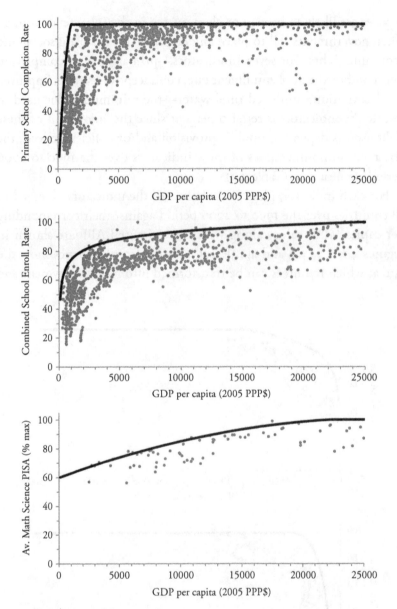

FIGURE 4.2 Right to Education Frontiers

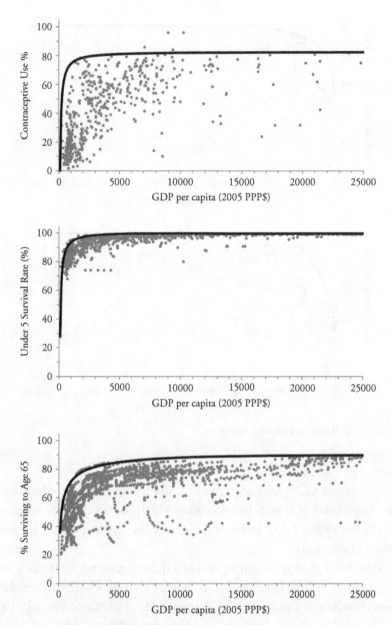

FIGURE 4.3 Right to Health Frontiers

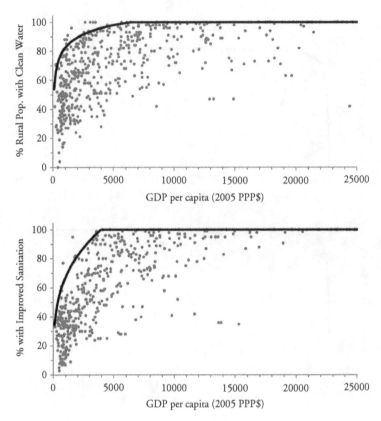

FIGURE 4.4 Right to Housing Frontiers

the per capita GDP level required to fulfill the right aspect concerned, Yp. These rates of transformation vary widely across the indicators, as do the per capita GDP levels at which the indicators reach their peak values (Table 4.5).

This indicates that certain aspects of a right require substantially fewer resources to fulfill. It is feasible to ensure that all children complete primary school at a per capita GDP level of just over $1,000 (2005 PPP$), to ensure that no one lives on less than $2.00 (2005 PPP$) per day at just over $3,800 (2005 PPP$), and to ensure that everyone has access to improved sanitation at just under $4,000 (2005 PPP$). At the other extreme, the APF never peaks for the contraceptive prevalence rate, and a per capita income level exceeding $25,000 (2005 PPP$) is required to enable 90 percent of the population to survive to age sixty-five.[12]

TABLE 4.5 International Social and Economic Rights Fulfillment Index Frontier Equations and Xp and Yp Values

Right and Index Version	Indicator	Frontier Equation	Peak Indicator Value (Xp)	Income Level When Indicator Reaches Peak (Yp)
Right to Food				
Core countries	Not Stunted (NS)	% NS = −2.158 + 11.175(LN_GDPpercap); 98% for GDPpercap ≥$7,806	98%	$7,806
High-income OECD countries	Normal (Not Low) Birth Weight (NBW)	% NBW = 95.8%	95.8%	$16,000
Right to Education				
Core countries	Primary School Completion Rate (capped at 100%) (PC)	% PC = −7.2382 + 0.16414(GDPpercap) − 0.000059159(GDPpercap_squared); 100% for GDPpercap ≥$1,076	100%	$1,076
Both versions	Combined School Enrollment (CS)	% CS = −56.591 + 67.622LN(LN_GDPpercap); 100% for GDPpercap ≥$25,112	100%	$25,112
High-income OECD countries	Average of Average Math and Science Programme for International Student Assessment Scores (PISA)	PISA = 332.345 + 0.017203(GDPpercap) − 0.00000023068(GDPpercap_squared); 555 for GDPpercap ≥$22,190	555	$22,190
Right to Health				
Core countries	Prime-Aged Couples Using Contraceptives (CU)	% CU = 82.753 − 8,507.686/GDPpercap	82.753	Peaks asymptotically
Both versions	Child (Under 5) Survival Rate (U5S)	% U5S = 100.895 − 7,334.1/GDPpercap; 99.74% for GDPpercap ≥$6,350	99.74%	$6,350

(Continued)

TABLE 4.5 (Continued)

Right and Index Version	Indicator	Frontier Equation	Peak Indicator Value (X_p)	Income Level When Indicator Reaches Peak (Y_p)
Both versions	% Surviving to Age 65 (65S)	% 65S = −90.820 + 35.481(LN_GDPpercap) − 1.742(LN_GDPpercap_squared); 89.85% for GDPpercap ≥$26,450	89.85%	$26,450
Right to Housing				
Core countries	Rural Population with Access to Improved Water (RW)	% RW = −22.905 + 19.634(LN_GDPpercap) − 0.641(LN_GDPpercap_squared); 100% for GDPpercap ≥$6,453	100%	$6,453
Core countries	Access to Improved (Good) Sanitation (GS)	% GS = 9.04405(GDPpercap)$^{0.289997}$; 100% for GDPpercap ≥$3,970	100%	$3,970
Right to Work				
Core countries	Not Poor (NP) = With Income >$2.00 (2005 PPP$) per Day	% NP = −1,869.552 + 471.876(LN_GDPpercap) −28.289(LN_GDPpercap_squared); 98% for GDPpercap ≥$3,824; 0% if percapGDPpercap ≤$730	98%	$3,824
High-income OECD countries	Not Relatively Poor (NRP) = With Income ≥50% Median of Income	% NRP = 95.8%	95.8%	$16,000
High-income OECD countries	Unemployed Not Long-Term Unemployed (NLTU)	% NLTU = 94.7%	94.7%	$16,000

Note: OECD = Organisation for Economic Co-operation and Development, LN = the natural log of, GDPpercap = Gross Domestic Product per capita measured in 2005 Purchasing Power Parity dollars, LN_GDPpercap = the natural log of GDPpercap, GDPpercap_squared = the square of GDPpercap, LN_GDPpercap_squared = the natural log of the square of GDPpercap.

Source: Adapted and updated from Adapted from Table A.3 in Fukuda-Parr, Lawson-Remer, and Randolph 2011b.

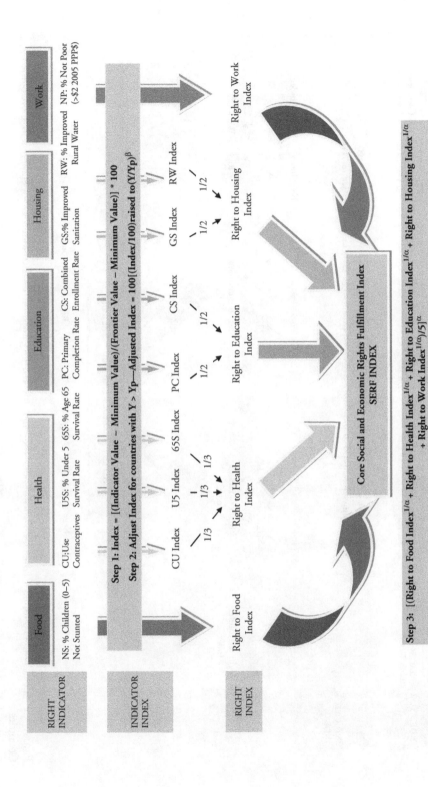

FIGURE 4.5 Social and Economic Rights Fulfillment Index for Core Countries

Source: Fukuda-Parr, Lawson-Remer, and Randolph 2011b, Figure A.1. Reproduced with permission.

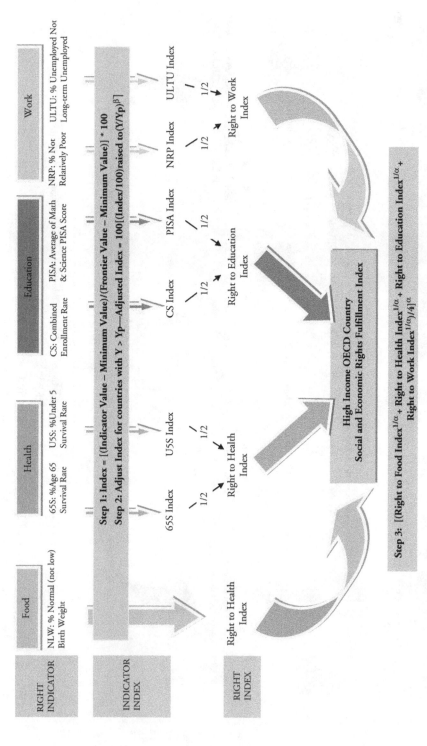

FIGURE 4.6 Social and Economic Rights Fulfillment Index for High-Income Organisation for Economic Co-operation and Development Countries

Source: Fukuda-Parr, Lawson-Remer, and Randolph 2011b, Figure A.2. Reproduced with permission.

TABLE 4.6 Alternative Indicators for the International Social and Economic Rights Fulfillment Index Historical Trend Series Frontier Equations and Peak, Maximum, and Minimum Values

Right and Indicator	Frontier Equation	Peak Value (Xp)	Income Level at Xp (Yp)	Minimum Value
Right to Health				
Life Expectancy at Birth (LE)	% LE = 1.895 + 13.051(LN_ GDPpercap) −0.51045(LN_ GDPpercap_ squared)	Asymptotic	n.a.	23 years
Right to Education				
Gross Secondary School Enrollment Rate (GSE)	% GSE = −322.563 + 54.860(LN_ GDPpercap); 100% for GDPpercap ≥$2,214	100%	$2,214	0%
Right to Housing				
% Population with Access to Improved Water Source (GW)	% GW = −151.879 + 56.139(LN_ GDPpercap) − 3.098886(LN_ GDPpercap_ squared); 100% for GDPpercap ≥$3,580	100%	$3,580	0%

Note: LN = the natural log of, GDPpercap = Gross Domestic Product per capita measured in 2005 Purchasing Power Parity dollars, LN_GDPpercap = the natural log of GDPpercap, GDPpercap_squared = the square of GDPpercap, LN_GDPpercap_squared= the natural log of the square of GDPpercap.

Source: Randolph and Guyer 2012a.

These different transformation rates underscore the importance of assessing the extent to which different aspects of a right are fulfilled prior to aggregating across right aspects or across rights. Averaging all the indicator scores reflecting different rights before constructing a frontier would give substantially different results than a rights fulfillment index, such as the SERF Index, that first creates indices reflecting the extent to which each right aspect is fulfilled and then averages. Figures 4.5 and 4.6 provide a schematic representation of the steps to construct the SERF Index for core countries and for high-income OECD countries, respectively.

Tracking historical trends in the international SERF Index presents two challenges.[13] First, historical data going back several decades on several of the indicators used in the annual international SERF Index are either not available for any country or not available for a large number of countries. As noted in the discussion on indicator sets, this required that we change three indicators in the historical series. The frontier equations, peak values, and maximum and minimum values of the substituted indicators are shown in Table 4.6.

Second, while data on some of the indicators used in the construction of the international SERF Index are annual series, data on many of the indicators are collected less frequently, with only a subset of countries collecting the data in the same year. As such, our International SERF Index Trend Data are constructed for "waves" spanning a decade so as to ensure that the data used in constructing the index are unique to that decade. In the event data on a given indicator for a given country are available for more than one year in the decade, the observation closest to the midpoint of the decade is used. Thus, if data on the child stunting rate are available for 1982, 1986, and 1989, the data from 1986 are used in constructing the series for the 1981 to 1990 wave, since that data point is closest to 1985.

Concluding Remarks

With an understanding of the SERF Index's construction in place, we move in the next chapter to applying the SERF Index to reveal the current status of social and economic rights fulfillment across and within nations and to evaluate countries' progress (or lack thereof) in fulfilling their obligations over time. This is followed by an examination of the factors and policies that promote economic and social rights fulfillment in chapter 6. Our discussion of the construction of the SERF Index in this chapter highlights a number of choices made in the construction of the index. Chapter 7 explores the robustness of the SERF Index as regards several of these choices and extends the analysis in several directions.

5

A Global Picture of Social
and Economic Rights Fulfillment

ACROSS THE WORLD, IN ALL regions, governments have made significant progress toward meeting their obligations to fulfill the substantive social and economic rights of their citizens. However, most countries can do much more, and these broad improvements mask troubling trends. Overall rights performance varies widely across countries, and some countries have even regressed. At the same time, the data reveal significant differences in countries' performance on each social and economic right, with progress in fulfilling some rights, such as the right to work, lagging behind other rights, such as the right to education. Equally troubling, aggregate country-level scores hide significant disparities in rights enjoyment among racial, ethnic, and other demographic groups, and mask serious discrepancies in performance among states and regions within the same country. Finally and notably, there are some strong SERF performers and poor SERF performers at every income level, at every level of human development, and in every region of the world.

This chapter describes the global and historical patterns in social and economic rights fulfillment as revealed by the SERF Index. We examine both the historical SERF Index, which reveals trends across time, and the most recent annual SERF Index scores, which provide insight into the state of human rights fulfillment in the world today. As discussed previously, the SERF Index is specified for two groups of countries. First, there is the core SERF Index, which is used for most countries. Second, there is a supplemental index, the high-income

OECD country SERF Index. These country groups are analyzed separately due to the significant differences in data availability, as detailed in chapter 4.

Progress and Retrogression in Social and Economic Rights Fulfillment over Time

On average, countries are increasingly meeting their obligations to fulfill social and economic rights with each successive decade. The historical SERF data, as measured over two decades from 1985 to 2005, reflect this general upward trend. While core countries generally score much lower than high-income OECD countries on the SERF Index, the core countries are improving at a faster rate, steadily approaching the high SERF scores of those included in the high-income OECD sample (see Figure 5.1).

Looking more closely at SERF Index scores, we find that, on average, SERF Index scores for core countries have increased by more than ten

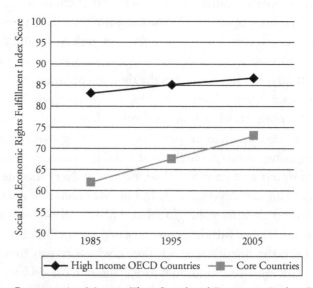

FIGURE 5.1 Countries Are Meeting Their Social and Economic Rights Obligations to an Increasing Degree

Note: Social and Economic Rights Fulfillment Index score averages calculated for all countries for which a 2005 index score is available.

Source: www.SERFindex.org.

points over the past three decades, but much progress still remains to be made. Only a handful of core countries currently achieve a SERF Index score of 90 percent or higher, and well over half achieve scores below 80 percent.

Although the high-income OECD countries' gains have been less pronounced over the past three decades, they have still been steady, and today only a third of the high-income OECD countries' SERF Index scores fall below 80 percent, with none below 70 percent (see Table 5.1).

Rights Remain Unfulfilled for Many

The average SERF trends, however, mask wide variation in performance across countries, with many countries still falling very short of their rights obligations, and some even regressing. The data reveal that many countries continue to struggle to fulfill social and economic rights for their citizens. Five countries have SERF Index values of less than 50, while another seventeen countries only achieve SERF Index scores from 50 to 59.9, as seen in Table 5.1. The average score for the bottom 10 percent of core countries is 45.5, in contrast to an average score for the top 10 percent of 91.8 (see Figure 5.2).

Equatorial Guinea, at the bottom of the core SERF Index distribution, fulfills only 27 percent of the rights that it feasibly could. Oil sales generate a per capita GDP of more than US$30,000, placing Equatorial Guinea squarely in the family of high-income countries. Yet, despite its high income, the government of Equatorial Guinea has failed to provide its citizens with even the most basic rights. In Figure 5.3, we see that Equatorial Guinea fails to score above a 30 on four of the five rights indices.

Despite a general trend of gains in SERF Index values, more than half of the global population continues to live in countries where rights fulfillment falls below 70 percent of what is feasible—a dismal performance in respecting, protecting, and fulfilling universal human rights guaranteed under international law (see Figure 5.4). Sadly, some countries, scoring at both the top and bottom of the distribution, on both supplemental and core SERF indices, are actually performing worse today than they did thirty years ago. The human rights principle

TABLE 5.1 Countries' Fulfillment of Social and Economic Rights Obligations Varies Widely

Sample	Score on the Social and Economic Rights Fulfillment Index (%)					
	90–100	80–89.9	70–79.9	60–69.9	50–59.9	<50
Core countries	Ukraine, Belarus, Uruguay, Moldova, Croatia, Bulgaria, Kyrgyz Republic, Jordan, Costa Rica, Argentina, Chile, Serbia, Islamic Republic of Iran	Turkey, Brazil, Thailand, Russian Federation, Tunisia, Sri Lanka, Mexico, Kazakhstan, Georgia, Jamaica, Armenia, Guyana, Maldives, Dominican Republic, Albania, Ecuador, Bosnia and Herzegovina, Romania, Colombia, Paraguay, Syrian Arab Republic, Arab Republic of Egypt, Liberia, Belize, Macedonia FYR, Venezuela RB, El Salvador, Vietnam, Honduras	Tajikistan, Malawi, Morocco, Uzbekistan, Suriname, Peru, Nicaragua, Azerbaijan, Togo, Panama, Philippines, Democratic Republic of Congo, São Tome and Principe, Nepal, Ghana, Iraq, Burundi, Bolivia, The Gambia, Mongolia, Bhutan, Comoros	Indonesia, Guatemala, South Africa, Uganda, Senegal, Cameroon, Kenya, Rwanda, Cambodia, Guinea, Mozambique, Bangladesh, Lesotho, Central African Republic, Ethiopia, Guinea-Bissau, Namibia, Lao PDR	Mauritania, Timor-Leste, India, Pakistan, Djibouti, Burkina Faso, Côte d'Ivoire, Sudan, Niger, Mali, Madagascar, Benin, Zambia, Tanzania, Republic of Yemen, Swaziland, Gabon	Republic of Congo, Nigeria, Angola, Chad, Equatorial Guinea
High-income Organisation for Economic Co-operation and Development countries	Finland, Republic of Korea, Sweden, Norway, Denmark	Canada, Poland, Australia, Austria, Slovenia, Switzerland, Czech Republic, Estonia, France	Italy, United Kingdom, Greece, Ireland, Israel, United States, Luxembourg			

Source: www.SERFIndex.org/data, 2013 Update.

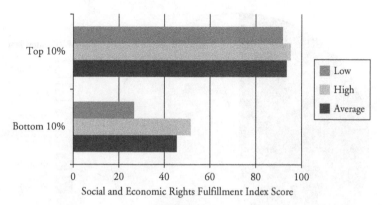

FIGURE 5.2 Average, Minimum, and Maximum Social and Economic Rights Fulfillment Index Scores for Best- and Worst-Performing Core Countries
Source: www.SERFindex.org/data, 2013 Update.

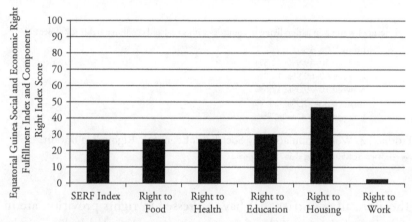

FIGURE 5.3 Equatorial Guinea Could Do Much More to Fulfill Social and Economic Rights
Source: www.SERFindex.org/data, 2013 Update.

of nonretrogression prohibits states from undertaking any deliberately retrogressive measure to undermine rights fulfillment. Specifically, the Committee on Economic, Social and Cultural Rights' *General Comment 3: The Nature of States Parties' Obligations* states: "Any deliberately retrogressive measures. . . would require the most careful consideration and would need to be fully justified by reference to the totality of the rights provided for in the covenant and in the context of the full use of the maximum available resources" (1990, para. 10).

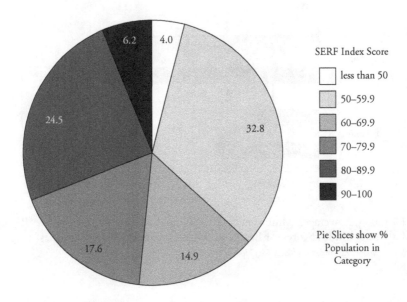

Percent of world population living in countries with social and economic rights fulfillment ...

below 50%: 4%
between 50–59.9%: 32.8%
between 60–69.9%: 14.9%
between 70–79.9%: 17.6%
between 80–89.9%: 24.5%
between 90–100%: 6.2%

FIGURE 5.4 World Population by Social and Economic Rights Realization
Source: www.SERFindex.org/data, 2013 Update.

Therefore all countries that have regressed in rights provision are in violation of the principle of nonregression, unless the decline can be justified.

Nevertheless, nine of the twenty-two high-income OECD countries for which we can observe a trend over time regressed at some point between 1975 and 2005. Though Sweden, Finland, and the Netherlands all saw an increase in the extent to which they met their social and economic rights commitments from 1995 to 2005, all three regressed prior to 1995. The United States, by contrast, was experiencing an increase in social and economic rights fulfillment prior to 1985 but then saw rights fulfillment plunge. The Czech Republic and Switzerland saw a dramatic downturn in the extent to which they fulfilled their social and economic rights obligations to their citizens from 1995 to 2005.

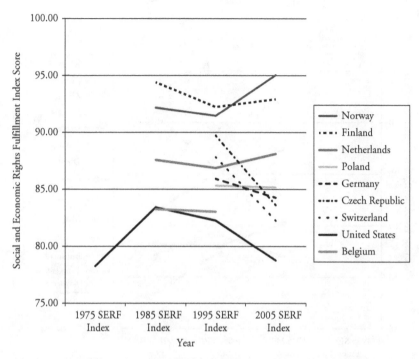

FIGURE 5.5 High-Income Organisation for Economic Co-operation and Development Countries Violating the Principle of Nonretrogression
Source: SERF High-Income OECD Country Historical Trend Data Variant A, www.SERFindex.org.

Poland, Germany, and Belgium have also seen a slight decline in the extent to which they are meeting their obligations (see Figure 5.5).

Though most core countries can boast at least some progress in the extent to which they meet their social and economic rights obligations, thirteen core countries for which we can observe a historical trend violated the principle of nonretrogression at some point between 1975 and 1985. China, though it experienced significant gains in rights provision from 1995 to 2005, was regressing from 1985 to 1995. Likewise, Côte d'Ivoire regressed from 1985 to 1995 but saw a small recovery from 1995 to 2005. While Mali's performance improved between 1985 and 1995, it subsequently declined from 1995 to 2005. Countries at both the top and the bottom of the distribution saw a decline from 1995 to 2005, with Armenia's SERF Index score falling from 92.7 to 85.5 and Burkina Faso's falling from 54.9 to 46.8 (see Figure 5.6).

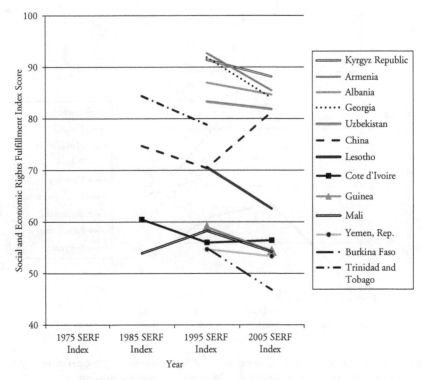

FIGURE 5.6 Core Countries Violating the Principle of Nonretrogression
Source: SERF Core Country Historical Trend Data, www.SERFindex.org.

Rights Fulfillment Varies Significantly across Rights

While average SERF scores provide helpful insights regarding the seriousness of rights deprivation in countries, the disaggregated scores for each component reveal that some apparently high performers may actually be doing poorly in some rights areas while poor performers may actually be doing well in certain categories. In short, rights fulfillment within countries can vary significantly, even though the general pattern is that countries performing well on one right also tend to perform well on the other rights.

As noted previously, in general, the performance of countries in the core SERF Index sample has been steadily improving. The greatest gains have been made in the right to education. Performance on the right to health has backtracked some, but has remained relatively steady around

85. Performance on the right to work has also declined and stagnated (see Figure 5.7).

Tracking high-income OECD countries' component rights scores over time, we see that performance has also generally been improving, but this progress has been uneven across the component rights. For example, the right to work component has stagnated or declined in many countries, while large gains have been made in the right to education (see Figure 5.8).

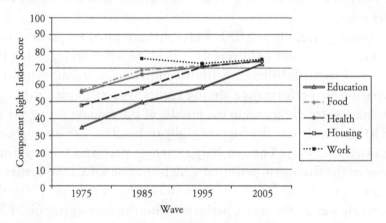

FIGURE 5.7   Core Country Performance on Component Rights Indices Is Improving
Note: Countries with data for any wave.
Source: Adapted from Randolph and Guyer 2012b, Figure 3.

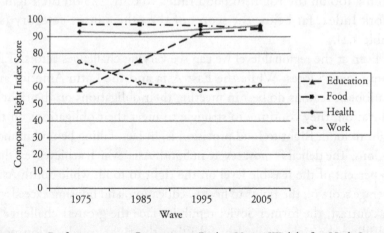

FIGURE 5.8   Performance on Component Rights Varies Widely for High-Income Organisation for Economic Co-operation and Development Countries
Note: Countries with data for any wave.
Source: Adapted from Randolph and Guyer 2012b, Figure 4.

Greece's performance on the right to education steadily improved
from 1975 to 2005, climbing from 48 to 100. However, from 1995
to 2005, its performance on the right to work remained low, stuck
at barely 40. Likewise, Ireland's performance on the right to work
has fluctuated but remained relatively low, falling from 43 in 1985 to
36 in 1995 and then climbing again back to 45 in 2005. Meanwhile,
Ireland's performance on the right to education, which began at 68
in 1975, was up to 100 by 1995 and has remained at that strong level
ever since.

Looking carefully at SERF scores disaggregated by performance
on each component right reveals critical information regarding the
status of rights fulfillment within countries, including surprising
variation in performance among rights. For example, although
Vietnam currently scores in the middle of the road on the aggregate
SERF Index, it has the highest right to health score among core
countries, at 99.3. Though Italy's current performance is among
those of the five worst-performing high-income OECD countries, it
is among the top three on the right to health, scoring 99.5. Nigeria,
currently one of the worst performers on the core aggregate SERF
Index with a score of 43.6, has a right to education score of 68. The
Republic of Korea, one of the best-performing high-income OECD
countries, secures a SERF Index score of 92.8, with scores ranging
from a 100 on the Right to Food Index to only 75.8 on the Right to
Work Index, far below the scores of the others in its category (see
Table 5.2).

Even at the regional level we can see varying challenges across SERF
component scores. While the East Asia and the Latin America and
Caribbean regions do best in meeting their obligations on the right to
education, they continue to struggle to meet their obligations on the
right to food. Right to food provision is, in fact, falling behind in most
regions. The deficit is most severe in South Asia, which achieves less than
50 percent of the feasible level on the right to food, while South Asia's
average score on the rights to health, education, and housing exceeds 75.
In contrast, the former Soviet republics face the greatest challenge in
fulfilling the right to health; fulfilling the right to education poses
the greatest challenge for most of the Eastern European region (see
Figure 5.9).

TABLE 5.2 Best and Worst Performers on the Social and Economic Rights Fulfillment (SERF) Index Overall and on Component Right Indices

Country	SERF Index Score	Right to Education Index Score	Right to Health Index Score	Right to Housing Index Score	Right to Food Index Score	Right to Work Index Score	Per Capita Gross Domestic Product (2005 PPP$)
Core Countries							
Best Performers							
Ukraine	95.25	97.23	83.40	95.61	100.00	100.00	6,029
Belarus	94.93	99.91	85.72	93.26	95.76	100.00	12,505
Uruguay	94.23	97.22	94.43	100.00	79.52	100.00	12,642
Moldova	94.16	85.03	88.71	97.06	100.00	100.00	2,793
Croatia	93.68	80.21	91.52	96.67	100.00	100.00	15,917
Bulgaria	93.31	92.22	86.16	100.00	88.17	100.00	11,506
Kyrgyz Republic	93.30	94.70	81.76	97.52	100.00	92.54	2,026
Jordan	92.01	81.97	85.62	95.67	96.77	100.00	5,250
Costa Rica	91.91	84.36	97.96	90.35	93.41	93.49	10,453
Argentina	91.76	99.62	92.74	78.09	88.33	100.00	14,363
Ukraine	95.25	99.91	85.72	93.26	95.76	100.00	6,029
Worst Performers							
Zambia	51.60	79.18	54.83	59.30	43.90	20.78	1,401
Tanzania	50.88	82.04	64.62	32.85	51.30	23.58	1,293
Republic of Yemen	50.64	58.83	63.23	56.60	13.22	61.32	2,373
Swaziland	50.45	63.76	54.21	59.09	40.93	34.28	5,338

(Continued)

TABLE 5.2 (Continued)

Country	SERF Index Score	Right to Education Index Score	Right to Health Index Score	Right to Housing Index Score	Right to Food Index Score	Right to Work Index Score	Per Capita Gross Domestic Product (2005 PPP$)
Gabon	50.27	53.58	55.95	20.12	52.30	69.42	13,611
Republic of Congo	45.97	58.32	56.93	25.88	62.30	26.41	3,812
Nigeria	43.58	67.98	39.82	42.45	49.49	18.16	2,137
Angola	42.54	46.32	30.41	46.22	61.85	27.88	5,172
Chad	42.18	45.92	35.50	34.73	46.65	48.09	1,337
Equatorial Guinea	26.65	30.03	27.04	46.71	26.91	2.57	30,493

High-Income Organisation for Economic Co-operation and Development Countries

Best Performers

Country	SERF Index Score	Right to Education Index Score	Right to Health Index Score	Right to Housing Index Score	Right to Food Index Score	Right to Work Index Score	Per Capita Gross Domestic Product (2005 PPP$)
Finland	93.11	98.09	98.80	—	99.76	75.78	31,310
Korea, Rep.	92.80	97.17	97.81	—	100.00	76.23	26,774
Sweden	91.56	81.44	99.89	—	99.53	85.40	34,125
Norway	91.50	82.85	99.74	—	97.93	85.49	46,906
Denmark	90.94	86.56	96.74	—	99.24	81.22	32,379

Worst Performers

Country	SERF Index Score	Right to Education Index Score	Right to Health Index Score	Right to Housing Index Score	Right to Food Index Score	Right to Work Index Score	Per Capita Gross Domestic Product (2005 PPP$)
Greece	79.11	80.58	99.23	—	92.31	44.31	23,982
Ireland	79.02	85.64	99.04	—	96.28	35.13	35,993
Israel	78.98	73.80	99.40	—	91.54	51.19	25,995
United States	76.38	83.01	94.96	—	90.00	37.55	42,079
Luxembourg	74.73	59.05	98.53	—	88.77	52.58	68,679

Source: SERFindex.org, 2013 Update.

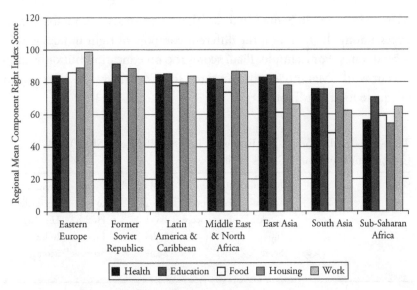

FIGURE 5.9 Component Right Indices Mean Scores by Region—Core Countries
Source: www.SERFIndex.org/data, 2013 Update.

Aggregate Scores Hide Variation at the Subnational Level among Regions and among Genders, Races, and Ethnic Groups

SERF Index scores at the country level can hide serious discrepancies in rights performance at the subnational level—among populations as well as across regions. These differences in rights provision are often linked to one another as different populations may live predominately in different geographic areas within a country. In short, a high country score does not mean that all populations within the country are receiving adequate rights provision. In order to highlight these differences, we look carefully at three case studies: Brazil, the United States, and India.

Brazil

Brazil receives a high aggregate SERF score, ranking fifteenth of 104 countries. However, disaggregation using Brazil-specific data reveals a wide variation in rights provision along regional and ethnic lines.

We find significant variation across regions in rights performance disaggregated by state within Brazil. SERF scores range from 74, in

Maranhão, to 96, in Santa Catarina. There are also several notable differences among the scores on the different component right indices within several states. For example, Piauí scores 100 on education but only 44 in decent work. Maranhão, which scores 40 in decent work, scores 93 in adequate food (see Table 5.3).

TABLE 5.3 Brazilian Social and Economic Rights Fulfillment (SERF) and Component Right Index Scores by State

State	SERF Index Score	Right to Decent Work Index Score	Right to Education Index Score	Right to Adequate Food Index Score	Right to Health Index Score	Right to Adequate Housing Index Score
Santa Catarina	96	97	97	90	99	95
São Paulo	93	89	95	86	96	98
Minas Gerais	92	87	92	86	99	94
Paraná	92	86	96	89	96	91
Espirito Santo	91	83	93	91	95	91
Rio Grande do Sul	91	83	95	87	99	94
Goiás	90	84	97	92	98	80
Mato Grosso do Sul	90	88	98	92	98	74
Rio de Janeiro	90	84	87	86	92	98
Distrito Federal	89	85	88	83	95	97
Rondônia	88	80	92	95	93	80
Mato Grosso	86	78	93	93	94	72
Rio Grande do Norte	86	67	96	93	91	80
Sergipe	86	60	94	91	92	93
Amapá	85	76	98	91	91	71
Amazonas	84	66	91	93	91	77
Paraíba	84	56	96	94	90	83

(Continued)

TABLE 5.3 (Continued)

State	SERF Index Score	Right to Decent Work Index Score	Right to Education Index Score	Right to Adequate Food Index Score	Right to Health Index Score	Right to Adequate Housing Index Score
Roraima	84	59	94	91	90	87
Pará	83	61	92	90	97	74
Acre	82	70	91	93	94	61
Bahia	82	53	93	91	95	78
Ceará	82	53	98	93	92	75
Piauí	82	44	100	94	90	80
Tocantins	82	60	98	94	93	65
Pernambuco	81	58	94	92	86	75
Alagoas	78	56	93	93	81	68
Maranhão	74	40	91	93	85	63

Source: Adapted from Fukuda-Parr et al. 2010, Table 3.

There is also a strong negative relationship between the percentage of the population that is Afro-Brazilian and SERF scores. The state with the highest score on the Brazilian SERF Index, Santa Catarina, has the smallest proportion of Afro-Brazilians, while Maranhão, the state with the lowest score on the Brazilian SERF Index, is among the states with the highest population of Afro-Brazilians (see Figure 5.10).

United States

The United States, a relatively low performer among high-income OECD countries, also demonstrates a wide range of scores on the U.S. SERF Index across states, ranging from 69 in Louisiana to 85 in North Dakota. And there are significant differences among states across component right scores as well. For example, the United States meets its obligations on the right to education—with an average score of 95 on the U.S. Right to Education Index, ranging from 85 in Nevada to

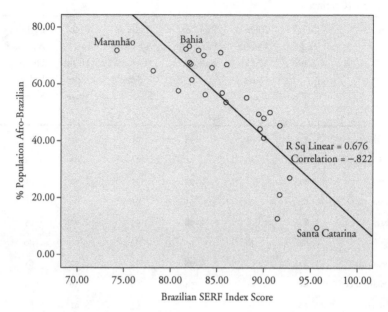

FIGURE 5.10 States with the Most Afro-Brazilians Do the Worst in Fulfilling Social and Economic Rights Obligations

98 in Maine—to a dramatically greater extent than on the right to housing—with an average score of 50, ranging from 11 in California to 79 in Wyoming on the U.S. Right to Housing Index (see Table 5.4 and Figure 5.11).

When scores are disaggregated by ethnic background, we see even larger differences in rights provision. Across all component rights, the lowest score for whites in any state is higher than the highest score in any state for both blacks and Hispanics. Within each state, the differences between the scores of whites and the most marginalized ethnic group on the SERF Index and component right indices are reported in the final column of Table 5.5. Overall, the largest difference in rights provision among ethnic groups is in Wisconsin, with a difference of 18.33 between whites and the most marginalized ethnic groups.

India

India has realized strong growth over the past decade, but the benefits have not been evenly distributed across states, and many groups have

TABLE 5.4 U.S. Social and Economic Rights Fulfillment (SERF) and Component Right Index Score Ranges

Index	Index Score Range)	Mean Across States	Number of States with Index Score >90	Number of States with Index Score <75
SERF	69.1 (Louisiana)–84.8 (North Dakota)	77.4	0	13
Right to Food	68.1 (Texas)–86 (North Dakota)	76.4	0	20
Right to Education	85.2 (Nevada)–97.7 (Maine)	92.6	41	0
Right to Health	85.9 (Louisiana)–94.2 (North Dakota)	91.2	37	0
Right to Work	62.7 (Connecticut)–79.5 (North Dakota)	71.6	0	9
Right to Housing	11.2 (California)–79.1 (Wyoming)	46.7	0	49
Right to Social Security	74.2 (Alaska)–93.1 (Maine)	86.1	9	2

Source: Adapted from Randolph, Prairie, and Stewart 2012, Table 4.

been left out and left behind even while India's per capita GDP has skyrocketed. For example, the variation in performance across Indian states on the right to food component of the SERF Index is substantial. Some states do remarkably well, especially relative to their state per capita income and food production per capita; among them are Kerala and Tamil Nadu, with scores of 77 and 65, respectively. By contrast, Punjab, which produces more food per capita than any other state, does not do nearly as well. Uttar Pradesh produces more than ten times more food per capita than Kerala and twice as much as Tamil Nadu, yet its performance on the right to food component of the SERF Index is the worst among the Indian states, at a disgraceful 17. In short, while the overall volume of food available may be sufficient to feed India's

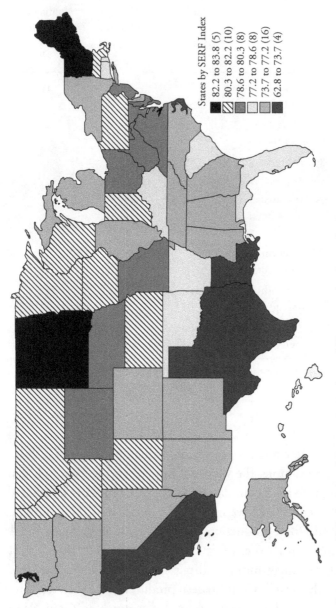

Figure 5.11 U.S. Social and Economic Rights Fulfillment Index Scores by State

Source: Randolph, Prarie and Stewart 2012.

States by SERF Index

82.2 to 83.8 (5)
80.3 to 82.2 (10)
78.6 to 80.3 (8)
77.2 to 78.6 (8)
73.7 to 77.2 (16)
62.8 to 73.7 (4)

TABLE 5.5 U.S. Social and Economic Rights Fulfillment (SERF) and Component Right Index Score Ranges by Ethnic Group

Index (Number of States with Data by Ethnic Group)	Index Score Range for Whites	Index Score Range for Blacks	Index Score Range for Hispanics	Range of State Score Differences between Whites and Marginalized Group
SERF (26)	86.9 (Nevada)–90.9 (Maryland)	60.7 (Missouri)–74.6 (Maryland)	64.7 (North Carolina)–77.4 (Florida)	2.69 (California) –18.33 (Wisconsin)
Right to Education (36)	90.8 (Nevada)–100 (15 states)	64.7 (Wisconsin)–80.2 (Texas)	68.3 (California)– 87.8 (Florida)	6 (New Mexico)–30.1 (West Virginia)
Right to Health (42)	89.6 (Delaware)–94.5 (Washington and Minnesota)	73.7 (Delaware)–87.0 (Oregon)	88.8 (Hawaii)–95.3 (Alaska)	4.9 (Hawaii)–12.6 (Wisconsin)
Right to Work (35)	64.9 (Oregon)–81.7 (Mississippi)	15.4 (Washington)–58.3 (Maryland)	30.7 (Oregon)–63.1 (Mississippi)	6.5 (California)– 44.68 (Missouri)
Right to Social Security (32)	86.1 (Louisiana)–94.8 (Wisconsin)	60.3 (Louisiana)–81.5 (Maryland)	50.2 (North Carolina)–73.3 (Missouri)	12.18 (California) –33.94 (Delaware)

Source: Randolph, Prairie, and Stewart 2009.

hungry, distribution occurs with substantially differing levels of transparency and effectiveness state by state and locally. At the same time, social norms and cultural practices affect intrahousehold utilization of food. Therefore right to food scores vary widely within India by state (see Table 5.6).

TABLE 5.6 Indian Right to Food Index Scores by State

State	Right to Food Index Score
Kerala	77.38
Tamil Nadu	65.18
Goa	63.70
Jammu and Kashmir	62.65
Manipur	61.14
Tripura	58.19
Nagaland	53.48
Sikkim	52.05
Punjab	51.44
Mizoram	50.04
Himachal Pradesh	48.72
Rajasthan	45.11
Andhra Pradesh	43.21
Arunachal Pradesh	42.94
Orissa	42.13
Karnataka	40.81
Uttarakhand	40.35
West Bengal	39.70
Assam	38.50
Delhi	37.04
Haryana	34.09
Maharashtra	33.29
Madhya Pradesh	32.17
Jharkhand	31.05
Chhattisgarh	23.95
Gujarat	23.54
Bihar	23.43
Meghalaya	18.53
Uttar Pradesh	17.28

SERF Scores Are Diverse for Countries with Similar Levels of Income and Human Development Performance and Within Regions

Income

There is a wide range of performance on the core SERF Index at every per capita income level. For example, the Kyrgyz Republic and the Republic of Yemen both have per capita income levels just over $2,000 (2005 PPP$), yet the Kyrgyz Republic achieves a score of 93 percent on the core SERF Index, while the Republic of Yemen only achieves a score of 50 percent. India, with a slightly higher per capita GDP, only scores 58 percent on the core SERF Index. At a per capita income level of roughly $5,000, Jordan scores 92 percent, Bhutan scores 71 percent, and Angola scores just under 43 percent on the core SERF Index. We find similar variation in scores on the core SERF Index for countries at a per capita income level of roughly $13,000 (2005 PPP$), with Uruguay scoring 94 percent; Panama, 76 percent; and Gabon, just barely over 50 percent (see Figure 5.12).

While high-income OECD countries seem to have a floor on SERF Index scores, given that their current SERF Index scores all exceed 70, we do witness high and low performers at all income levels. For example, the Republic of Korea, with a per capita GDP of $26,774 (2005 PPP$), has a SERF Index score of 92.8, while Italy, with a slightly higher per capita GDP ($27,083, measured in 2005 PPP$), only achieves a score of 79.5.

Looking at the individual right index scores for core countries, one continues to observe wide variation in country scores across the per capita income range (see Figure 5.13).

When we disaggregate SERF scores for high income Organization for Economic Cooperation and Development countries into component right scores, we see even more clearly that income is not the sole determinant of social and economic rights performance. Indeed, among the high-income OECD sample, no relationship at all is observable, positive or negative, between per capita income and SERF Index or component right index scores (see Figure 5.14).

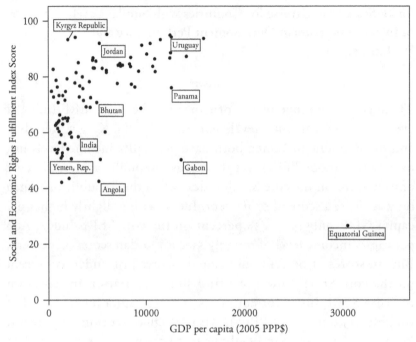

FIGURE 5.12 Core Social and Economic Rights Fulfillment Index Scores by Per Capita Income Level

Source: www.SERFindex.org 2013 Update.

Human Development Index

The SERF Index differs fundamentally from the Human Development Index because social and economic rights fulfillment takes into account resource availability, allowing apples-to-apples comparisons across similarly situated countries, unlike the HDI. As a result, scores on these two indices diverge significantly. For example, while the United States scored third overall in the 2013 HDI, it places twentieth among high-income OECD countries in the SERF Index. Uruguay places only fifty-first overall on the HDI but comes in third among core SERF countries. Likewise, the Kyrgyz Republic places 125th on the HDI but seventh on the core SERF Index. Guyana, which scores 104th overall in the HDI, has a SERF Index score of 89.25, placing it eleventh among core SERF countries (see Table 5.7).

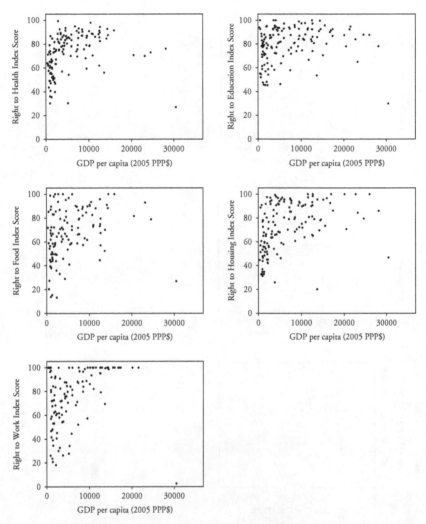

FIGURE 5.13 Performance on Each Right Varies Widely for Core Countries at the Same Income Level

Source: www.SERFindex.org, 2013 Update.

Regions

There are likewise strong and poor performers in each region and a wide dispersion of SERF Index scores globally. For example, Laos and Timor-Leste stand out as poor performers in the otherwise moderately successful region of East Asia. Liberia, the best performer in sub-Saharan Africa, performs well above the median of all countries (83 compared with about 76). While

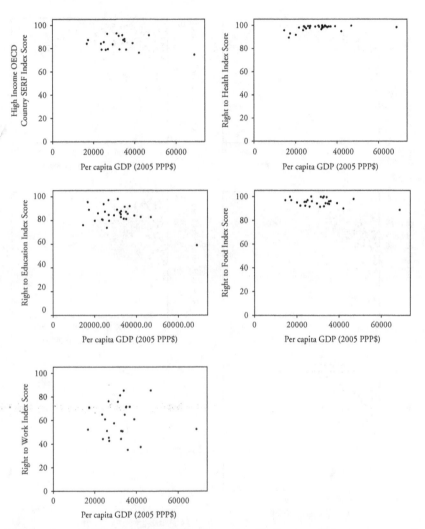

FIGURE 5.14 High-Income Organisation for Economic Co-operation and Development Country Social and Economic Rights Fulfillment and Component Right Index Scores by Per Capita Income Level

Source: www.SERFindex.org, 2013 Update.

regional averages range from nearly 90 to nearly 60, within every region there are countries with high scores above 80. Only Eastern Europe and the former Soviet republics avoid scores below 70 (see Figure 5.15).

Take the case of performance on the Right to Education Index within sub-Saharan Africa. By 1985, Mozambique achieved over 90 percent of the feasible value given its resource capacity but then regressed dramatically to

TABLE 5.7 Social and Economic Rights Fulfillment (SERF) Index and Human Development Index (HDI) Rank Countries Differently

Country	2013 HDI Score (Rank)	2013 SERF Index Score (Rank)
United States	93.7 (3rd overall)	76.4 (20th among 21 high-income Organisation for Economic Co-operation and Development countries)
Uruguay	79.2 (51st overall)	94.2 (3rd among 104 core SERF countries)
Guyana	63.6 (118th overall)	85.1 (25th among 104 core SERF countries)
Brazil	73.0 (85th overall)	88.1 (15th among 104 core SERF countries)
Kyrgyz Republic	62.2 (125th overall)	93.3 (7th among 104 core SERF countries)
Ireland	91.6 (7th overall)	79.0 (18th among 21 high-income Organisation for Economic Co-operation and Development countries)

Source: U.N. Development Programme, *2013 Human Development Report* statistical tables, http://hdr.undp.org/opendata/, and http://www.SERFindex.org, 2013 Update.

half that score. Malawi, on the other hand, showed steady progress, raising its score from less than 30 percent of the feasible value to over 80 percent. At the same time, Lesotho's score hardly budged over the forty years and remained around 55 percent of the feasible value (see Figure 5.16).

Concluding Remarks

The SERF Index allows us to see much more clearly both general trends and nuanced variations in social and economic rights fulfillment around the world. Looking across time, over the past three decades there has been relatively steady progress in rights realization. However, for many

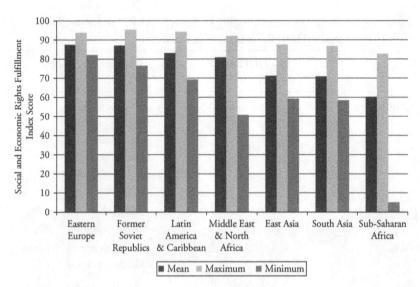

FIGURE 5.15 Social and Economic Rights Fulfillment Index Performance by Region: Best, Worst, and Average

Source: www.SERFIndex.org, Core Countries, 2013 Update.

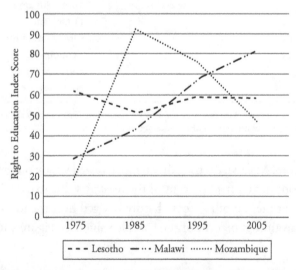

FIGURE 5.16 Countries in the Same Region Perform Very Differently on the Right to Education

Source: Adapted from Randolph and Guyer 2012b, Figure 5.

people in the world, in rich and poor countries alike, rights remain unrealized. These patterns of exclusion and marginalization are strikingly clear when we examine countries in depth, such as the United States and Brazil, as discussed in this chapter. Similarly, overall aggregate trends mask significant variations among rights, and understanding these variations is crucial from a policy perspective. In short, the SERF Index provides a global picture of social and economic rights fulfillment, giving policymakers, advocates and activists, and scholars the ability to analyze and improve the economic and social rights situation in countries and communities around the world.

6

What Matters for Strong Performance?

THE SERF INDEX PROVIDES A new and powerful tool to describe social and economic rights performance globally, but what can we learn from this new lens?* Are democracies more or less likely to fulfill the social and economic rights of their citizens? Do legal guarantees on paper correspond with rights fulfillment in practice? Do countries face trade-offs between growth and social and economic rights fulfillment? These are critical questions as we seek to understand and foster social and economic rights fulfillment around the world.

In this chapter we examine country characteristics associated with strong performance in fulfilling social and economic rights, and characteristics associated with countries that do poorly in fulfilling their rights obligations. Areas of inquiry include governance, democracy and civil rights, legal guarantees, gender equality, social spending, and growth versus rights fulfillment trade-offs.

What Roles Do Governance, Democracy, and Civil Rights Play?

At first glance, a democratic and accountable government, along with robust civil and political rights, would seem to be required for, or at least greatly beneficial to, the fulfillment of social and economic rights. Although the relationship between governance and economic outcomes has been widely researched, there is little empirical work examining the relationship between quality of governance and social and economic rights fulfillment. Addressing this gap is particularly important given that many theorists argue that civil and political rights and social and economic rights are mutually reinforcing and inextricably intertwined (Agbakwa 2002; Howard 1983; Kibwana 1993; Rukooko 2010).[1]

Analysis of the SERF Index shows that there is, in fact, a clear empirical relationship between democratically accountable governance and the fulfillment of social and economic rights. Higher levels of democratic accountability and political freedoms place a "floor" on social and economic rights achievement—all of the poorest performers on the SERF Index are also countries with low levels of democracy, accountability, and political freedom. Although some autocratic countries do relatively well in fulfilling economic and social rights, many fail abysmally. On the other hand, the relationship between social and economic rights and individual civil rights is ambiguous, with no clear connection, and is sensitive to which indicator is used for the comparison.

Background

The majority of research on the relationship between political accountability and economic growth has found a positive association, although debates remain as to whether democracy improves economic performance or whether rising wealth creates the necessary conditions for a functioning democracy (Teorell 2010). Theoretically, a government that is more accountable to its citizens should do a better job of meeting those citizens' needs (UNDP 2002). For example, it has long been argued that democratic accountability and political rights prevent famines and other severe catastrophes (Sen 1999; UNDP 2002). Others contend that inclusive political institutions, which are accountable to more citizens, generate better economic policies, which foster economic growth that is more inclusive and sustainable in the longterm (Acemoglu et al. 2001, 2002). In this vein, many argue that more democratic political systems lead to improved economic performance (Acemoglu et al. 2002, 2008, 2009; Aixalá and Fabro 2009; Engerman and Sokoloff 1994; Rodrik and Wacziarg 2005; Sokoloff and Engerman 2000).

In addition to electoral democracy, other aspects of "good governance," such as voice and accountability, political stability and absence of violence, government effectiveness, regulatory quality, rule of law, and control of corruption, have been found to be correlated with rising income per capita, falling infant mortality, and improvements in literacy rates (Kaufmann and Kraay 2002; Kaufmann et al. 2005; Kaufmann, Kraay, and Zoido-Lobaton 1999). Some researchers have found that this causal relationship flows from governance improvements to better socioeconomic outcomes but not the other way around (Kaufmann and Kraay 2002; Kaufmann et al. 2005).

Others disagree, however, arguing that efforts to strengthen democracy and civil and political rights should come only after economic development is well advanced. In this view, termed the "modernization hypothesis" (Lipset 1959), rising incomes per capita and greater prosperity within a country lead to democracy (Przeworski and Limongi 1993), not the other way around. Adherents of the modernization hypothesis argue that policymakers should focus first on growing economies and raising per capita income; only after wealth is realized should attention be turned to improving governance. Proponents of this "economic development first" view sometimes even argue that there are benefits from autocracy in terms of spurring economic growth, citing examples such as China and Singapore to contend that autocracy can be beneficial for economic growth if the autocrat is the "right" kind of leader (Jones and Olken 2005).

However, foreshadowing our findings here, others argue that while there may be some anomalous instances of fast growth under autocracies, there are also more instances of economic failure (Almeida and Ferreira 2002; Easterly 2011; Rodrik and Wacziarg 2005; Quinn and Woolley 2001). Democracy appears to allow more stable growth because it is more capable of dealing with exogenous shocks (Easterly 2011).

Still others find a mutually reinforcing, "virtuous cycle" of bidirectional causality between governance and growth (Coleman and Lawson-Remer 2013; Persson and Tabellini 2006). And some research has failed to find any relationship at all between governance and growth (Barro 1996; Farr, Lord, and Wolfenbarger 1998; Przeworski and Limongi 1993).

But what about the relationship between discrimination and lack of civil and political rights, on the one hand, and economic development outcomes, on the other? Much research has found that civil and political rights guarantees improve human development outcomes. For example, in South Asia, discrimination against women exacerbates the malnutrition of children and generates radically unequal intrahousehold allocation of food and other resources (UNDP 2002). Similarly, people who do not have birth certificates in some countries are unable to attend schools or use public health clinics, and it is often children from the most marginalized groups or areas who lack birth certificates (UNDP 2002). Still, other research has found that political inclusion is positively related to a range of improved social and economic outcomes, such as declines in infant mortality (Gerring, Thacker, and Alfaro 2012; Kudamatsu 2007). And political inclusion appears to be related to public policies that can lead to social and economic rights fulfillment, such as increases in spending on public education (Brown and Hunter 2004) and health and employment insurance (Box 6.1).

SERF Findings

But what about social and economic rights specifically? Our research finds that social and economic rights fulfillment, as measured by the SERF Index, is positively correlated with democracy, political competition,

---

Box 6.1 Values and Rights

Some analysts argue that civil and political rights are "Western values" and that an insistence on this framework represents a sort of cultural intrusion on other countries, particularly African or Asian countries. These arguments were perhaps most famously made by Singapore's Lee Kuan Yew, who argued for an "Asian Model" that puts a greater emphasis on communal advancement and stability, as opposed to individual rights (Lee 2001). A similar argument has at times been made regarding Africa, where focusing on universal individual rights rather than social and economic improvements and local context has been said to serve the interests of the powerful and to be Western or Eurocentric (Mohan and Holland 2001); others argue that civil and political rights should be adapted to the local context (see, for example, Cobbah 1987 on "African values" and human rights). Opponents of this latter argument insist that human rights are indeed universal values (see, for example, Donnelly 2003, 119–123) and that these types of freedoms are in fact becoming more widely shared, regardless of geographic region (Sen 1999).

government accountability, rule of law, and other aspects of good governance. The relationship is not linear, however. Instead, the range (also called the "variance" in statistical terms) of social and economic rights outcomes decreases as countries realize improvements in democracy, accountability, and political freedom. The correlation between good governance and social and economic rights fulfillment therefore reflects a rising "floor" on social and economic rights performance as governance improves. In other words, while countries with low levels of democracy and accountability can sometimes do very well at fulfilling the social and economic rights of their citizens, they are also much more likely to do very poorly. In contrast, democracies and countries with good governance more generally avoid the worst social and economic rights–related outcomes (see Table 6.1).

The data reveal significant positive correlations between the SERF Index and multiple measures of democracy and political accountability. These include the Polity autocracy and democracy measure (Marshall and Jaggers 2010),[2] which is the most highly correlated with the SERF Index, with a Spearman's rank correlation coefficient of about 0.24 (statistically significant at 5 percent).[3] The World Bank's Worldwide Governance Indicators on "Voice and Accountability" and

TABLE 6.1 Relationship between Social and Economic Rights Fulfillment (SERF) Index Scores and Democracy

Polity Quintile	Average Core SERF Score	Lowest Core SERF Score	Highest Core SERF Score	No. of Countries
Most Autocratic				
1st quintile	71.49	20.22	93.41	17
2nd quintile	61.99	34.75	93.65	17
3rd quintile	71.12	42.51	90.69	24
4th quintile	74.22	52.50	92.15	26
Most Democratic				
5th quintile	80.92	56.06	94.05	13

Note: Democracy/autocracy scores on a scale of –10 to 10. The range in SERF scores within the most autocratic countries is almost double that of the range within the most democratic countries—73 versus 38. The floor on SERF achievement is almost three times higher in the most democratic countries compared with the most autocratic countries—56 versus 20.

Source: Democracy/autocracy scores from Polity 2010 (Marshall and Jaggers). Core SERF Index scores from http://www.SERFindex.org/data, 2011 Update.

"Rule of Law" (2013c) and the scores given by Freedom House (2013) on political rights and civil liberties were also positively correlated with SERF scores.[4]

As noted, however, this positive correlation is driven not by the highest performers but by the worst performers. Figure 6.1 and Table 6.1 demonstrate that as governance improves in country groups arranged by Polity score quintiles, what actually changes is the range of scores. This same pattern is also visible with the other measurements of governance in Figures 6.2 and 6.3. Although there are countries that do quite well at fulfilling social and economic rights obligations regardless of their political systems, better governance guards against extremely poor social and economic rights outcomes. In short, social and economic rights fulfillment varies more under autocracies than in democracies, just as economic growth does: Sen's (1999) hypothesis about democracies being able to avoid the worst catastrophes in social and economic rights outcomes is borne out by the empirical data.

On the other hand, the relationship between social and economic rights and individual civil liberties is ambiguous. Civil liberties such as

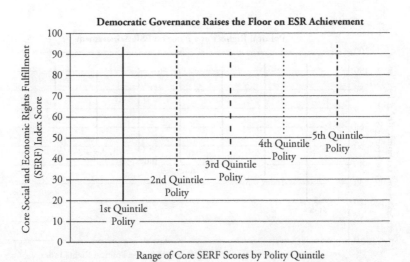

FIGURE 6.1 Relationship between Core Social and Economic Rights Fulfillment (SERF) Index Scores and Polity's Measure of Democracy

Note: Democracy/autocracy scores range on a scale of –10 to 10. The 1st quintile is the most autocratic; the 5th quintile is the most democratic.

Source: Democracy/autocracy scores from Polity 2010 (Marshall and Jaggers) 2010. Core SERF scores from http://www.SERFindex.org/data, 2011 Update.

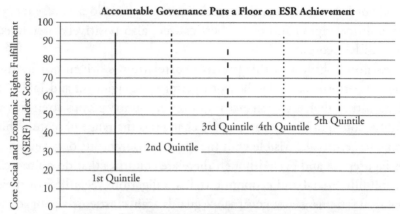

Range of Core SERF Scores by World Bank Voice and Accountability
Index Quintiles

FIGURE 6.2 Relationship between Core Social and Economic Rights Fulfillment Index Scores and the World Bank's Measure of Accountable Governance

Note: Voice and accountability scores range from approximately –2.5 to 2.5 (for our sample, approximately –2 to 1.15). The 1st quintile is the most autocratic; the 5th quintile is the most democratic.

Source: Voice and accountability scores from the World Bank's (2010) Worldwide Governance Indicators. Core SERF scores from http://www.SERFindex.org/data, 2011 Update.

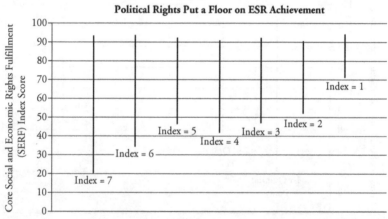

Range of Core SERF Scores by Freedom House Political Rights Index

FIGURE 6.3 Relationship between Core Social and Economic Rights Fulfillment Index Scores and Freedom House's Political Rights Index

Note: Political Rights Index scores range from approximately 1 to 7. Higher scores reflect greater political rights.

Source: Political Rights Index scores from Freedom House (2012). Core SERF scores from http://www. SERFindex.org/data, 2011 Update.

freedom of speech and religion, as measured by Freedom House, are positively correlated with SERF outcomes (Spearman's rank correlation coefficient of 0.25, 1 percent significance). However, the correlation is not robust for comparisons with other measures of civil rights, specifically those from the Cingranelli–Richards (CIRI) Human Rights DataSet (2010).[5] This dataset assigns countries rankings for several different types of rights categories. No clear pattern or relationship is discernible between the rights measured in these indices and social and economic rights fulfillment.[6] Since the Freedom House and CIRI indices are highly correlated with each other (as would be expected), it is not clear whether this different result is caused by some artifice of the indices or scoring choices made by the creators of the indices or perhaps by the different types of rights in each. At best, though, all we can say is that, empirically, the relationship between individual civil rights and social and economic rights fulfillment remains uncertain. As data improve in the area of access to justice and civil and political rights, through, for example, the World Justice Project Rule of Law Index, this is an area for fruitful future research.

Do Legal Commitments to Fulfill Social and Economic Rights Matter?

Many countries have legal guarantees for social and economic rights built into their domestic laws. The majority of countries in the world have also ratified international treaties guaranteeing social and economic rights. However, the extent to which these legally guaranteed rights have a concrete effect on human rights fulfillment on the ground remains a matter of much dispute. Do international treaty commitments actually affect a state's behavior, translating into greater rights enjoyment by citizens? Do domestic legal guarantees protecting a social or economic right increase the likelihood that the right will be fulfilled? Or does causality run in the other direction, with any such legal guarantees merely reflecting, without transforming, existing practices? And, of course, it is possible that such paper rights commitments are just used as "cover" by repressive regimes to whitewash their behavior and avoid real accountability for actually fulfilling the rights of citizens. As legal realists have long acknowledged (Llewellyn 1931; Pound 1910), there is often a gap between the law on the books and the law in action, especially in countries where the tools to enforce laws are weak. If legal protections for human rights are not enforced or upheld, then perhaps human rights work that concentrates on establishing legal commitments on paper is a waste of precious time and energy.

In our analysis, we set out to answer the critical question of whether or not legal guarantees are at all associated with actual social and economic rights fulfillment, at least from a statistical perspective. While our findings should not be interpreted to imply a causal relationship, and should not be applied blindly to any specific country since circumstances differ substantially in every situation, this analysis provides important insight into whether there are any generalizable associations between legal guarantees on paper and rights fulfillment in practice. To sum up our results succinctly, we find no clear relationship between ratification of international treaties and social and economic rights outcomes, but we do find that countries with domestic legal guarantees for social and economic rights protections in their domestic/national laws generally perform better at fulfilling those rights. Correlation does not imply causation, however, since it could be that countries that are already more likely to pursue policies to fulfill social and economic rights are also more likely to enshrine those social contract commitments into law.

Background

Much of the literature addressing the effectiveness of international treaties in changing states' behavior focuses on civil and political rights, not social and economic rights. For example, Landman (2004) and Simmons (2009) find that, for a select set of civil and political rights, treaty ratification is associated with improved rights protections even when controlling for other factors. In contrast, while Keith (1999) found a strong correlation between ratification of the International Covenant on Civil and Political Rights and states' relevant behavior, the association seemed to disappear when controlling for other factors. Other research has even found that although human rights practices of countries that have ratified human rights treaties are generally better than the practices of those that have not, once other related factors are controlled for, treaty ratification is actually associated with weaker rights performance (Hathaway 2002). Hathaway explains this perverse relationship by positing that domestic politics influence the effect of a treaty on a state: democratic countries with poor human rights records may be less likely to ratify a human rights treaty, since there is a greater chance that the government will be held accountable to said treaty. Conversely, states with poor human rights records but fewer democratic institutions may be more likely to ratify, since the chance of enforcement is small (Hathaway 2002, 2007). It should be noted that the model and methods of some of these various studies have been criticized, and the findings, disputed (Goodman and Jinks 2003). Taking a different approach, Smith-Cannoy (2012) argues that governments often ratify human rights treaties insincerely, in response to domestic pressures or to secure international economic assistance, but that once ratified, civil and political rights treaties can surprise oppressive regimes by providing previously powerless individuals a new global venue to challenge patterns of government repression.

Some more recent studies have turned to address the possible impacts of international social and economic rights treaties on state behavior. For example, Boyle and Kim (2009) find that the ratification of children's rights treaties, when controlling for other relevant factors, has no effect on outcomes such as child labor, levels of immunization, and primary and secondary enrollment; however, they find that ratification of the ICESCR positively affects health and education variables. Other research suggests that the effect of social and economic rights treaties on state action depends on country characteristics. For example, ratification of the CRC is correlated with a subsequent increase in child immunization rates in upper-middle- and high-income countries but not in lower-income countries (Gauri 2011). Related work focuses on the domestic political processes that take place between ratification of a treaty and domestic implementation. Case studies of Ecuador, Argentina, and Chile after each ratified the CRC show new legislation or other central government action meant to benefit children (Grugel and Peruzzotti 2012).

Turning to domestic laws, social and economic rights are enshrined in the constitutions and laws of many countries, particularly the rights to health, to an adequate standard of living, and to social security (Vidar 2006). There have been few systematic attempts to quantify the effects of these domestic legal protections, but an important emerging literature is beginning to examine the different consequences of domestic human rights legislation on government policies and priorities. For example, Keith (2011) conducts a series of econometric investigations and finds that human rights provisions in domestic legal frameworks can constrain state repression, even when controlling for other factors. Approaching the question from a different perspective, Sikkink (2011) analyzes the impacts of using legal prosecutions to hold political leaders criminally accountable for human rights violations, arguing that this litigation is generating a "justice cascade" (improving democracy and reducing repression) by affecting the behavior of political leaders worldwide.

Some case studies similarly attribute state policies to the existence of legally recognized social and economic rights. One example is found in Malawi, which guaranteed education, health services, food, and employment and included human rights–based language in poverty-reduction strategies and other development documents following the first multiparty elections in 1994 (Banik 2010). While litigation on social and economic rights in Malawi has been limited, members of the government claim that legal guarantees have had an impact on issues related to employment and wages and to education (Banik 2010). However, it should also be noted that the same case study argues that pressure from outside donors forced a human rights–based approach to development on Malawian elites, which may not be best for the country (Banik 2010).

The research also suggests that the efficacy of legal guarantees and legal strategies for social and economic rights fulfillment fundamentally depends on context—while in many circumstances legal engagement is positive, litigation and other legal approaches also sometimes have perverse effects. For example, when judicial decisions will have broad applicability, legal strategies tend to serve the interests of the poor, while judicial domains characterized by individualized effects are significantly less likely to have pro-poor outcomes (Brinks and Gauri 2012). Studies suggest that legal strategies have been pro-poor in India but distribution-neutral in Indonesia and Brazil and sharply anti-poor in Nigeria (Brinks and Gauri 2012). In terms of health rights specifically, case studies reveal that litigation has had a nuanced and

Box 6.2 India: Legally Guaranteed Rights and Subpar Outcomes

India is often studied regarding legally guaranteed social and economic rights, particularly the right to food (Drèze 2004; Gaiha 2003; Hertel forthcoming; Hertel and Randolph 2015; Vidar 2006). It has been argued that the right to food has the potential to provide governments with an imperative to support poverty-alleviation programs, and in India a 2001 Supreme Court decision that upheld the right to food did in fact order action by both state and federal governments to alleviate hunger. Drèze (2004) explains that one of the directives of the Indian Supreme Court in 2001 was that the state governments had to provide midday meals for schoolchildren. Within a few years India's midday meal program became the largest public nutrition program in the world—certainly a concrete result. Drèze (2004) also mentions concrete benefits of the right to information, attributes a rapid expansion of schooling in India in the 1990s partially to the widespread acceptance of the right of every child to an education, and cites the lack of acceptance of a right to healthcare as contributing to insufficient state action in that arena. However, the right to food is nowhere near realization in India. India's right to food SERF score of 33 percent is worse than those of all but five of the 127 countries for which a SERF right to food was calculated. On education, the story is better, at least comparatively; India's right to education SERF score of 86 percent is just about at the median. Its overall SERF score, however, is lower than that of 80 percent of the countries for which the SERF was calculated. These poor outcomes do not mean that legally guaranteeing rights definitely did not generate specific concrete state actions to promote rights fulfillment. It is very possible that the guarantee of these rights has had positive yet insufficient effects. However, it is clear that despite the constitutional guarantees, India is not fulfilling the social and economic rights of its citizenry to the maximum of its available resources.

varied impact on health equity, with very different implications for systemic change and varying winners and losers in different countries (Yamin and Gloppen 2011). One example of these nuanced effects is evident in India (see Box 6.2), where the constitution contains a right to life and a duty of the state to improve nutrition and public health. The Indian Supreme Court formally recognized the right to food in 2001, and in 2013 the government passed major legislation on this issue, the National Food Security Bill. Yet enjoyment of the right to food continues to fall short for large segments of the Indian population. The South African constitution, considered to be a "model" for guaranteeing universal human rights, contains a justiciable right to food and other social and economic rights. However, there have been major shortcomings in implementation, with significant segments of the South African population still food insecure (Fukuda-Parr and Greenstein 2012; Koch 2011). Beyond their questionable effectiveness, some researchers even argue that justiciable social and economic rights can have deleterious effects by giving courts the power to reallocate, perhaps inefficiently, limited state resources (Ferraz 2011). Clearly, whether a legally guaranteed social or economic right has the desired effect remains controversial.

SERF Findings

We find a statistical association between domestic legal guarantees of rights and fulfillment of those rights obligations, but no evidence of a relationship between international treaty ratification and fulfillment of social and economic rights. Looking first at domestic law, countries that have a legally justiciable guaranteed right tend to do a better job of fulfilling that right. For example, countries that give a legal status to the right to health perform better on the right to health SERF score. The same pattern holds for the rights to work, education, and housing. In every case, the average SERF score for a right is higher in countries that have legally guaranteed that right, and in every case except the right to food, the difference is statistically significant (see Figure 6.4 and Table 6.2). In addition, countries that have incorporated the ICESCR into domestic law also on average perform better on the aggregate SERF Index, and the difference is statistically significant (see again Figure 6.4 and Table 6.2).

Countries' domestic legal guarantees of economic and social rights were measured using ratings from the Toronto Initiative for Economic and Social Rights (Jung 2010), which assigns a score to each country based on whether a particular right is constitutionally enshrined and whether citizens have legal recourse concerning its fulfillment.[7] Statistical association was analyzed using a Wilcoxon rank-sum test, a nonparametric test to measure whether the distribution of a variable in one group (in this case, countries with a legally guaranteed right)

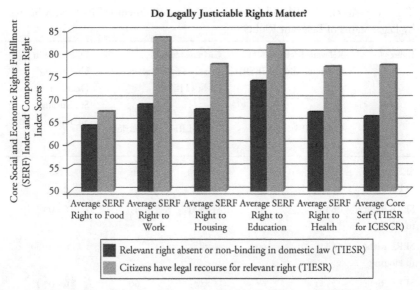

FIGURE 6.4   Average Social and Economic Rights Fulfillment (SERF) Index Scores by Legal Status of Relevant Rights

Source: Relevant rights classification from the Toronto Initiative for Economic and Social Rights (TIESR) (Jung 2010). Core SERF scores from http://www.SERFindex.org/data, 2011 Update.

tends to be higher than the distribution of that variable for a second group (countries without such guarantees). It should be reiterated that these results indicate a correlation, not necessarily a causal relationship. It is possible that legally guaranteed rights do lead to actions and policies by the state that improve the fulfillment of social and economic rights, but it is equally plausible that the same countries that would be more likely to implement policies to fulfill social and economic rights would also be more apt to adopt legal guarantees of these rights.

Table 6.3 further illustrates the strong association between legal rights guarantees and social and economic rights fulfillment. Countries that have a legally justiciable right to health are overrepresented in the upper quintile of good SERF health scores. Almost half of the countries with this legally justiciable right are in the top two quintiles in the entire sample. And very few of these countries perform poorly, as they are extremely underrepresented in the bottom quintile of the sample.

TABLE 6.2 Average Social and Economic Rights Fulfillment (SERF) Index Scores by Legal Status of Relevant Rights

Index	Relevant Right Absent or Nonbinding (TIESR)		Citizens Have Legal Recourse for Relevant Right (TIESR)		Difference in Underlying Distributions Statistically Significant?
	Average Core SERF Score	No. of Countries	Average Core SERF Score	No. of Countries	
SERF Right to Food	64.47	99	67.59	16	No
SERF Right to Work	69.38	67	84.23	43	Yes (1%)
SERF Right to Housing	68.13	90	78.12	30	Yes (10%)
SERF Right to Education	74.32	61	82.33	60	Yes (1%)
SERF Right to Health	67.67	67	77.79	49	Yes (1%)
Core SERF (TIESR for the ICESCR)	66.58	56	78.07	38	Yes (1%)

Note: TIESR =Toronto Initiative for Economic and Social Rights. Statistical significance measured using the Wilcoxon rank-sum test.

Source: Relevant rights classification from the Toronto Initiative for Economic and Social (Jung 2010). Core SERF scores from http://www.SERFindex.org/data, 2011 Update.

Turning now to the relationship between international treaty obligations and SERF performance, the data do not indicate a correlation between international legal guarantees and rights outcomes on the ground. Almost all of the countries in the sample have ratified all three of the relevant economic and social rights treaties, so it is not possible to make a meaningful comparison based on a simple bivariate "ratified or not" metric.[8] However, years since ratification can potentially serve as a useful proxy for countries' commitments to these treaties. At first glance it appears that there is a positive and statistically significant correlation between years since ICESCR ratification and SERF scores

TABLE 6.3 Legal Right to Health and Social and Economic Rights Fulfillment (SERF) Index Right to Health Score

SERF Right to Health Quintile	Countries with a Legally Justiciable Right to Health	
	No. of Countries	%
Top	13	27
4th	10	20
3rd	14	29
2nd	8	16
Bottom	4	8
Total	49	

Source: Relevant rights classification from the Toronto Initiative for Economic and Social Rights (Jung 2010). Core SERF scores from http://www.SERFindex.org/data, 2011 Update.

(Spearman's rank coefficient 0.22, statistically significant at 5 percent), but the relationship is highly nonlinear, suggesting that other historical and political factors are the main drivers of the relationship. And there is no relationship whatsoever between SERF performance and years since ratification of CEDAW or CRC.[9] It would of course be preferable to examine whether countries' improved their social and economic rights outcomes after ratifying relevant treaties; data limitations make this a difficult question to study, but it could be a fruitful line of future inquiry. In short, our analysis does not indicate that international treaty ratification matters for social and economic rights outcomes, but our analysis is constrained by lack of sufficiently nuanced data.

Does Gender Equality Matter?

What is the relationship between gender inequality and social and economic rights fulfillment? A careful look at the data reveals that societies with greater gender equality achieve higher fulfillment of social and economic rights for all members.

Improving gender equality is in itself a goal with clear, intrinsic value. However, there has also been significant research regarding relationships between gender equality and other development outcomes, including economic growth. It is possible, for example, that increasing girls' access to education may have a different effect on a society than increasing educational access for boys only. Similarly, increased economic opportunities and political representation for women can have ripple effects on fertility, savings rates, child mortality, and socioeconomic outcomes for the next generation. Gender equality is also directly relevant to the fulfillment of social and economic rights: a country that allows more of its members to have access to basic rights such as education, and that empowers its members to make decisions affecting themselves and their families, is already fulfilling rights obligations for more of its citizens.

Background

The effect of gender equality on economic growth has been the subject of a great deal of empirical research, focusing mostly on educational inequality and to a lesser extent on labor force participation. One common theoretical argument is that reducing gender inequality leads to growth through the channels of human capital and fertility rates. In this view, improving access to education for women increases the level of human capital in a society, and, conversely, barriers to female education reduce a society's human capital. Likewise, improving gender equity can lower fertility rates (Mason 2001), generating a positive effect on per capita income and other development outcomes by spurring a demographic transition from households with many children to households with fewer, allowing economic growth to outpace population growth (Galor and Weil 1996). While some research has not found a positive relationship between female education and growth (Barro and Lee 1994), many studies do find a negative effect on growth from gender inequality in education or a stronger effect on growth from female than from male educational attainment (Dollar and Gatti 1999; Forbes 2000; Klasen and Lamanna 2009; Knowles et al. 2002).

The effects of labor market inequality are more controversial. Some research finds a negative effect on growth from labor force participation inequality or wage discrimination (Klasen and Lamanna 2009). However, other research suggests that inequality in pay for women can have positive effects on economic growth (Blecker and Seguino 2002), with low wages for women leading to lower-cost exports and the attraction of foreign investment. Gender inequality in labor markets may also affect growth through the effect of women's relative income on the total savings rate (Seguino and Floro 2003).

The relationship between gender inequality and economic growth is likely not unidirectional. Gender inequality appears to decrease with per capita income (Dollar and Gatti 1999). An increase in women's labor force participation associated with growth, a recent finding, can be interpreted causally in either direction, as economic growth may draw more women into the workplace (Klasen and Lamanna 2009). Recent research also indicates that women may be disproportionally hurt by global economic downturns: in developing countries, where women are concentrated in export manufacturing and tourism, job losses for women may be greater than for men when these industries collapse (Seguino 2009).

Of course, economic growth is not the only development goal— and also not the only one that correlates with gender equality. A substantial body of research suggests that gender equality and the achievement of other development goals are inseparable. Higher levels of female education and literacy have also been found to reduce child mortality (Anyanwu and Erhijakpor 2007; Caldwell 1994; Filmer and Pritchett 1997; Hill and King 1995) and improve educational attainment for the next generation (Hill and King 1995; Thomas, Schoeni, and Strauss 1996), though not all research agrees on this point (Behrman and Rosenzweig 2002). Other research suggests that female education can have an effect on age of fertility in the next generation (Breierova and Duflo 2003) and that having women in political leadership positions increases schooling for girls (Beaman et al. 2012). The U.N. Development Programme (2011) also points to a correlation between gender inequality and human development, finding that low-HDI countries in general perform much more poorly on gender inequality measurements than do high-HDI countries.

SERF Findings

There is a clearly observable and statistically significant correlation between gender equality and social and economic rights fulfillment. To test the relationship between the SERF Index scores and gender equity, two measurements of gender equality were compared with SERF Index outcomes: Social Watch's Gender Equity Index (GEI)[10] and the UNDP's Gender Inequality Index (GII).[11] The GEI is an annual ranking that assigns a gender equality score to each country and region, with a higher score reflecting greater gender equality. The GEI takes into account three vectors of equality between men and women: education equality, economic equality, and political empowerment. The GII focuses on three dimensions of inequality—reproductive health, empowerment, and the labor market—with a higher score indicating greater gender inequality.

Both of these gender equity indices are highly correlated with the SERF Index. The GEI and the SERF have a Spearman's correlation coefficient greater than 0.5, while the negative correlation between the SERF and the GII is even stronger, with a Spearman's correlation coefficient of –0.7 (both significant at less than 1 percent). In short, there is a clear correlation between gender equality and social and economic rights fulfillment. Figure 6.5 illustrates the relationship between the SERF Index and the GEI for a sample of ninety-three countries, and Figure 6.6 illustrates the relationship between the SERF Index and the GII for eighty-four countries.

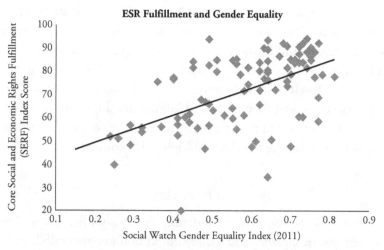

FIGURE 6.5 Social and Economic Rights Fulfillment and Gender Equality

Source: Gender Equality Index from Social Watch (2011). Core SERF scores from http://www.SERFindex. org/data, 2011 Update.

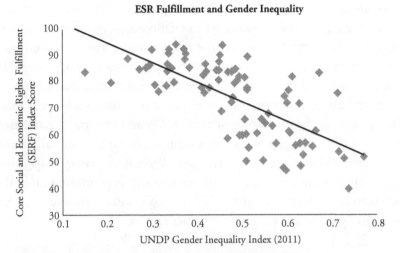

FIGURE 6.6 Social and Economic Rights Fulfillment and Gender Inequality
Source: Gender Inequality Index from U.N. Development Programme 2011. Core SERF scores from http://www.SERFindex.org/data, 2011 Update.

It should not be a surprise that gender equity correlates more closely with SERF scores than any other factor tested. In a sense, improved gender equality must necessarily be associated with the fulfillment of social and economic rights: a society that excludes half of its population cannot possibly be said to be fulfilling the rights of all of its members. Moreover, previous research suggests that increased gender inclusion may also affect the fulfillment of social and economic rights indirectly through other channels. A causal relationship cannot be identified, but the correlation is clear. Societies that are more equal in terms of gender opportunities do a better job of fulfilling the social and economic rights of all their members.

Are High Government Expenditures Necessary to Ensure Social and Economic Rights?

At first glance it seems obvious that the amount a government spends on public goods such as health and education should be an important factor in determining SERF outcomes. After all, shouldn't a country that devotes more resources toward, for example, doctors and vaccines than another country at a similar income level realize better health results for its citizens? Examining this relationship carefully for the right to health, however, reveals that the relationship between expenditures and outcomes is far more attenuated than policymakers might hope. By some measures, there is indeed a correlation between levels of expenditures and SERF Index performance, but it is at best weak—and other factors such as the prevalence of HIV/AIDS and malaria, the effectiveness of service delivery, and government accountability are often more significant. When such factors are controlled for, the effect of spending is mitigated or disappears. In short, government expenditures on health do correlate with health rights fulfillment, but this positive relationship is relatively weak and swamped by other factors.

Background

The effect of public expenditures on health outcomes has been widely studied. Several studies have found a positive effect of public health spending or services provided by more extensive welfare states on health outcomes in developed nations (Brady 2005; Chung and Muntaner 2007; Conley and Springer 2001; Kim and Jennings 2009). However, other work extending this analysis to different parts of the world has produced more ambiguous results (Karim, Eikemo, and Bambra 2010). In short, the literature directly assessing the effect of public health spending in developing countries has not been conclusive. In one well-known article, Filmer and Pritchett (1997) find virtually no effect of public health spending on child mortality, instead arguing that other factors such as GDP per capita, income distribution, female education, and culture are the primary determinants of health outcomes. The authors suggest that these factors influence the efficacy of public health policy, which varies greatly across countries. A body of research likewise argues that local and domestic context, delivery systems, and the efficacy of government interventions matter most for health outcomes (Ablo and Reinikka 1998; Lindelow 2006). Other studies in developing countries, though, have indeed found a positive effect from health and education spending on outcomes (Gupta et al. 2002) and a high correlation between public health spending and improvements in child or infant mortality in low- and middle-income countries generally

(Anand and Ravallion 1993); between education and health spending and outcomes in Africa (Anyanwu and Erhijakpor 2007); and between specific interventions, such as bed nets, and relevant health improvements (Demombynes and Trommlerová 2012). Some research finds a positive effect of government health expenditure, not only on health but on growth as well, in Africa and Latin America in the 1980s and 1990s (Fan and Rao 2003).

In the developing world, and sub-Saharan Africa in particular, the burden of HIV/AIDS and malaria must be taken into account when analyzing the impact and efficacy of health expenditures. The global cost of effectively treating and controlling these diseases in developing countries has been estimated at several billion dollars annually—amounts far outside the reach of developing country budgets (see, e.g., Bertozzi et al. 2004 on HIV; and Teklehaimanot, McCord, and Sachs 2007 on malaria). In addition to the direct impact on health, these disease burdens tend to degrade human capital and thus are likely to have an effect on broader economic outcomes (Dixon, McDonald, and Roberts 2002; Gallup and Sachs 2001). Further, a high prevalence of HIV and malaria may strain public health systems or draw money away from other needed health services. For example, Easterly (2006) has argued that international aid dollars spent on AIDS could save many more lives if directed toward diarrhea or measles. These types of trade-offs clearly exist on the national level as well. Although interventions targeting both diseases often attract foreign aid, the vast majority of public health spending in developing countries is from domestic governments themselves (Kenny and Sumner 2011). Empirically, HIV prevalence rates have a positive correlation with domestic health spending per capita (Youde 2010), since treating HIV can be more costly than many other types of ailments (Hansen et al. 2000). In sub-Saharan Africa, where HIV/AIDS rates are high, a significantly larger proportion of health spending is HIV/AIDS related than in other low- and middle-income countries (Amico, Aran, and Avila 2010)—Zambia and Uganda are spending more than 40 percent of their health budgets on HIV/AIDS, and Lesotho and Kenya are both spending more than 60 percent (Amico et al. 2010).

SERF Findings

So what is the relationship between government expenditures and social and economic rights outcomes? Here we look carefully at health expenditures and right to health fulfillment.

In attempts to assess the impact of public health spending on health outcomes, researchers generally use either public health spending per capita (see Anand and Ravallion 1993; Anyanwu and Erhijakpor 2007) or public health spending as a share of GDP (see Filmer and Pritchett 1997) as the independent variable. Public spending per capita is an absolute measure that tends to be correlated with GDP per capita itself, while public spending as a share of GDP, like the SERF Index, measures a government's actions relative to the country's resources. We test the relationship between both variables and the SERF right to health outcomes here (see Box 6.3).

The results are not promising for those who think that greater spending alone will make a society healthier. Cross-country regressions do not show a statistically significant relationship between public health spending per capita and the SERF right to health score. And when controlling for disease burden (HIV and malaria), the already statistically insignificant expenditure coefficient shrinks even further. In fact, the relationship between disease burden and SERF health outcomes is strongly negative, while there is no significant relationship between spending and health. And while there is a strong correlation between

---

Box 6.3 High Spending, Poor Result

Botswana, Burundi, Djibouti, and Lesotho are in the bottom quartile of SERF health scores yet in the top quartile of public health spending as a percent of GDP. For example, Botswana spent more than 8 percent of its GDP on health, more than all but two countries in our 133-country sample. However, it also had the second-highest HIV prevalence of the group, second only to Swaziland, and its right to health score is in the bottom quartile. Turning to expenditure per capita, Equatorial Guinea has the second-highest government health spending per capita and the lowest right to health score among the countries for which data are available. It also has a 5 percent HIV prevalence rate and a malaria death rate of 150 per 100,000, among the highest in the sample.

public health expenditure as a percent of GDP and the SERF right to health score (0.54, significant at less than 1 percent), other factors, particularly the prevalence of HIV/AIDS and malaria, actually correlate more closely with SERF right to health scores. However, these findings represent only a cross-section of countries at a given point in time and could be explained by any number of invisible, country-specific factors. It is quite possible that increasing or decreasing health spending in a country could improve or undermine that country's health outcomes over time, but such changes within countries over the course of years or decades cannot be tested here with a simple cross-section of countries.

Table 6.4 shows regression results for expenditure per capita, where numbers for each variable are coefficients indicating the effect of independent variable change (for example, HIV prevalence) on the mean of the distribution of the independent variable—the SERF right to health score—when all other dependent variables are unchanged. The "R-squared" is the proportion of the variability of the dependent variable that is explained in that regression. A graphical depiction of the relationship (see Figure 6.7) indicates that there is a wide dispersion in SERF outcomes for countries at low levels of public health spending per capita, and any positive relationship that does exist is largely driven by a few high-spending outliers.

Table 6.5 shows positive and statistically significant relationships among the SERF right to health score and public health spending as a share of GDP, HIV prevalence, malaria deaths per one hundred thousand people, and rural population.[12] The size and statistical significance of the coefficient on public health spending fluctuates depending on the control variables included. Whenever both diseases were controlled for, expenditure loses its statistical significance and has a much smaller coefficient (see Figures 6.7 and 6.8).

We can further illustrate the relationship among public health spending, disease burden, and the fulfillment of the right to health by calculating the median health spending and SERF right to health scores for our sample. We then place each country for which data are available into one of four categories: above median in both categories, above-median right to health and below-median spending, below-median right to health and above-median spending, and below median on both. Countries that spend large amounts for low right

Table 6.4 Public Expenditure Per Capita and Health Right Outcomes

Variable	(1)	(2)	(3)	(4)	(5)	(6)	(7)	(8)	(9)	(10)	(11)	(12)
	Dependent Variable: 2011 Social and Economic Rights Fulfillment (SERF) Health											
Public health expenditure per capita	0.0181 (0.0142)					0.0172 (0.0185)	-0.00371 (0.0212)	-0.00676 (0.0116)	-0.00212 (0.0175)	-0.00709 (0.00709)		
HIV		1.516*** (0.219)				-2.102 (1.437)	-0.887* (0.461)	-1.170 (0.753)	-0.857 (0.671)	-1.168 (0.826)	0.980*** (0.211)	1.106*** (0.231)
Rural population			0.339*** (0.0675)				-0.0545 (0.0987)	0.0146 (0.118)				
Population at risk of malaria				30.02*** (2.816)				39.56*** (5.979)		39.31*** (5.206)		29.88*** (3.030)
Malaria death rate					0.246*** (0.0239)		0.271*** (0.0400)		0.275*** (0.0423)		0.262*** (0.0192)	
Constant	64.25 (3.115)	75.32 (1.919)	89.33 (3.224)	83.71 (1.439)	78.32 (1.705)	67.56 (4.700)	83.37 (7.656)	91.82 (7.979)	80.26 (3.684)	92.51 (2.738)	81.95 (1.346)	87.00 (0.804)
Observations	64	108	131	116	91	49	41	45	41	45	79	104
Adjusted R^2	0.0471	0.1533	0.1644	0.5012	0.5308	0.1320	0.6959	0.6696	0.7018	0.6775	0.7085	0.6539

Note: "Population at risk of fatal malaria" estimates the percentage of the population at risk of contracting falciparum malaria, the most fatal species of malaria, in a country. Bootstrapped standard errors in parentheses; *** $p < .01$, * $p < .1$.

Source: Public expenditure on health per capita (PPP int. $) (2010) from the World Health Organization. HIV prevalence ages 15–49 (2009), malaria death rate per 100,000 (2008), and rural population as a percentage of total population (2009) all from World Development Indicators. Sachs Malaria Data Set (Sachs 2003). Core SERF scores from http://www.SERFindex.org/data, 2011 Update.

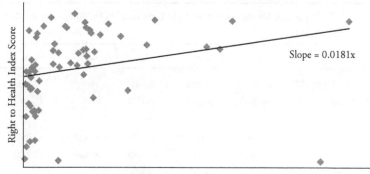

Simple Correlation between SERF Right to Health and Per Capita Government Health Expenditure

Slope = 0.0181x

Right to Health Index Score

Public Health Expenditure Per Capita

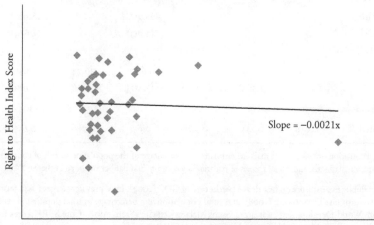

Partial Correlation between SERF Right to Health and Public Health Expenditure, controlled for Disease Burden

Slope = −0.0021x

Right to Health Index Score

Public Health Expenditure Per Capita

FIGURE 6.7 Change in Correlation between Right to Health and Public Health Expenditure Per Capita When Controlling for Disease Burden (Controlled for HIV Prevalence and Malaria Deaths per 100,000)

Source: Public expenditure on health per capita (2009), HIV prevalence ages 15–49 (2009), and malaria death rate per 100,000 (2008) from World Development Indicators. Core SERF scores from http://www. SERFindex.org/data, 2011 Update.

to health scores tend to have a large disease burden. This relationship holds true for either measure of public health spending, as depicted in Tables 6.6 and 6.7. The logic of this observed relationship is hard to ignore: high disease burden is both expensive and damaging to health results and may absorb or otherwise mitigate the positive effects of increased public spending on health outcomes. The relationship is

TABLE 6.5 Public Expenditure as a Percentage of Gross Domestic Product (GDP) and Health Right Outcomes

Variable	Dependent Variable: 2011 Social and Economic Rights Fulfillment (SERF) Health					
	(1)	(2)	(3)	(4)	(5)	(6)
Public expenditure as % GDP	2.077***	3.082***	0.704	0.645	0.762	0.738
	(0.711)	(0.705)	(0.944)	(0.588)	(0.807)	(0.495)
HIV		−1.703***	−1.042***	−1.133***	−1.053***	−1.166***
		(0.367)	(0.239)	(0.229)	(0.196)	(0.252)
Rural population			−0.0212	−0.0425		
			(0.0644)	(0.0583)		
Malaria death rate			−0.256***		−0.258***	
			(0.0203)		(0.0201)	
Population at risk of malaria				−28.25***		−28.92***
				(2.913)		(2.684)
Constant	65.26	65.56	80.96	86.37	79.74	84.31
	(2.805)	(2.562)	(3.274)	(3.412)	(2.706)	(2.100)
Observations	131	108	79	104	79	104
Adjusted R^2	0.038	0.233	0.705	0.653	0.708	0.655

Note: "Population at risk of fatal malaria" estimates the percentage of the population at risk of contracting falciparum malaria, the most fatal species of malaria, in a country. Standard errors in parentheses; *** $p<.01$.

Source: Public expenditure on health as a percentage of GDP (2009), HIV prevalence ages 15–49 (2009), malaria death rate per 100,000 (2008), and rural population as a percentage of total population (2009) all from World Development Indicators. Sachs Malaria DataSet (Sachs 2003). Core SERF scores from http://www.SERFindex.org/data, 2011 Update.

most striking in the case of HIV prevalence. The difference in malaria death rates between countries spending above median and achieving good results and those spending above median and underachieving is again stark. Countries with larger disease burdens have much greater difficulty fulfilling the right to health for their citizens with a similar, or even larger, amount of public resources.

There are, of course, countries with high health budgets, which indeed performed very well on the right to health SERF. Cuba, for example, had the highest health expenditure per capita in our

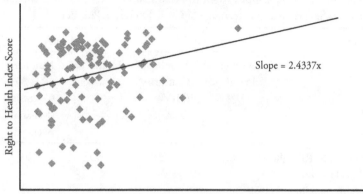

Simple Correlation between SERF Right to Health and Public Health Expenditure

Slope = 2.4337x

Right to Health Index Score

Public Health Expenditure (% GDP)

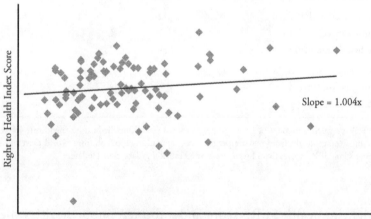

Partial Correlation between SERF Right to Health and Public Health Expenditure, controlled for Disease Burden

Slope = 1.004x

Right to Health Index Score

Public Health Expenditure (% GDP)

FIGURE 6.8 Change in Correlation between Right to Health and Public Health Expenditure as a Percentage of Gross Domestic Product When Controlling for Disease Burden (Controlled for HIV Prevalence and Malaria Deaths per 100,000)

Source: Public expenditure on health per capita (2009), HIV prevalence ages 15–49 (2009), and malaria death rate per 100,000 (2008) from World Bank (2012). Core SERF scores from http://www.SERFindex.org/data, 2011.

sample and also performed very well on the health SERF, obtaining the third-highest score. Costa Rica, number two on the list of health SERF scores, is also among the highest health spenders, with about 7 percent of its GDP spent on health in 2009. Singapore has a top

TABLE 6.6 Disease Burden by Above- or Below-Median Social and Economic Rights Fulfillment (SERF) Index Right to Health and Above- or Below-Median Public Health Spending as a Percentage of Gross Domestic Product

SERF Score	HIV		Malaria	
	Average Prevalence	Number of Countries (HIV Averages)	Deaths per 100,000	Number of Countries (Malaria Averages)
Above-median SERF right to health, below-median public health spending	0.35	25	0.22	23
Above-median SERF right to health, above-median public health spending	0.46	30	0.00	11
Below-median SERF right to health, above-median public health spending	7.92	20	62.54	24
Below-median SERF right to health, below-median public health spending	2.17	33	69.58	33

Source: HIV prevalence total (% of population ages 15–49) (2009), public health expenditure (%GDP) (2009), and average deaths from malaria per 100,000 population (2008) all from World Development Indicators. Core SERF scores from http://www.SERFindex.org/data, 2011 Update.

ten right to health SERF score and a top ten public health expenditure per capita. However, there exist perhaps an equal number of countries that do well without such spending. Paraguay, the recipient of a top ten SERF right to health score, spent $110 per capita on health: less than about half of the countries in the sample and well below the average. Vietnam, the recipient of the highest SERF right to health score, spent only 2.8 percent of its GDP on health in 2009, well below average for the sample. The ultimate conclusion is that while a high level of public health spending certainly can be associated with fulfillment of the right to health, it is neither necessary nor sufficient, as health outcomes also depend on a variety of other factors.

TABLE 6.7 Disease Burden by Above- or Below-Median Social and Economic Rights Fulfillment (SERF) Index Right to Health and Above- or Below-Median Public Health Spending Per Capita

SERF Score	HIV		Malaria	
	Average Prevalence	Number of Countries (HIV Averages)	Deaths per 100,000	Number of Countries (Malaria Averages)
Above-median SERF right to health, below-median public health spending	0.22	25	0.50	23
Above-median SERF right to health, above-median public health spending	1.16	6	2.45	11
Below-median SERF right to health, above-median public health spending	5.23	6	50.29	6
Below-median SERF right to health, below-median public health spending	2.13	19	83.24	25

Source: HIV prevalence total (% of population ages 15–49)(2009) and average deaths from malaria per 100,000 population (2008) from World Development Indicators. Per capita government expenditure on health (PPP int. $) (2010) from the World Health Organization, 2010. Core SERF scores from http://www.SERFindex.org/data, 2011 Update.

Does Attention to Social and Economic Rights Impede Economic Growth?

Countries face trade-offs in resource allocation.[13] A key question is whether countries that devote more resources to fulfilling their commitments under the ICESCR and accordingly perform better on the SERF Index and component right indices endure slower growth as a result, thereby reducing the resources available to further social and economic rights enjoyment in the future. That is, do countries face a trade-off between fulfilling social and economic rights today and promoting per capita income growth to enable higher social and economic rights attainment tomorrow? Our analysis reveals that there is no necessary trade-off. Quite the contrary, fulfilling social and economic rights and economic growth can be synergistic; countries with policies and institutions promoting social and economic rights tend to enjoy a virtuous cycle in which social and economic rights promote growth and growth promotes the further extension of social and economic rights.

Background

There are reasons to suspect that the allocation of resources, as well as the policies and institutions, that best secure social and economic rights in the short term may differ from those best supporting per capita income growth. Economic theory and empirical evidence suggest capital investment and technological change as key forces for growth (see, for example, Aghion and Howitt 1998; Domar 1946; Easterly and Levine 2003; Grossman and Helpman 1991; Levine and Renelt 1992; Romer 1990; Solow 1956, 1957). Neither the levels of capital investment nor the kinds of capital investment that are frequently advocated to promote per capita income growth are likely to simultaneously optimally promote current enjoyment of social and economic rights. Investments promoting small-scale, geographically dispersed, labor-intensive industry tend to foster the expansion of social and economic rights enjoyment, whereas investments fostering large-scale, capital-intensive industry and supportive infrastructure (export processing zones, ports, highways linking major cities, etc.) are often the quickest route to per capita income growth. Policies attracting foreign capital inflows, such as capital account liberalization, augment domestic savings; these effects promote growth but tend to concentrate income and do not directly further the expansion of social and economic rights enjoyment. Further, devoting the "maximum of available resources" to expand the enjoyment of economic and social rights may entail reducing current investment so as to augment current consumption.

Similarly, many of the policies and institutional arrangements thought to foster technological change are not those that best support the expansion of social and economic rights. Ensuring universal primary and secondary education and providing financing to facilitate investments and innovations by small-scale producers are likely to extend the enjoyment of social and economic rights more rapidly than educational policies targeted to develop a cadre of highly trained technical experts skilled at adapting foreign technologies and developing new technologies, yet the latter are more likely to rapidly promote technological change (Vandenbussche, Aghion, and Meghir 2006). Foreign direct investment and trade are channels for technological change, and their potential to accelerate growth is well documented (Borensztein, De Gregorio, and Lee 1998; Dollar 1992), yet in many contexts, and particularly when a country's comparative advantage lies in natural resources, trade liberalization and the policies used to attract foreign direct investment can undermine social and economic rights (Deva 2003; Lawson-Remer 2012; U.N. CESCR 1989).

On the other hand, the available evidence documents channels through which the extension of social and economic rights directly fosters economic growth, setting up a virtuous cycle. An abundance of empirical studies document the direct positive impact of improvements in the general level of health and education on growth (see, for example, Bloom, Canning, and Sevilla 2004; Krueger and Lindahl 2001; Weil 2007). Several empirical studies find that investments in primary education and basic health are critical to growth (Behrman 1993; Sala-i-Martin, Doppelhofer, and Miller 2004), perhaps because they foster the ability to exploit the new opportunities that arise in the course of growth (Schultz 1975). The available evidence also indicates the effectiveness of other policies supporting economic growth, such as trade liberalization and the adoption of improved technologies, tend to increase with the level of health and education enjoyed (see, for example, Miller and Upadhyay 2000 regarding trade; and Wozniak 1984, 1987, regarding technology). Furthermore, the new conventional wisdom is that equity facilitates rather than impedes economic growth (Aghion et al. 1999; Perry et al. 2006, chap. 1). Some evidence to date suggests that the expansion of social and economic rights need not impede growth—it is possible to craft policy regimes that simultaneously enhance growth and the expansion of social and economic rights enjoyment—and in fact, there is evidence to suggest that rather than imposing an obstacle to growth, the expansion of social and economic rights can serve as a handmaiden to growth (Ranis et al. 2000).

SERF Findings

In order to learn whether countries face a trade-off between fulfilling their social and economic rights in the future and fulfilling them today, we adapt the Ranis et al. (2000) methodology. Beyond enabling a comparable test of whether their results can be generalized, this methodology does not require us to impose a specific functional relationship between social and economic rights fulfillment and economic growth. Our goal here is to learn whether there tends to be synergy between social and economic rights fulfillment and economic growth, not whether a specific linear or nonlinear relationship exists between them.

We begin by dividing countries into two groups—those with scores above versus those with scores below the median—along each of two dimensions—their per capita income growth rate over the decade of the 1990s and their SERF Index score in 1995 (using the SERF Index Trend Data)—and classifying them according to whether they are

- In the vicious quadrant, with below-median per capita income growth and a SERF Index score below the median;
- In the virtuous quadrant, with above-median per capita income growth and a SERF Index score above the median;
- In the growth-lopsided quadrant, with above-median per capita income growth but a SERF Index score that is below the median; or
- In the SERF-lopsided quadrant, with a SERF Index score that is above the median but below-median per capita income growth.

We classify countries in the same manner for the decade of the 2000s. We then look at the transition pattern of countries between decades. Specifically, we look at how likely countries that fell into one of the quadrants, say, the vicious quadrant, in the first decade were to end up in each of the quadrants in the subsequent decade.

Box 6.4 shows our results. The table cell quadrants in each panel indicate countries' starting positions in the decade of the 1990s. The bubbles show where countries starting in a given quadrant ended up a decade

Box 6.4 Fulfilling Social and Economic Rights Promotes Growth

(*Continued*)

Box 6.4 Continued

The diagram above tracks where countries that started out in a particular position in the 1990s ended up in the first decade of the 2000s. The cells show where countries' starting positions. The bubbles show where countries that started in a particular position ended up in the subsequent decade. For example, looking at the northwest panel, we see that among those countries that were SERF lopsided in 1995—above-median SERF Index score in 1995 but below-median per capita income growth rate over the decade of the 1990s—25 percent remained SERF lopsided in 2005 (above-median SERF index score in 2005 and below-median per capita income growth in the first decade of the 2000s), 68 percent advanced to the virtuous quadrant (with above-median SERF Index scores and per capita income growth rates), 6 percent fell into the vicious quadrant (with below-median SERF Index scores and per capita income growth rates), and none converged to the growth-lopsided quadrant (with below-median SERF Index score in 2005 and above-median per capita income growth rate in the first decade of the 2000s). The results indicate that countries with policies and institutions that promote social and economic rights are likely to end up in the virtuous position and stay there, while countries with policies and institutions that promote growth while neglecting social and economic rights face a high risk of getting trapped in the vicious quadrant.

Source: Adapted from Randolph et al. 2011.

later. As can be seen, by far the majority of countries that found themselves in the vicious quadrant in the 1990s, 67 percent, got stuck there.
But a virtuous cycle emerged as well. By far the majority of countries
that had achieved the virtuous quadrant in the 1990s maintained their
status in the 2000s, indicating that those in the virtuous quadrant were
able to continue or even expand their fulfillment of rights obligations
while simultaneously pursuing economic growth. In short, countries can
both fulfill obligations under the ICESCR today and stimulate growth,
so as to enable expansion of the enjoyment of social and economic rights
in the future.

But what about countries that seek to escape the vicious cycle? Are
they better off renewing their efforts to stimulate per capita income
growth or devoting the maximum of available resources to promoting
social and economic rights? Here the transition patterns of the countries that began in the lopsided quadrants are instructive. Countries
with above-median growth but below-median SERF Index scores in
the 1990s—in the growth-lopsided quadrant—with few exceptions
either remained growth lopsided (44 percent) or regressed to the
vicious quadrant (44 percent) in the 2000s. Only 6 percent managed
to transition to the virtuous quadrant. In contrast, countries with
above-median scores on the SERF Index but below-median per capita
growth in the 1990s—in the SERF-lopsided quadrant—well over half
(68 percent)—succeeded in achieving the virtuous cycle, where growth
and the enjoyment of social and economic rights reinforce each other.
A quarter (25 percent) remained in the SERF-lopsided quadrant, with
better prospects for transitioning to the virtuous quadrant in a future
decade. Only 6 percent fell into the vicious cycle. Thus, countries
renewing their efforts to fulfill their obligations under the ICESCR
need not fear that their efforts to improve social and economic rights
enjoyment today will undermine economic growth and hence their
ability to improve social and economic rights enjoyment in the future.

Concluding Remarks

The preceding sections give some insight into the descriptive traits of
countries that do well in fulfilling the social and economic rights of their

citizens, as measured by the SERF Index, and those that do not. The key findings of this chapter include the following:

- Democracy and accountability are related to better fulfillment of social and economic rights, but the relationship is not straight-forward. We see a higher floor of achievement for countries with more robust democratic accountability; and while countries ruled by autocrats can still perform well on social and economic rights fulfillment, they are also more likely to do poorly. The relationship between social and economic rights and individual civil liberties is tenuous and depends on the indicators used.
- Although international treaties are unrelated to a country's social and economic rights performance, countries with legally enforce-able rights guarantees in domestic law do perform better at fulfill-ing the rights guaranteed by law, although this correlation does not imply causation.
- While increasing public social expenditure may have a positive effect on social and economic rights fulfillment, the relationship is much more complicated than "higher spending equals superior fulfillment of rights." Higher spending may be the result of other factors, especially a higher disease burden.
- Most strikingly, gender equity is highly correlated with greater ful-fillment of social and economic rights.
- Finally, there is no necessary trade-off between a country's ful-fillment of social and economic rights today and economic growth rates.

7

Responding to Critics

Trade-Offs, Policy Choices, Historical Legacies, and Discrimination

THIS CHAPTER EXAMINES THE ROBUSTNESS of the SERF Index by exploring some assumptions and choices that were made in its construction and provides extension of the methodology to address compliance with the principle of nondiscrimination.* First, as noted in chapter 3, in constructing the Achievement Possibilities Frontier for each right separately, the SERF Index methodology assumes that countries could achieve the frontier results without compromising achievement on other rights. This raises the critical question: Does best practice with regard to a given right depend on a country prioritizing that right over others, thus setting unreasonably high standards for achievement? Second, are the APFs robust compared with alternative methodologies one might use to econometrically specify the frontiers? Third, what is the effect of countries' structural characteristics and historical policy legacies on the fulfillment of their social and economic rights obligations, and what insights can we gain from these effects regarding policies to promote social and economic rights? Fourth, if one takes into account policy choices that cause a country's per capita income to grow either faster or slower than is typical, would this substantively alter the SERF Index scores? Relatedly, does the choice of using per capita GDP as a measure of resources, rather than other measures of countries' wealth that account for international resources such as development aid, lead to a systematic bias in the SERF

Index scores? Finally, how can the SERF Index be modified to take into account the extent to which a country or region is upholding the fundamental human rights principle of nondiscrimination?

Does Excellent Performance on One Right Come at the Expense of Neglecting Other Rights? Or Are Rights "Interdependent" and Mutually Reinforcing?

Theoretically it is possible that countries that perform well on one substantive right do so at the expense of poor performance on other substantive rights. Although the human rights framework holds that rights are interdependent and mutually reinforcing (Vienna Declaration 1993), in a real world of limited resources, it could be plausible that countries face trade-offs in rights fulfillment, as they choose to allocate scarce resources toward one right and not others. Since we have constructed the SERF Index by aggregating performance across the five substantive rights indices, our methodological approach implicitly assumes that countries can realize each right to the maximum extent feasible given available resources, without compromising achievement on other rights. However, whether rights are interdependent and mutually reinforcing, or subject to trade-offs given resource constraints, is an empirical question worth interrogating. The SERF Index opens up the opportunity to examine these competing possibilities.

Testing for the possibility of "trade-offs" in rights fulfillment involves first finding the correlations among component right indices and then regressing each of the individual component right indices against all the other component right indices. The results of these analyses for the core SERF Index are reported in Tables 7.1 and 7.2, respectively. All of the right indices are positively and significantly (1 percent level) correlated with each other. None of the regression coefficients in Table 7.2 is significantly negative, and by far the majority of the coefficients are significantly positive. Countries that perform better on meeting their obligations with regard to one right tend to perform better, not worse, with regard to meeting their obligations toward other rights.

We use the same approach to test the possibility that, in high-income OECD countries, excellent performance with regard to one social and economic right might come at the expense of poorer performance on other rights. Table 7.3 presents the correlation coefficients among the

TABLE 7.1 Correlation Matrix for International Social and Economic Rights Fulfillment Index Components—Core Countries

Index	Index			
	Right to Food	Right to Health	Right to Education	Right to Housing
Only Countries with Data on All Five Components				
Right to Health	0.43***			
Right to Education	0.32***	0.65***		
Right to Housing	0.35***	0.61***	0.50***	
Right to Work	0.35***	0.31***	0.34***	0.37***
All Available Data				
Right to Health	0.48***			
Right to Education	0.37***	0.67***		
Right to Housing	0.40***	0.66***	0.52***	
Right to Work	0.35***	0.30***	0.34***	0.35***

*** significant at the 1% level on the Pearson correlation test.

TABLE 7.2 Regression of Each Right Index on All Other Right Indices in the International Social and Economic Rights Fulfillment Index—Core Countries

Independent Variable	Dependent Variable				
	Right to Food Index	Right to Health Index	Right to Education Index	Right to Housing Index	Right to Work Index
Right to Food Index		0.187**	−0.01	0.062	0.230**
Right to Health Index	0.326**		0.543***	0.451***	−0.052
Right to Education Index	−0.014	0.436***		0.129	0.198
Right to Housing Index	0.081	0.339***	0.12		0.217*
Right to Work Index	0.221**	−0.029	0.136	0.160*	
R^2	0.245	0.565	0.459	0.420	0.211

Note: Beta coefficients in cells; *** significant at the 1% level, ** significant at the 5% level, * significant at the 10% level.

four rights indices making up the SERF Index for high-income OECD countries, while Table 7.4 summarizes the results of regressions of the rights on each other. The rights to health and education are significantly positively correlated with the right to food, and none of the component right indices is significantly negatively correlated with any other component right index. The results are strongly supportive of the conclusion that to the extent there is a relationship between countries' performance on one right versus another, the relationship is a positive one, rather than a negative one. That is, good performance with regard to fulfilling one right does not come at the expense of good performance on other rights. Quite the contrary, good performance on one right tends to go hand in hand with good performance on other rights. This likely reflects differences in commitments across countries to fulfilling social and economic rights as well as mutual reinforcement among rights.

These results provide empirical evidence to support the principle of "indivisibility and interdependence" of rights. Affirmed in the 1993 Vienna Declaration and Programme of Action, the equal importance of each right has tremendously important implications for human rights practice and public policy. These findings indicate that different

TABLE 7.3 Correlation Matrix for International Social and Economic Rights Fulfillment Index Components—High-Income Organisation for Economic Co-operation and Development Countries

Index	Index		
	Right to Food	Right to Health	Right to Education
Only Countries with Data on All Five Components			
Right to Health	0.18		
Right to Education	0.65***	−0.12	
Right to Work	0.64***	0.02	0.31
All Available Data			
Right to Health	0.17		
Right to Education	0.52***	−0.06	
Right to Work	0.63***	0.03	0.32

*** significant at the 1% level on the Pearson correlation test.

TABLE 7.4 Regression of Each Right Index on All Other Right Indices in the International Social and Economic Rights Fulfillment Index—High-Income Organisation for Economic Co-operation and Development Countries

Independent Variable	Dependent Variable			
	Right to Food Index	Right to Health Index	Right to Education Index	Right to Work Index
Right to Food Index		0.644*	−0.225	0.833***
Right to Health Index	0.239*		−0.268	−0.167
Right to Education Index	0.535***	−0.458		−0.254
Right to Work Index	0.468***	−0.253	0.845***	
R^2	0.691	0.168	0.513	0.450

Note: Beta coefficients in cells; *** significant at the 1% level, * significant at the 10% level.

component social and economic rights are likely mutually interdependent and that an investment in promoting one social and economic right is simultaneously an investment in promoting others.

Comparing Alternative Methodologies for Specifying Achievement Possibilities Frontiers

The approach we use to specify the APFs is both simple and flexible, but how does it compare with alternative approaches, notably Data Envelopment Analysis (DEA) (Charnes, Cooper, and Rhode 1978), the residuals approach (Cingranelli and Richards 2007; Duvall and Shamir 1980; Foweraker and Landman 1997; Kimenyi 2007; Landman et al. 2012), and techniques for estimating stochastic frontier production functions (Kumbhakar and Lovell 2000)? DEA is a nonparametric approach;[1] it does not require one to assume or fit a particular functional form to the data, a clear advantage. However, because the construction of the DEA frontier entails fitting linear cords between observations defining the outer boundary of the frontier plot, the envelope can be driven by outliers— meaning that DEA is prone to setting unrealistically high benchmarks. The residuals approach is a parametric approach, and as such, a particular distribution and functional form must be assumed when estimating the frontiers. The approach assumes a two-sided error structure and as such is less sensitive to outliers than the DEA approach, provided the sample is large and fully covers the relevant income range. As noted in chapter 3, however, the residuals approach benchmarks a country's performance relative to the average performance given the country's per capita income level, and accordingly the benchmark set is well below the level reflecting the use of maximum available resources and best practices.

The econometric estimation of stochastic frontier production functions, in contrast, is a parametric approach that assumes the data follow a particular distribution and a particular functional form when estimating the frontier, and it uses statistical methods to screen out the effects of measurement error. As in the approach we use, the estimation of Stochastic Achievement Frontiers (SAFs) assumes that the boundary of the production function is defined by "best practice" observations—in our application, countries using best practices. Since the estimation procedures are stochastic, some white noise is statistically accommodated when identifying best practice outcomes, and the approach incorporates an additional one-sided error term to capture any other reason why country performance might deviate from (within) the boundary. Although this is more sophisticated and somewhat less dependent on researcher judgment than the approach we use, it imposes more assumptions when estimating the frontier. The results of the two approaches are compared below.

Specifying a translog functional form, we estimate SAFs for a given indicator as specified by the following equation:

$$\text{Log}\,(y_{it}) = \beta_0 + \beta_1 \log\!\left(\text{GDP}_{it}\right) + \beta_2 \left[\log\!\left(\text{GDP}_{it}\right)\right]^2 + v_{it} - u_{it} \quad (7.1)$$

Here y_{it} is the observed indicator score for country i in year t. Following Battese and Coelli (1992), the statistical disturbance term v is assumed to be an independently and identically distributed random variable that follows a normal distribution, $N(0,\sigma_v^2)$, and is independent of the inefficiency error term, u. The one-sided error is assumed to follow a truncated normal distribution with $N(0,\sigma_u^2)$. The model is assumed to be time invariant, and the βs are the parameters to be estimated using the Maximum Likelihood estimation method. While the example above specifies a translog functional form, alternative functional forms were also estimated, and the best-fit form was selected using both statistical goodness-of-fit criteria and researcher judgment.

Figures 7.1 and 7.2 compare the frontiers specified using the SAFs (solid lines) with our APFs specified as described in chapter 3 (dashed lines). The observed data values are also superimposed on the graphs. As can be seen, the two approaches yield very similar frontiers, and neither approach is observed to fit the data better across all indicators. Table 7.5 shows the correlation in the scores between the two approaches. We calculate the correlation over all observations available on a given indicator for all countries over all years between 1990 and 2006. For half the indicators, the correlation coefficient is between 0.98 and 1.0, indicating that nearly identical scores result from the two approaches. The lowest correlation coefficient is at 0.87, still indicating a tight correspondence between the scores obtained using the two approaches. This lowest correlation occurred for the percentage of the rural population with access to improved sanitation. A look back at the graph comparing the frontiers indicates that over the per capita GDP level where the two frontiers diverge, two outliers heavily influence the SAF, and accordingly, our estimated APF from our original approach provides a more realistic benchmark.

Do Countries' Structural Characteristics and Historical Policy Legacies Matter?

The SERF Index does not explicitly take into account the particular structural or geographical characteristics of a country that might increase the resources required to achieve a given level of rights enjoyment. For example, one might expect the per capita cost of extending basic healthcare access to less densely populated rural areas to be higher than extending access to urban areas, especially if rural infrastructure is limited. To be sure, policy choices influence settlement patterns as well as the density of rural road networks, and to the extent they do, countries can be held accountable for those choices. However, a country cannot rapidly change the historical legacy of many previous policy choices, and this legacy affects the resources required to achieve a given level of rights enjoyment. Here we explore the relationship between a country's

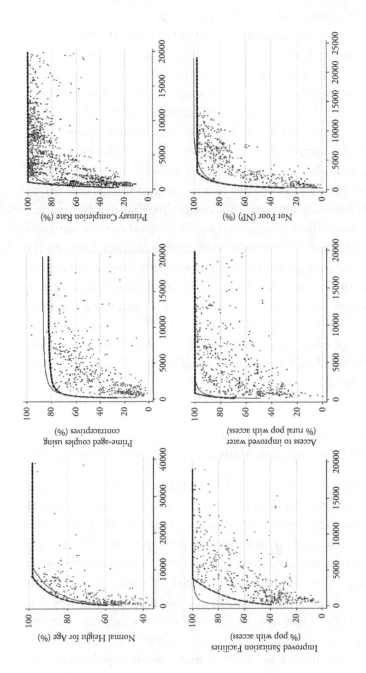

FIGURE 7.1 Comparison of the Original Achievement Possibilities Frontier Approach with the Stochastic Achievement Frontier Approach—Social and Economic Rights Fulfillment (SERF) Index for Core Countries Only

Note: The x-axes are gross domestic product per capita (2005 PPP\$).

Key: - - - original Achievement Possibilities Frontier; —— Stochastic Achievement Frontier; • observation.

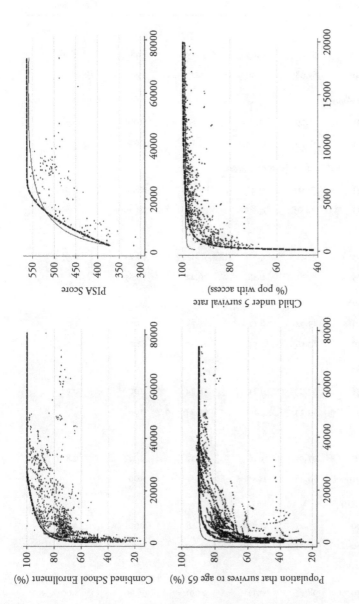

FIGURE 7.2 Comparison of the Original Achievement Possibilities Frontier Approach with the Stochastic Achievement Frontier Approach—Social and Economic Rights Fulfillment (SERF) Index for both Core Countries and High-Income Organisation for Economic Co-operation and Development (OECD) Countries or for High-Income OECD Countries Alone.

Note: The x-axes are gross domestic product per capita (2005 PPPs).

Key: - - - original Achievement Possibilities Frontier; —— Stochastic Achievement Frontier; • observation.

TABLE 7.5 Correlation of Stochastic Achievement Frontier (SAF) with Achievement Possibilities Frontier (APF) Performance Indicator Scores

Indicator	Number of Observations	Mean	Standard Deviation	Minimum	Maximum	Correlation Coefficient
Normal Height						
SAF	246	80.53	11.89	51.75	98	0.99
APF	246	85.08	10.30	59.23	98	
Combined School Enrollment						
SAF	1,625	85.29	12.37	48.80	100	0.98
APF	1,625	87.79	10.23	55.15	100	
Programme for International Student Assessment Score						
SAF	133	521.07	41.43	370.50	558.45	0.98
APF	133	522.03	53.87	373.41	561.50	
Age 65 Survival Rate						
SAF	1,905	87.31	4.37	52.47	90.23	0.93
APF	1,905	89.81	0.58	76.22	80.85	
Contraceptive Use Rate						
SAF	501	89.92	8.12	25.75	87.53	1.00
APF	501	87.56	7.54	40.55	82.75	
Improved Rural Water						
SAF	2,935	97.95	4.81	48.74	100	0.92
APF	2,935	99.24	3.13	69.23	100	
Improved Sanitation						
SAF	480	97.91	3.46	63.37	100	0.87
APF	480	86.96	15.56	39.51	100	
Primary Completion Rate						
SAF	1,660	95.67	8.75	25.58	100	0.91
APF	1,660	97.13	9.00	29.29	100	
Child Survival Rate						
SAF	1,070	98.77	0.32	94.91	98.96	1.00
APF	1,070	97.62	4.33	44.52	99.74	
Not Poor (≥$2.00, 2005 purchasing power parity dollars)						
SAF	1,213	85.52	15.57	0.00	100	0.95
APF	1,213	76.23	31.91	0.00	98.00	

particular structural features and SERF performance, revealing important insights regarding structural characteristics that either promote or impede the fulfillment of social and economic rights.

Data and Methodology

To determine how a country's performance on the SERF Index and underlying component right indices (education, health, housing, food, work) is related to structural characteristics, we estimate the following equation:

$$R_{ri} = \alpha_r + \beta_{rs}S_{si} + \varepsilon_{ri} \qquad (7.2)$$

Here R_r is the suite of r right indices, and the data source for the SERF Index and component right indices is the SERF Index Historical Trend Data. A set of variables, called S variables, reflecting countries' structural features related to their development level or the legacy of past policy choices, is regressed on the rights indices. As specified in the equation above, S_s is a vector of s structural characteristics reflecting the historical policy legacy, α is the intercept, β is the estimated coefficient of S that shows the impact of characteristic s on right r, ε is the error term, and i specifies the country.

We consider four factors that might be expected to affect the resources required to achieve a given level of rights enjoyment: economies of scale in infrastructure provision, women's empowerment and knowledge, income inequality, and malaria prevalence and risk. The percentage of the population living in rural areas (World Bank, World Development Indicators, 2012) is the proxy for economies of scale in infrastructure provision. The per-person cost of providing geographic accessibility to schools, health clinics, and improved water and sanitation is likely higher in rural areas or, in general, where population density is lower, especially if infrastructure is limited. While the impact of low population density is less clear with regard to the rights to work and food, one might conjecture that interactions in ensuring the rights to education, health, and work conspire to make it more costly to ensure the right to food in rural areas as well and, further, that the larger range of job opportunities with relatively higher labor productivity in urban areas additionally makes it more costly to ensure the right to work in rural areas.

The proxy for women's empowerment and knowledge is the ratio of the female-to-male primary school enrollment rate lagged ten years (World Development Indicators, 2012). Numerous empirical studies find that the more empowered women are to influence household expenditures, and the more knowledge they have or can acquire regarding how best to foster their family's health, nutrition, and education, the better the health and nutrition outcomes of their family members and the more education their children are likely to acquire (Agarwal 1997; Alderman et al. 1995; Anyanwu and Erhijakpor 2007; Caldwell 1986, 1994; Filmer and Pritchett 1997; Hill and King 1995; Hou 2011; Thomas 1990; Tolhurst et al. 2008).

At any given per capita income level, higher income inequality will make it more likely that a larger share of the population will be unable to purchase the goods and services necessary to secure their social and economic rights, while, at the same income level, lower inequality will make economic and social rights goods more broadly accessible across the population. The proxy for income inequality is the Gini coefficient, a widely used broad gauge of income inequality that takes into account the entire income distribution (extracted from the UNU-WIDER World Income Inequality Database, Version 2.0c [United Nations University World Institute for Development Economics Research 2008], supplemented with data from World Development Indicators, 2012).

Malaria raises morbidity and mortality, thereby increasing spending on the healthcare necessary to achieve good health outcomes. It is estimated that anywhere from 30 to 50 percent of outpatient visits and hospital admissions in much of sub-Saharan Africa result from malaria (Barofsky et al. 2011). The increase in morbidity due to malaria also impedes school attendance and can impose deficits that reduce a child's ability to learn. The reduced utilization of nutrients when malaria is active compounds this effect. Malaria is associated with reduced labor productivity while on the job as well as a reduction in the number of days those afflicted are able to work. While malaria can be eradicated over the medium term, eradication is costly, and accordingly, the spending necessary to achieve good health outcomes increases with the current level of malaria risk, even in the face of a successful eradication program. The proxy for malaria risk is the percentage of the population living in areas with malaria (Gallup, Mellinger, and Sachs 2007).

Results

Table 7.6 shows the estimated coefficients of each structural factor on the SERF Index and each component right index. The results indicate that all four structural factors influence a country's performance on the SERF Index as well as the component right indices. More specifically,

- Countries with a larger percentage of the population living in rural areas are disadvantaged. The relationship is statistically significant for the SERF Index and each of the component right indices, with the exception of the Right to Education Index. The impact is largest for the Right to Housing Index.
- Countries with greater gender equality are advantaged. Enhancing women's empowerment and knowledge promotes the fulfillment of social and economic rights. The impact is statistically significant for the SERF Index and each of the component right indices, with the exception of the Right to Work Index; the largest impacts are observed for the Right to Health and Right to Education indices.
- Income inequality handicaps countries when it comes to fulfilling each of the substantive rights; the impact is statistically significant for each of the component right indices as well as the SERF Index.
- Countries with a greater percentage of their population living in areas with endemic malaria face a greater challenge in meeting their obligations as assessed by the SERF Index and each of the component right indices; the disadvantage is greatest with regard to the Right to Work Index.

One can gain insight into the magnitude of the impediment these structural features pose to ensuring social and economic rights, and quantify the potential for policies redressing these structural features to improve social and economic rights outcomes, by examining the impact of a large change

TABLE 7.6 Structural Factors Influencing Performance on the Social and Economic Rights Fulfillment (SERF) Index and Component Right Indices

Variable	Index					
	SERF	Right to Education	Right to Health	Right to Housing	Right to Food	Right to Work
Rural population percentage	−0.180*** (0.0453)	−0.0365 (0.0583)	−0.159*** (0.0362)	−0.284*** (0.0464)	−0.273*** (0.0623)	−0.186** (0.0817)
Female-to-male primary school enrollment ratio lagged 10 years	0.254*** (0.0513)	0.402*** (0.0768)	0.405*** (0.0451)	0.318*** (0.0608)	0.204*** (0.0747)	−0.0737 (0.0974)
Gini coefficient	−0.418*** (0.0896)	−0.788*** (0.109)	−0.307*** (0.0670)	−0.592*** (0.0866)	−0.239* (0.126)	−0.411** (0.162)
% population living in areas with malaria	−9.051*** (2.210)	−11.82*** (3.427)	−12.65*** (1.986)	−13.25*** (2.725)	−5.551* (3.197)	−13.57*** (4.419)
Constant	80.54*** (6.493)	69.24*** (8.637)	65.59*** (5.136)	89.38*** (6.827)	82.50*** (9.177)	115.3*** (11.65)
Observations	169	308	278	319	215	230
R^2	0.507	0.417	0.670	0.599	0.274	0.154

Note: Standard errors in parentheses; ***p <.01, **p <.05, *p <.10.

in structural variables on the index scores. For example, we can analyze the projected impact of moving a country from the median score on a variable to the twenty-fifth percentile of the variable score distribution (in the case of indicators with a negative impact) or the seventy-fifth percentile of the variable score distribution (in the case of indicators with a positive impact).

Table 7.7 shows the impact on the SERF Index and component right indices of moving a country from the median score on the indicator to the variable score corresponding with the seventy-fifth percentile of the variable score distribution, in the case of the women's empowerment indicator, and to the twenty-fifth percentile of the variable score distribution in the case of the other three indicators. The number in parentheses below the name of the variable is the change in the variable score between the median and the twenty-fifth percentile of the distribution (or in the case of the women's empowerment indicator, the seventy-fifth percentile). For example, a country with the median score for the percentage of the population living in rural areas (52 percent rural), compared with a country with a score at the seventy-fifth percentile (36 percent rural), would be expected to have its score on the SERF Index rise by 2.77 percentage points. As explored in greater detail in chapter 6, the large role played by women's empowerment and knowledge in securing social and economic rights is striking; the women's

TABLE 7.7 Impact of a Twenty-five-Percentile Improvement in Structural Variable Scores

Variable	Index					
	Social and Economic Rights Fulfillment	Right to Education	Right to Health	Right to Housing	Right to Food	Right to Work
Rural population percentage (−15.65)	2.77	—	2.61	4.12	3.99	2.72
Female-to-male primary school enrollment ratio lagged 10 years (+21.2)	5.34	8.44	8.76	6.38	4.16	—
Gini coefficient (−6.5)	2.6	4.94	2.28	3.27	1.18	2.11
% population living in areas with malaria (−0.567)	5.14	5.88	7.01	6.90	3.12	7.58

Note: Numbers in parentheses indicate the change in the variable score between the median and the 25th percentile of the distribution (or in the case of the women's empowerment indicator, the 75th percentile).

empowerment indicator has the largest impact on the SERF Index, as well as on most of the component right indices. The results demonstrate that by crafting policies that reduce inequality, empower women, eradicate malaria, and improve rural infrastructure or promote more efficient settlement patterns, countries can enjoy high dividends with regard to advancing social and economic rights.

Policy Choices and Resource Capacity: Some Alternative Formulations

As detailed previously, the SERF Index uses GDP per capita as a proxy for a country's resource capacity. This section explores the assumptions embedded in this indicator choice and examines whether the SERF Index is robust compared with alternative approaches to measuring resource capacity. We begin with a discussion of the potential bias resulting from endogenous growth rates. Specifically, policy choices can result in exceptionally fast or exceptionally slow growth rates, and since the level of a country's social and economic rights obligations is determined by per capita GDP, the policy choices that affect growth rates impact the level of rights obligations. We present a strategy for dealing with this bias and consider whether in practice the bias is likely to be large. We then examine whether using options other than per capita GDP to measure economic wealth, such as per capita gross national income (GNI), changes SERF Index scores.

Policy Choices and Resource Capacity: Dealing with Endogeneity

The total available resources in a country, as measured by GDP per capita, are endogenous to policy choices.[2] This could cause countries with low growth rates resulting from poor policy choices, such as the Democratic Republic of Congo and Liberia, to appear to perform well on social and economic rights outcomes because of depressed resource availability, while causing countries with exceptionally strong recent growth rates resulting from good policy choices, such as China and Vietnam, to appear to perform poorly on social and economic rights realization due to expanded resource availability. In other words, countries making bad recent choices that undermine growth rates could potentially be rewarded with higher SERF scores, while strong-growth performers would be unfairly penalized with low scores. This is because in countries that enjoyed exceptionally rapid per capita GDP growth rates in the recent past, SERF Index scores will underestimate the extent to which the country is meeting its obligation of progressive realization, while in countries that endured exceptionally slow per capita GDP growth rates in the recent past, SERF Index scores will overestimate the enjoyment of social and economic rights relative to what is reasonably feasible. The purpose of this section is to empirically examine the practical magnitude of the bias in SERF Index scores due to the endogeneity of per capita GDP.

We examine this question by developing a measure of economic resources that is not affected by the government's short-term policy choices. Stated succinctly, instead of measuring resource availability in terms of *actual* available resources, resource availability is measured using *predicted* resource availability. The predictions are based on the characteristics of a country that remove the impact of recent policy choices that could be affecting growth rates. Many such measures can be created, and there is no consensus in the economic literature on a best method. The method used here to test the robustness of SERF Index scores is one of many possible approaches.

Figure 7.3 helps one visualize how the use of predicted per capita GDP rather than actual per capita GDP as a proxy for economic resources could theoretically affect SERF Index performance for a given country. The x-axis measures economic resources available to a country; the y-axis measures the level of social and economic rights enjoyment available to its citizens. $SERF_C$ denotes the computed SERF Index score based on predicted GDP, while $SERF_A$ represent the actual SERF Index score. Figure 7.3 illustrates a hypothetical situation where the predicted economic resource availability of a country is less than its actual GDP per capita—the case where a country enjoys exceptionally rapid growth. For a given level of social and economic rights enjoyment in that country, predicted economic resource availability less than actual GDP per capita causes the computed SERF Index score to exceed the actual SERF Index score.

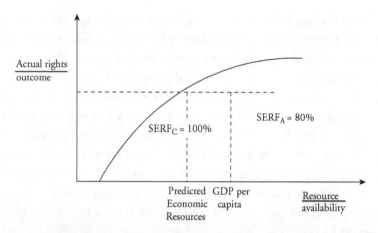

FIGURE 7.3 Comparison of Social and Economic Rights Fulfillment (SERF) Index Scores Using Predicted versus Actual Resource Availability

Key: SERF$_C$ = computed SERF Index score based on predicted gross domestic product; SERF$_A$ = actual SERF Index score.

Data and Methodology

The computation of predicted resource availability requires the specification of a set of variables that are independent of a government's recent policy choices, have continuous and reliable data available, and are widely accepted as robust predictors of economic growth. Following Sala-i-Martin et al.'s (2004) careful analysis and tests for the most robust predictors of economic growth rates, five variables are selected that predict a country's economic resources. Definitions and sources of data for each variable are summarized in Table 7.8. A panel data set of 105 countries covering the twenty-nine-year period 1980–2008 is used to compute predicted economic resource availability per capita. A linear model for panel data with between effects is employed, regressing GDP per capita on the five selected regressors. Between effects, rather than fixed effects, are used since the variation between countries is of primary importance. We divide the countries into the two categories of current high-income OECD countries (twenty-five) and core countries (eighty) and run separate regressions due to the significant economic and structural differences between the two groups of countries.

TABLE 7.8 Predicted Gross Domestic Product (GDP) Per Capita: Variable Names, Descriptions, and Data Sources

Category	Variable	Description	Source
Initial income level	Natural log of GDP per capita in 1970	Purchasing power parity–converted GDP per capita at current prices	Penn World Table Version 7.2
Initial health conditions	Life expectancy in 1970	Number of years a newborn infant is expected to survive following prevailing patterns of mortality	World Bank World Development Indicators
Geography and sanitary conditions	Malaria prevalence in 1966	Percentage of country area with malaria in 1966	Gallup and Sachs 2001
Effects of wars	War deaths in a year	Total number of deaths in armed conflicts in a given year, using the low estimate of casualties	Uppsala Conflict Data Program/ Peace Research Institute Oslo data set
Natural resource wealth	Oil rents per capita	Ratio of oil rents and population; oil rents are defined as the difference between the value of crude oil production at world prices and total costs of production	World Bank World Development Indicators

The following set of multivariate linear equations is estimated:

Core countries:

$$\ln (\text{GDP per capita}_t) = \beta_1 + \beta_2 \ln(\text{GDP per capita}_{1970}) \\ + \beta_3 \text{life expectancy}_{1970} \\ + \beta_4 \text{Net oil rents per capita}_t \\ + \beta_5 \text{domestic war deaths}_t \\ + \beta_6 \text{Malaria prevalence}_{1966} \qquad (7.3)$$

High-income OECD countries:

$$\ln (\text{GDP per capita}_t) = \beta_1 + \beta_2 \ln(\text{GDP per capita}_{1970})$$
$$+ \beta_3 \text{life expectancy}_{1970} \qquad (7.4)$$
$$+ \beta_4 \text{Net oil rents per capita}_t$$

The two equations differ because for OECD countries, war deaths and malaria prevalence in 1966 have a value close to zero during the period 1980–2008. Most variables were lagged to reflect preexisting structural characteristics and policies; contemporaneous oil rents per capita and contemporaneous war deaths are used because those variables reflect the accumulation of past policies. The estimated results find that all variables are significant at the 95 percent confidence level, with the exception of war deaths per year, which is significant at the 90 percent confidence level. Moreover, the signs of all variables, except life expectancy for high-income OECD countries, are as expected.[3] The R-squared values for both regressions are greater than 0.85, demonstrating that the variables have high predictive capability in determining the log of GDP per capita.

We use the estimated coefficients to predict GDP per capita for each country for each year, 1980–2008. We compute this measure of economic resources, henceforth referred to as predicted economic resource availability, for each country for each year to construct the "predicted SERF Index" score. With the exception of the use of the predicted GDP per capita instead of actual GDP per capita, the computation of the predicted SERF Index score is as described in chapter 3.

Findings

The results indicate that the use of the actual GDP per capita data does not lead to a significant bias, except in a few cases of countries with extremely rapid or extremely low per capita income growth rates in the recent past. For most countries, the difference between the SERF Index using actual per capita GDP and the computed SERF Index using predicted per capita GDP as the measure of economic resources is less than five points. Figure 7.4 plots the two versions of the SERF Index (one using actual per capita GDP and the other using predicted economic resource availability). Each dot on the graph represents a country. If the actual and predicted SERF Index scores are the same, then the dots will trace out the forty-five-degree line, and the slope coefficient of the predicted SERF Index will equal 1.0. The actual regression line has a slope of 0.9, signifying that the two methods give very similar, although not identical, results. It can be seen that most countries are located on or within one standard deviation of the forty-five-degree line, illustrating that the two proxies of economic resources are quite similar. To the extent that the actual and predicted SERF Index scores differ, the actual SERF Index scores tend to be biased downward. The predicted SERF Index score exceeds the actual SERF Index score in almost 80 percent of countries, indicating that most countries followed policies that enabled them to increase their per capita GDP more rapidly than predicted.

While the difference between the predicted and actual SERF Index scores tends to be quite small, there are exceptions. The problem is limited to countries with exceptionally high growth rates rather

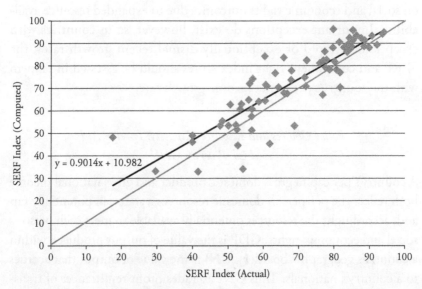

FIGURE 7.4 Correlation between Computed and Actual Social and Economic Rights Fulfillment (SERF) Index Scores

than exceptionally low growth rates. The actual and predicted SERF Index scores never differ by more than two standard deviations in the twenty-five OECD countries studied. The difference between the actual and predicted SERF Index scores only exceeds two standard deviations in seven of the eighty non-OECD countries studied: Botswana, China, India, Cameroon, Swaziland, Senegal, and Liberia. Liberia is the only country for which the predicted SERF Index score is more than two standard deviations below the actual SERF Index score.

Analysis

Overall, the endogeneity of the indicator of resource availability, GDP per capita, does not bias the results. SERF Index scores using actual per capita GDP do not diverge substantially from scores using predicted GDP per capita as the measure of resource availability; in fact, for approximately 90 percent of the countries there is no significant difference. As a general rule, therefore, the SERF Index is *not* rewarding countries with low growth rates resulting from poor policy choices by making them appear to perform well on social and economic rights outcomes because of depressed resource availability, or penalizing countries with strong recent growth rates by making them appear to perform poorly on social and economic rights outcomes due to expanded resource availability. Important exceptions do exist, however, so in countries with exceptionally rapid or exceptionally dismal recent growth rates, the SERF and component right index scores should be assessed in tandem with the country's per capita income growth rate.

Policy Choices and Resource Capacity: Foreign Aid and GDP versus GNI

A country's per capita gross domestic product and gross national income both reflect the per-person domestic resources a state can potentially tap and, accordingly, the resources potentially available to meet each person's social and economic rights. GDP is the value of output produced within a country's geographic boarders. GNI is the value of output that accrues to a country's nationals. Thus GNI excludes profit remittances of transnational corporations (TNCs) and includes remittances from a country's nationals. The difference in per capita GDP and GNI is not insubstantial for a few countries, but for most countries it is negligible.

In our view, there is no clear advantage in selecting GNI over GDP as the indicator of a country's resource capacity, and there is stronger historical precedence for using per capita GDP as a measure of a country's national product.[4] A country's policies strongly influence its ability to attract TNCs as well as the ease with which TNCs can remit profits. The policies a country adopts and the agreements it negotiates also play a role in the ability of its nationals to work abroad and the ease with which they can send remittances home. That is, factors that would lead to GNI exceeding GDP reflect policy choices. Accordingly, GDP per capita is specified as the indicator of a state's resource capacity for the SERF Index. While in some countries per capita GDP exceeds per capita GNI, in other countries the opposite is true. The question that arises is whether there is a systematic bias in choosing per capita GDP over GNI.

We based our decision to exclude the value of per capita aid flows when specifying resource availability on both conceptual and measurement grounds, as discussed in greater detail in chapter 3. To an important degree, the aid flows a country attracts reflect policy choices, and data on the value of foreign aid are problematic. A similar question arises regarding the decision not to include the value of aid flows in our tally of per capita resource availability: Does the exclusion of aid flows introduce a systematic bias since some countries attract much larger aid flows than other countries?

To address these questions, the following relationship is estimated:

$$S_i = \alpha + \beta \, (\text{GNI per capita} - \text{GDP per capita})_i \\ + \gamma \, (\text{ODA \% GDP})_i + \varepsilon_i, \qquad (7.5)$$

where S is the SERF Index score, i is an index for country, α is the intercept term, β and γ are estimated coefficients, and ε is the error term; ODA%GDP stands for official development assistance as a percentage of GDP. Here, the estimated β coefficient tests whether countries whose per capita GNI exceeds their per capita GDP tend to score higher or lower on the SERF Index, while the estimated γ coefficient tests whether

TABLE 7.9 Effect of Alternative Resource Indicators

Independent Variable	Estimated Coefficient	Standardized Coefficient	t Value	Significance Level
Constant	72.95***		43.326	.000
Gross national income per capita – gross domestic product per capita	0.000	−0.011	−0.0109	.913
Net official development assistance (% GDP)	−0.028	−0.040	−0.0382	−.703
R^2: 0.002				
F value: 0.087				.917

*** significant at the 1% level.

countries that attract more foreign aid (relative to their GDP) tend to score higher or lower on the SERF Index.

The results are shown in Table 7.9. The estimated β and γ coefficients are near zero, and neither is even close to being statistically significant. These results imply that countries' scores on the SERF Index are *not* systematically affected or biased as a result of the choices to use GDP per capita rather than GNI per capita and to exclude aid flows from the tally of resource availability.

Addressing Nondiscrimination

The principle of equal rights of all individuals is a core human rights norm. It is a fundamental ethical principle with important implications for the design of public policy. Moreover, the obligation of nondiscrimination is not subject to progressive realization; discrimination must be eliminated with immediate effect, as discussed in chapter 2. Although a country's or subnational unit's score on the SERF Index will inherently be reduced in the face of inequalities of sex, race, or other factors that undermine aggregate performance on rights outcome indicators, a high SERF Index score is not inconsistent with the persistence of discrimination. As shown in chapter 5, a country can achieve a high SERF

Index score even while systematically and persistently denying a small minority the enjoyment of social and economic rights because the socio-economic data used in the construction of the index reflect the overall situation in a country and do not specifically reflect disparities among groups. Adapting the SERF Index to account for disparities among groups would offer a more comprehensive and accurate assessment of the extent to which countries are meeting their social and economic rights obligations. Here we explain one way the SERF Index can be adapted to account for disparities, in order to incorporate attention to those vulnerable groups that face discrimination limiting their ability to enjoy their social and economic rights. Our approach to adjust the SERF Index is outlined here and applied to the U.S. context.

The strategy used to take into account discrimination relies on disparities in rights enjoyment outcomes among groups as prima facie evidence of discrimination (see Department of Justice, Section IV.A.2, for detail on the use of prima facie evidence of discrimination). Although outcome disparities often reflect the legacy of historical discrimination rather than ongoing discrimination, the focus on outcome disparities gives attention both to population subgroups facing current discrimination and to those for whom proactive policies are necessary to redress past injustices.

Methodology

Several conceptual and practical factors pose a challenge to adapting the SERF Index to account for discrimination. The contours of discrimination differ not only across countries but also across regions and states within a country and across rights dimensions. In the U.S. context, for example, discrimination may limit Native Americans' opportunity to claim social and economic rights in the Southwest, while opportunities may be the most limited for Hispanics in the American West and for blacks in the South. Women may particularly suffer discrimination with regard to the right to work. Further, data constraints necessarily limit how finely the contours of discrimination can be detailed. For example, while Hispanics as a group may not be the target of discrimination in some regions of the United States, Puerto Rican or Mexican Hispanics may well be, but data are too sparse to trace out these distinctions.

Our approach to addressing discrimination is to compute performance indicator scores separately for mutually exclusive but exhaustive population subgroups and then aggregate across population subgroups in a manner that weights the performance indicator score for the most marginalized group most heavily. Specifically, the following formula is used to aggregate the performance indicator scores across population subgroups:

$$A^D = (1 - \omega) \sum p_i A_i + \omega A_1, \qquad (7.6)$$

where A^D is the performance indicator score after adjusting for discrimination, A_i is the performance indicator score for subgroup i (specifying $i = 1$ as the subgroup with the lowest performance indicator score), and p_i denotes the proportion of the population in subgroup i. The extent to which we care about inequality is denoted by ω and can range between 0 and 1. Specifying $\omega = 1$ imposes the maximum penalty for disparities; in this case, A^D collapses to the performance indicator score for the most marginalized group. Specifying $\omega = 0$, no account is taken of disparities, and A^D collapses to A, the population performance indicator score. Thus, as the value of ω decreases from 1 to 0, inequality aversion decreases.

Below we summarize the findings for sex discrimination and racial discrimination in the United States, comparing the U.S. SERF Index scores for $\omega = 0$ and $\omega = 1$. (A more detailed analysis can be found in Randolph, Prairie, and Stewart 2009, 2012.)

Accounting for Sex Discrimination in the United States

Although the state-level U.S. SERF Index takes into account all six social and economic rights, the U.S. SERF Index adjusted for sex discrimination excludes the right to food and the right to decent housing because the indicators used to capture these rights rely on household-level data that cannot be differentiated by sex. In addition, given data constraints, it is only possible to take into account one aspect of the right to health— the child survival rate. These limitations aside, the overall picture that emerges is that efforts to redress sex discrimination over the past several decades have enjoyed considerable success.

Although females continue to be a marginalized group in twenty-nine of the fifty states, the difference in the U.S. SERF Index value adjusted for sex discrimination (setting $\omega = 1$) compared with the index ignoring discrimination (setting $\omega = 0$) is less than one percentage point in each of the fifty states. A more nuanced understanding of sex discrimination in the United States emerges from an examination by right and right aspect.

Women continue to suffer discrimination when it comes to the right to work in all but fourteen states, but overall, the difference between men and women in the U.S. Right to Work Index never exceeds four percentage points. However, women suffer most when it comes to gaining access to work that pays a living wage; women are marginalized in all fifty states along this dimension of the right to work, and the difference exceeds ten percentage points in half the states. In contrast, when it comes to obtaining work of any kind, young men are disadvantaged compared with young women in all but sixteen states, and the difference is pronounced (exceeding ten percentage points) in a third of the states.

Women have come to be advantaged, and men disadvantaged, with regard to the right to education. Although the advantage of girls over boys in gaining access to education is quite small, along the quality dimension, girls' advantage is not inconsequential.

Although there is no vestige of discrimination apparent when one looks at the right to social security overall, this result hides marked offsetting differences in outcomes across right aspects. Men are disadvantaged when it comes to gaining access to health insurance, but women continue to bear the greater burden of poverty. In all states, the difference is offsetting and comes to roughly five percentage points.

Accounting for Race and Ethnic Discrimination in the United States

Accounting for race and ethnic discrimination in the United States poses additional data challenges, only one of which is the ethnic/racial breakdown.[5] The results for the three major ethnic groups—whites, Hispanics, and blacks—are summarized below. Data limitations prevent incorporating the full set of rights and right aspects when adapting the U.S. SERF Index for race and ethnic discrimination. The right to social security is the only right for which all aspects considered in the basic U.S. SERF Index can be included. Only two of the three right aspects could be included in the health and work component right indices.[6] Only the quality component of the U.S. Right to Education Index could be included. Both the right to food and right to housing components must be omitted due to data constraints.

Unsurprisingly, the U.S. SERF Index reveals substantial disparities by race and ethnicity in those states for which data are sufficient to compute the full index. Table 7.10 shows the results.[7] The value of the index decreases by more than ten points on average across U.S. states as the value of ω is increased from 0 to 1. The reduction in the U.S. SERF Index upon adjusting for discrimination by race and ethnicity (setting ω = 1) is equivalent to over half the variation in the SERF Index for high-income OECD countries. Substantial cross-state differences are also revealed. In California and Texas, incorporating discrimination reduces the U.S. SERF Index score by only three points, whereas in Wisconsin and Missouri, states with relatively high U.S. SERF Index scores, the decline is precipitous—more than eighteen points.

Although whites uniformly enjoy their social and economic rights to a greater extent than blacks or Hispanics, the most marginalized race differs by state, with blacks enduring the most repressed enjoyment of social and economic rights in just over half the states. The difference in the U.S. SERF Index score for Hispanics and blacks only exceeds five points in Florida, Illinois, Michigan, Missouri, and Wisconsin, whereas the difference in the U.S. SERF Index score for whites and the most marginalized group, with few exceptions, is around twenty points.

Additional insight can be gained by focusing on the individual rights. Blacks suffer the greatest disadvantage when it comes to claiming the right to health; their score on the Right to Health Index is lower than that for any other ethnic group in every state. Hispanics fare best with regard to reproductive health. The component right index scores fall even more abruptly for the rights to education, work, and social security when comparing maximum (ω = 1) to minimum (ω = 0) inequality aversion. For the right to education, the average drop across the states is seventeen points; the average drop is twenty points for the rights to work and to social security. A gulf exists between whites and Asians, on the one hand, and blacks and Hispanics, on the other, with regard

TABLE 7.10 U.S. Social and Economic Rights Fulfillment (SERF) Index Score Adjusted for Ethnic and Racial Discrimination by State

State	2007 Gross Domestic Product Per Capita (2005 PPP$)	SERF Index Score				SERF Index Adjusted for Race Discrimination			
		Whites	Blacks	Hispanics	State	Marginalized Race	Score, $\omega = 0$	Score, $\omega = 1$	Difference, $\omega = 1 - \omega = 0$
Alabama	33,378	89.2	68.0		76.2		76.2		
Alaska	50,520	88.3			76.2		76.2		
Arizona	37,946	90.2		70.3	75.2		75.2		
Arkansas	31,323	89.2	66.8	71.0	77.6	Black	77.6	66.8	−10.81
California	47,779	87.5	69.7	68.5	71.2	Hispanic	71.2	68.5	−2.69
Colorado	46,008	88.1	69.3	65.8	75.5	Hispanic	75.5	65.8	−9.65
Connecticut	58,530	89.2	65.5	65.4	77.3	Hispanic	77.3	65.4	−11.90
Delaware	63,700	87.7	68.3		75.7		75.7		
District of Columbia	142,541		56.6	59.4	62.8		62.8		
Florida	37,678	90.1	70.3	77.4	77.7	Black	77.7	70.3	−7.42
Georgia	39,762	89.9	70.3	69.1	75.5	Hispanic	75.5	69.1	−6.43
Hawaii	43,804	87.1		78.3	78.0		78.0		
Idaho	33,648	89.7		71.1	81.2		81.2		
Illinois	44,613	88.8	65.1	73.2	76.1	Black	76.1	65.1	−10.99
Indiana	36,897	89.6	69.4	73.5	80.8	Black	80.8	69.4	−11.35
Iowa	40,381	89.5		72.9	81.7		81.7		
Kansas	39,204	89.8	70.6	69.9	80.7	Hispanic	80.7	69.9	−10.80

(Continued)

TABLE 7.10 (Continued)

State	2007 Gross Domestic Product Per Capita (2005 PPP$)	SERF Index Score				SERF Index Adjusted for Race Discrimination			
		Whites	Blacks	Hispanics	State	Marginalized Race	Score, ω = 0	Score, ω = 1	Difference, ω = 1 − ω = 0
Kentucky	34,236	85.9	68.0		77.8		77.8		
Louisiana	39,667	86.9	62.5		71.1		71.1		
Maine	34,143	89.8			82.8		82.8		
Maryland	44,645	90.9	74.6	73.8	79.1	Hispanic	79.1	73.8	−5.24
Massachusetts	53,389	89.5		68.0	80.8		80.8		
Michigan	37,034	88.3	63.8	71.8	76.4	Black	76.4	63.8	−12.60
Minnesota	46,626	90.6	65.7	66.8	81.0	Black	81.0	65.7	−15.34
Mississippi	27,598	91.3	68.0		75.3		75.3		
Missouri	36,746	88.8	60.7	73.5	79.0	Black	79.0	60.7	−18.25
Montana	31,797	89.6			81.4		81.4		
Nebraska	41,803	89.1	70.7	66.4	79.6		79.6		
Nevada	45,337	86.9		70.5	75.0	Hispanic	75.0	70.5	−4.52
New Hampshire	42,141	89.4			83.1		83.1		
New Jersey	50,797	90.3	70.8	70.9	78.8	Black	78.8	70.8	−8.00
New Mexico	34,889	89.4	69.6	74.8	73.7		73.7		
New York	55,291	87.5	69.6	69.5	74.7	Hispanic	74.7	69.5	−5.24
North Carolina	41,778	87.9	69.1	64.7	74.6	Hispanic	74.6	64.7	−9.90

North Dakota	39,118	90.7				83.1	83.1		
Ohio	38,381	89.0	66.8	70.3	Black	79.3	79.3	66.8	−12.47
Oklahoma	33,228	87.9	69.8	68.1	Hispanic	77.3	77.3	68.1	−9.17
Oregon	43,228	84.9		62.8		74.4	74.4		
Pennsylvania	39,635	90.0	69.0	70.3	Black	80.3	80.3	69.0	−11.38
Rhode Island	41,203	88.7	65.1	65.3	Black	77.6	77.6	65.1	−12.46
South Carolina	32,578	90.3	70.3	72.4	Black	77.2	77.2	70.3	−6.85
South Dakota	40,135	90.9		82.2		82.2	82.2		
Tennessee	38,045	86.5	68.8	69.2	Black	76.0	76.0	68.8	−7.28
Texas	42,612	89.2	69.7	69.6	Hispanic	72.7	72.7	69.6	−3.08
Utah	36,953	89.5		68.5		80.5	80.5		
Vermont	38,558	89.9		83.8		83.8	83.8		
Virginia	46,924	89.0	72.7	72.7	Hispanic	78.6	78.6	72.7	−5.98
Washington	45,508	87.2		67.9		76.3	76.3		
West Virginia	28,108	86.6		79.8		79.8	79.8		
Wisconsin	39,339	90.8	62.6	70.7	Black	80.9	80.9	62.6	−18.33
Wyoming	45,442	86.3		78.9		78.9	78.9		
Number of observations	51	50	32	37	26	51	51	26	26

Source: Adapted from Table 6 in Randolph, Prairie, and Stewart 2012.

to enjoyment of the right to education. When it comes to the right to work, the great divide is between whites, on the one hand, and blacks, Hispanics, and Asians, on the other. Blacks and Hispanics suffer the greatest disadvantage on the decent pay dimension; Asians suffer the most when it comes to gaining access to secure jobs with benefits. Hispanics are the most marginalized group when it comes to enjoying the right to social security, although the challenges faced by blacks are nearly as great.

Concluding Remarks

This chapter explores the robustness of the SERF Index compared with that of several methodological choices and adapts the index to assess nondiscrimination, revealing several surprising and important findings. First, although the APFs are specified with reference to specific rights, this does not result in standards that are unreasonably high for attainment of the full set of rights. Countries that perform well on one right do not do so by shortchanging attention to other rights. Quite the contrary, good performance on one right tends to go hand in hand with good performance on other rights; social and economic rights indeed appear to be indivisible and interdependent, empirically as well as normatively.

Second, although the SERF Index as constructed does not directly take into account differences in structural features among countries, the endogeneity of per capita income, or net international financial transfers, it is quite robust to these concerns. Four factors reflecting a country's historical policy legacy and structural characteristics impede a country's ability to fulfill its social and economic rights obligations—an adverse settlement pattern or inadequate infrastructure provision, women's disempowerment, income inequality, and the failure to control malaria. The median absolute deviation of the actual SERF Index score from the predicted score controlling for these factors is only 5.8 percentage points, indicating that the typical impact of these characteristics is not large. And although it is prudent to consider a country's per capita GDP growth rate alongside its SERF Index score, in general, policy choices that cause a country's per capita income to grow either faster or slower than is typical do not significantly bias the SERF Index scores. The few exceptions are cases where a country's growth is either exceptionally rapid or exceptionally slow. With regard to the specification of GDP as the indicator of resource availability for the SERF Index, our findings reveal that neither the choice of per capita GDP over GNI nor the exclusion of development aid leads to a systematic bias in the SERF Index scores.

Third, the nuanced analysis of social and economic rights fulfillment in the United States demonstrates one methodology that takes into account the principle of nondiscrimination and, specifically, disparities in rights enjoyment among groups. This analysis reveals that while sex discrimination is no longer an egregious problem in the United States, racial discrimination remains an entrenched challenge. This analysis also illustrates that high scores on the overall SERF Index do not ensure low levels of discrimination; troublingly, the states exhibiting the highest levels of disparities among racial and ethnic groups are among those that achieve the highest scores on the U.S. SERF Index.

This chapter has sought to address several questions related to the robustness of the SERF Index and, in so doing, explore some major issues in the theory and practice of human rights. In sum, our findings demonstrate the robustness of the SERF Index when compared with alternative methodological choices but also reveal the importance of taking into account the principle of nondiscrimination and, accordingly, an urgent need to expand the availability of data by population subgroup.

8

Conclusions

WE SET OUT TO DEVELOP the SERF Index with the following challenge: to discover what we learn if instead of judging the "success" of countries by the yardstick of per capita income and its growth, we flip the question on its head to judge the success of nations according to whether they translate available resources into expanded freedoms—the freedom for people to be and do the things they value and to pursue meaningful lives with dignity. We proposed to use international human rights, the global standard that defines these freedoms, as the yardstick to evaluate the success and failings of states and the progress of humanity.

What did we learn? The SERF Index helps us see the overall trends in government performance in fulfilling social and economic rights. Overall, the global picture is one of serious underperformance by most of the world's governments, a great deal of variation among countries and across rights, and inequities in rights fulfillment with marginalized people suffering the lowest levels of fulfillment in many instances. However, the good news is that, overall, across the world there has been steady improvement. The SERF Index provides government performance data for policymakers, advocates, activists and, scholars, that enhance their ability to identify successes and failures and pinpoint shortcomings in government performance in fulfilling social and economic rights. Moreover, our cross-country statistical analysis (chapter 6) contributes to the rich literature and debates concerning the types of social arrangements that facilitate the realization of rights and the role of democratic accountability, legal guarantees in national law, the ratification of international treaties, higher social spending in public expenditures, gender equality, and economic growth.

Beyond these findings, the SERF Index has several other implications for the study and practice of human rights—in furthering legal accountability, in designing public policies and advocating reforms, and in theorizing the principle of progressive realization. We highlight these points in this final chapter.

SERF Index Scores Further Legal Accountability

Information is the linchpin of accountability. Without information regarding the overall state of human rights realization in a country and its progress or regress, it is impossible to hold the government accountable for rights fulfillment. Information is required by international institutions to hold states accountable to their treaty obligations as well as to enable citizens to hold their governments accountable. The mechanisms for accountability at both levels, built up over the last half-century, have received increasing attention in the last decade and fostered a growing demand for quantitative information. The SERF Index scores fill an important informational gap in these accountability mechanisms; this summary measure of the extent to which a state is complying with its obligation to fulfill social and economic rights progressively supplements the contextually specific qualitative information and detailed indicators that presently dominate assessments of economic and social rights performance.

International Accountability

At the international level the principal accountability mechanism is the Committee on Economic, Social and Cultural Rights, the body of independent experts that examines state performance based on a narrative report submitted by the government and shadow reports submitted by civil society stakeholders.[1] Such reports typically focus on the steps being taken to fulfill rights, including new legislation and policy plans as well as data on the level of rights enjoyment using socioeconomic outcome indicators. Glaringly absent is the essential, central information regarding whether outcomes are adequate *relative to the level of resources available* in the country.

The recent CESCR review of Gabon in November 2013 illustrates the problem. The report (Government of Gabon 2012) submitted by the national government contains 252 paragraphs documenting the numerous efforts being made by that government to fulfill social and economic rights relevant to each of the thirty-one articles of the ICESCR. The report includes such details as new legislation passed on the age of retirement, proposals for a project on developing a labor market information system, and much more. Yet the details obscure the overall picture and, more fundamentally, tell us little about the effectiveness of these efforts and whether they can be evaluated as adequate. They do not reveal systematic patterns of progress and regress, violations, or actions to fulfill obligations. In the debates, committee members commented with concern, but without any systematic framework for assessment, that the evolution of Gabon's HDI scores was not in keeping with its GDP (U.N. OHCHR 2013a). Had they consulted the SERF Index, they would have seen evidence of the outrageous inadequacy of Gabon's efforts relative to the country's resources. The scores in Table 5.2 of chapter 5 show that Gabon is one of the ten worst performers, with an overall score of 50. In other words, Gabon is fulfilling only 50 percent of the potential level of rights enjoyment it could achieve given its available resources. Gabon falls far short of what other countries have achieved with the same level of economic resources. This poor performance calls for a fundamental re-examination of its policies, its strategies, and the scale of resources directed toward fulfilling social and economic rights.

Regional mechanisms for interstate monitoring—the Inter-American Commission on Human Rights,[2] the African Commission on Human and Peoples' Rights,[3] the European Committee of Social Rights[4]— proceed in a similar manner to the CESCR. Their monitoring strategies all require gathering information according to a systematic set of criteria that is broadly accepted as objective and nonpolitical and then interpreting and making judgments based on this information regarding violations and good practices. International organizations and treaty bodies charged with human rights monitoring face two key weaknesses in this regard: significant challenges of data collection and the absence of objective and consistent standards of performance or criteria for interpreting reports and complaints.

Self-reporting by states clearly does not provide adequate information and analysis, as states have every incentive to paint their own performance in the best light possible. Shadow reports from civil society groups and complaints by impacted individuals charging human rights violations are likely to be contested by implicated states and often are constrained by access to data in their ability to paint an accurate overall picture of the state of rights fulfillment in a given country.[5] Allegations leveled by other states can be suspect as politically motivated or seen as threats to the fundamental legal doctrine of state sovereignty. Without agreed criteria for evaluation, the assessments of bodies charged with monitoring human rights realization are vulnerable, contestable, and easily ignored. The SERF Index addresses this central challenge: governments can now use this index and underlying component right scores to report on their overall progress in their reports to treaty-monitoring bodies. Civil society groups can use the same information in shadow reports to highlight regress as well as progress. The CESCR itself can use index scores to scrutinize the government reports.

Accountability of the State to People

Long considered nonjusticiable, social and economic rights have been increasingly claimed and litigated in domestic courts. Civil society groups have increasingly initiated legal action to hold governments accountable for their constitutional and other legal commitments for ensuring access to healthcare, housing, water, and other rights. The first case was pioneered in India, where in a 1980 judgment, the Supreme Court ordered the municipality to comply with its duties to provide water, drainage, and sanitation systems. Subsequently, South Africa broke new ground when the Constitutional Court ruled in 2000 that the government had failed to take measures for the progressive realization of the right to housing. This was followed by several rulings in which the Constitutional Court ordered the government to take measures: to implement a treatment to prevent mother-to-child transmission of HIV/AIDS, to prevent urban displacement, and to extend social security benefits to noncitizens (Langford 2009). As Langford succinctly explains: "ESC [economic, social, and cultural] rights appeared to have been partly rescued from controversies over legitimacy, legality and justiciability, and in many jurisdictions have been accorded a more prominent place in advocacy, discourse and jurisprudence. If we were to speculate on the total number of decisions that have invoked constitutional and international ESC rights, a figure of at least one to two hundred thousand might be in order" (2009, 91).

These cases remain controversial among human rights advocates, who are often critical of their limited scope, ambition, and effectiveness, for example, recognizing rights only in cases of dire need. Yet they reflect an emerging trend in human rights activism to challenge public policies as sources of human rights violations. Arguments can only be strengthened with rigorous evidence using internationally sanctioned data on the performance of governments in achieving the progressive realization of social and economic rights.

Public Policies and Social Arrangements

Legal accountability on its own, without a strong understanding of how social and economic rights objectives can be achieved, is not very useful for furthering rights fulfillment. For this task, policymakers also need information on alternative approaches to fostering rights. Even the best-intentioned actors can falter in their efforts to design effective public policies in the absence of research and analysis providing policy guidance. A fundamental input required for conducting such policy analysis is quantitative data that can reveal the extent of—and trends in—rights realization and help identify causal relationships. Qualitative case reporting and narrowly focused indicators are inadequate in revealing systematic patterns of violations and motivating policy change. The SERF Index can be used in many analytical contexts. To start with, it can be employed to assess the scope for improving performance, identify the priorities for policy reform, and determine if there are trade-offs among competing policy priorities.

Exposing inadequate policy efforts

Hunger, premature death, illiteracy, and many other denials of social and economic rights are not single isolated events or actions affecting individuals. They are social phenomena that result from inadequate public policies and other social arrangements and affect vast numbers of people. Long-term deprivations are rooted in the structures of power, wealth, and resources. For example, recall the case of Fatimata, mentioned in chapter 1, whose five children did not survive to adulthood. Each of the five deaths had a proximate cause specific to Fatima's household, but all of them were also a part of the systematic pattern of high child mortality that affects many others in Sierra Leone.[6] The SERF Index gives evidence of the government's failure to fulfill its social and economic rights obligations and the magnitude of the problem. The country scores 27 percent on the SERF Index's Right to Housing Index and 33 percent on its Right to Health Index. The inadequacy of social arrangements is further highlighted when we compare these scores with those of Rwanda, in eastern Africa, which are considerably higher: 76 percent for housing and 61 percent for health. These scores provide quantitative evidence of the large scope for improvement through reforms in public policy. They open up questions about the causes of elevated child deaths and the failures of public policy and social arrangements, showing the need to advance social and economic rights through policy reform.

What might be the public policies that have been wanting in Sierra Leone? The country records the highest incidence of child mortality in Africa and in the world, at a rate of 185 per 1,000 live births (UNICEF 2012,12). Lack of access to healthcare, sanitation, and clean water in the slum settlement that was their home left Fatimata's family at high risk. But inadequate social infrastructure and services are only some of the wide-ranging preventable causes of high child death rates. Other causes include infectious diseases such as pneumonia and diarrhea and social variables such as maternal health, age, and education. A human rights analysis requires an exploration of these wide-ranging causes and the adequacy of government measures to address them. It requires particular attention be paid to identifying who—which population groups—are most affected and why. Is there discrimination that shapes these outcomes?

What are the root causes of preventable child deaths? It is essential to interrogate the effectiveness of a country's economic development strategy in generating equitable social and economic opportunities for people. High child mortality is only one of the interrelated issues of poverty and inequality in Sierra Leone that are embedded in structural obstacles to development. An analysis of state obligations for the creation of an enabling environment for development characterized by a constant and equitable improvement in human well-being has identified multiple policy requirements.[7] These include maintaining a stable economic and financial system through economic regulation and oversight to manage risk and encourage competition in the market; improving social conditions; promoting good governance, rule of law, and anticorruption measures; and much more (Randolph and Green 2013).

It is beyond the scope of this book to comprehensively review the systemic causes of child mortality as they relate to policy choices in Sierra Leone's economic strategy. But we highlight several issues raised in the country analysis report of the World Bank and African Development Bank (2010) to illustrate that state duties to fulfill social and economic rights require addressing a multiplicity of obstacles that lie in the household, national, and international spheres. First, improving poor people's productivity and access to social opportunities is an urgent priority, especially in rural areas. While two-thirds of the population of Sierra Leone live in rural areas and depend on subsistence agriculture, the country is increasingly dependent on food imports, and the rural poverty rate was 66 percent in 2011 (World Bank 2013b). Second, governance is a major obstacle. Rich in mineral resources—diamonds, iron ore, and more—the economy has long relied on extractive industries, and the country has faced major challenges in translating these resources into national development and widely shared benefits. Third, world market instability also plays a role. World market prices for these commodities, as well as the country's agricultural exports—cocoa and palm oil—are notoriously volatile. The economy was hard hit by the 2008 global financial crisis and the ensuing world recession. With sharply reduced demand for minerals, export earnings fell from 20.8 percent of GDP in 2007 to 16.3 percent in 2008 and 15.7 percent in 2009. Fourth, gender inequality is a major issue (World Bank and African Development Bank 2010, 6–7). Gender disparities in Sierra Leone are apparent in many socioeconomic indicators such as school enrollment rates and poverty rates, and these disparities are a source of underachievement in social indicators overall.

The obligation of progressive realization requires proactive policies to address these structural obstacles through appropriate economic institutions, policies, and practices. An aggregate analysis of state performance on fulfilling rights at the national or subnational level is a first step to identifying systemic failures that require priority attention. The SERF Index scores can be a starting point for pinpointing such systemic failures, which are manifested in low levels of human development across population groups.

Human Rights Obligations and Economic Policies

One of the most exciting developments of the last decade in human rights monitoring has been the new attention given to economic policies as a source of human rights abuses. The last decade has seen a rise in human rights advocacy directed at exposing the human rights consequences of national and international economic policies.

In this context, an issue that has dominated advocacy for policy reform is the inadequacy of social spending. For example, budget review has proliferated across the world as an innovative monitoring method (Blyberg 2009). It has been a major item on the agenda of the U.N. special rapporteur on extreme poverty, which has taken up diverse aspects of social spending: conditional cash transfer programs (2008), austerity measures (2011), and tax and fiscal policy (planned for 2014) (U.N. OHCHR 2013b). Rulings in cases of domestic litigation for social and economic rights have often led to orders by governments to provide services such as medications, healthcare, housing, and safe water. While these are important advances, and the essential role of welfare provisioning for the fulfillment of human rights is without question, they have raised concerns about the reconceptualization of human rights as rights to public services and resources and the consequences of litigation in distorting fiscal priorities (Biehl et al. 2009; Mahajan 2012). These trends also raise equal concern about the risks of misconceptualizing obligations as duties for direct provisioning and allocating maximum resources for social welfare spending. For both normative and empirical reasons, the obligation to advance economic and social rights is clearly *not* limited to the direct provisioning of welfare goods and services.

International legal instruments define obligations broadly, referring to all relevant legislative and policy measures to create an enabling environment for the realization of rights. Article 22 of the Universal Declaration of Human Rights articulates the right of individuals to economic, social, and cultural rights "through national efforts and international cooperation," while Article 28 states explicitly that "everyone is entitled to a *social and international order* in which the rights and freedoms set forth in this Declaration can be fully realized" (United Nations 1948, Arts. 22, 28; emphasis added). The 1986 Declaration on the Right to Development takes this further, explicitly calling on states to act collectively—through international cooperation—as well as individually, to create an enabling environment for development, particularly by removing obstacles and creating opportunities (1986, Preamble, Articles 1, 2, 4, 7). These principles are further articulated in *General Comment 12*, on the right to adequate food, which states:

> The obligation to fulfill incorporates both an obligation to facilitate and an obligation to provide. . . . The obligation to fulfill (facilitate) means the State must proactively engage in activities intended to strengthen people's access to and utilization of resources and means to ensure their livelihood, including food security. Finally, whenever an individual or group is unable, for reasons beyond their control, to enjoy the right to adequate food by the means at their disposal, States have the obligation to fulfill (provide) that right directly. This obligation also applies for persons who are victims of natural or other disasters. (U.N. CESCR 1999b, para. 15)

The General Comment goes on to explain that the "means" that the state must deploy include a wide range of policy instruments, in a coherent national strategy that "should address critical issues and measures in regard to all aspects of the food system, including the production, processing, distribution, marketing and consumption of safe food, as well as parallel measures in the fields of health, education, employment and social security" (U.N. CESCR 1999b, para. 25).

As the case of Fatimata in Sierra Leone illustrates, the lack of services is only a proximate cause of the denial of social and economic rights. The high incidence of child deaths arises from a systemic failure of the government to put in place policies, structures, and frameworks that are feasible within their resource constraints to advance rights realization. This might in some circumstances entail direct government provision of goods and services but far more often requires that the government play a catalytic or facilitating role in enabling rights realization—creating conditions for the "invisible hand" of the market to deliver equitable opportunities—by providing appropriate governance frameworks, regulations, investments, and other public goods. In other words, the realization of rights requires the creation of an enabling policy environment. And in the increasingly integrated global economy, it is not only the national but also the transnational environment that is a key driver of the economic health of countries and the well-being of people.

International human rights norms are intended to be neutral with respect to economic systems (U.N. CESCR 1990), not a recipe for a welfare state or a particular policy mix. A premise underlying the SERF Index is that the government obligation is to pursue an economic model that both generates resources and advances the realization of human rights. Developing such a strategy is a key challenge for all countries in this century.

The SERF Index scores provide an important research tool to motivate policy reforms. Aggregate measures of state performance—such as GDP or the HDI—help locate patterns of systemic problems that necessitate urgent and priority action in reform agendas. They can be used to further understanding of the relationship between social and economic rights and a wide array of other social arrangements and to explore trade-offs among competing priorities.

Trade-Offs among Competing Priorities

Governments face difficult choices regarding potential trade-offs. For example, is there a trade-off between meeting social and economic rights obligations and promoting economic growth, or phrased differently, is there a conflict between fulfilling social and economic rights today and expanding resource capacities to realize such rights more broadly in the long run? Are there some policies that simultaneously foster the realization of social and economic rights and economic growth? Does democratic accountability further social and economic rights fulfillment, or can democracy foster short-term patronage policies that impede rights realization? Do civil and political rights matter for social and economic rights? What about gender equality? How important are legal guarantees—should social and economic rights advocacy prioritize legal reforms or reforms to public policies? Do countries that spend more on social investments such as health and education do better in their provision? In this regard, the SERF Index provides an important new instrument to advance research and analysis regarding policies to promote economic and social rights realization. Our initial analyses in this regard reveal five major insights.

First, gender equity is highly correlated with greater fulfillment of social and economic rights. While improving gender equality is in itself a goal with clear, intrinsic value, it is also instrumental in the fulfillment of social and economic rights; societies where women have equal access to basic rights such as education, and women are empowered to make decisions affecting themselves and their families, achieve higher fulfillment of social and economic rights for all members.

Second, democracy and government accountability are strongly related to better fulfillment of social and economic rights. This relationship is not straightforward, however; the correlation reflects a rising "floor" on social and economic rights performance as governance improves. In other words, while countries with low levels of democracy and accountability can sometimes do very well at fulfilling the social and economic rights of their citizens, they are also much more likely to do very poorly. In contrast, democracies and countries with more accountable governments almost invariably avoid the worst social and economic rights–related outcomes.

Third, at first glance it seems obvious that the amount the government spends on public services such as health and education should be an important factor in determining SERF outcomes. Yet careful analysis reveals that spending money is not necessarily effective; the relationship between expenditures and outcomes is far more attenuated than policymakers might hope. Other factors such as the prevalence of HIV/AIDS and malaria, the composition of expenditures, the effectiveness of service delivery, and government accountability are often more significant than the level of public expenditures in predicting rights outcomes. In short, government expenditures on health do correlate with health right fulfill-ment, but this positive relationship is weak at best and swamped by other factors.

Fourth, there is no necessary trade-off between a country's fulfill-ment of social and economic rights today and economic growth rates. Countries with high levels of social and economic rights fulfillment and low levels of growth in the past tend to do much better at realizing *both* economic growth *and* rights fulfillment in the future than do coun-tries with low levels of rights fulfillment and high past growth rates. Conversely, countries with high levels of social and economic rights fulfillment and low growth rates are likely to achieve high growth rates in the near future. In other words, countries that are seeking to escape a low-growth, low-social-and-economic-rights trap are better off priori-tizing social and economic rights over growth. They are also more likely to achieve a virtuous cycle whereby high growth and high economic and social rights fulfillment reinforce each other.

Fifth, while international treaties are unrelated to social and economic rights outcomes, countries with legally enforceable rights guarantees in domestic law do indeed perform better at fulfilling the rights guaranteed in law. Correlation does not imply causation, however, since it could be that the same countries that for other reasons are already more likely to pursue policies to fulfill social and economic rights are also more likely to enshrine those social contract commitments into law. This issue bears further investigation.

"Progressive Realization to the Maximum of Available Resources"—The Empirical Approach to Building Theory

Normative versus Empirical Approach

A clear definition of a normative concept of human rights might appear to be a prerequisite for identifying indicators that reflect the essential elements of the concept. But in reality, the reverse can also be an effective approach in the study of human rights theory. Recent debates note that constructing human rights measurement tools can be a strategy to help clarify, not just implement, state obligations (Raworth 2001; Welling 2009). For example, in developing indicators for maternal mortality, Maine and Yamin write, "Without a sound understanding of the epidemiology of maternal mortality (and therefore, the interventions that can prevent it), the concept of a human right to be free from avoidable death during pregnancy and childbirth will remain meaningless. . . . Rather than starting with the abstract concept of the right to health and looking for indicators that might infuse substantive meaning into the progressive realization of that right,. . . [we] start with the very tangible problem of maternal mortality" (1999, 564).

In constructing the SERF Index, we start with the tangible evidence on well-being achievement and levels of economic resources available to give content to the abstract normative principle of "progressive realization to the maximum of available resources." In examining the historical experience of countries over twenty-five years, we can empirically document the maximum level of rights enjoyment that has been achieved over time at each different level of available resources. As seen in chapter 3 and explained further below, the shapes of the Achievement Possibilities Frontier boundaries show precisely the extent to which resource constraints operate on the realization of each substantive social and economic right. With this understanding, we clarify the concept of progressive realization, which has long been mired in controversy.

Controversy over the Principle of Progressive Realization

The principle of "progressive realization to the maximum of available resources" has been a major source of theoretical and policy controversy since its origins in the International Covenant on Economic, Social and Cultural Rights. Delegates negotiating the 1966 covenant were divided (Alston and Quinn 1987). Proponents argued that poor developing countries faced enormous constraints to achieving the full realization of social and economic rights and that the disparities in economic resources available to countries needed to be recognized in defining state obligations (Alston and Quinn 1987). Opponents argued that the principle of "progressive realization" posed a risk of weakening state obligations—characterized subsequently as opening up an "escape hatch" (Leckie 1998) for state accountability (Robertson 1994).

Furthermore, the principle of progressive realization has been used as an argument to challenge the legitimacy of social and economic rights as rights. Skeptics argue that these requirements set them apart from civil and political rights. However, Shue (1980), Alston (Alston and Quinn 1987), and others have argued that all rights require positive action to be fulfilled and therefore incur positive obligations for fulfillment. For example, guaranteeing the right not to be tortured requires training security personnel, setting up administrative oversight procedures, and many other investments, none of which can be achieved overnight and all of which require economic and organizational capacity to implement. While this argument has become well established in the human rights literature (see, for example, Chapman 2007; U.N. OHCHR 2012), the perception persists that social and economic rights are costly and, lacking hard standards against which violations can be identified and attributed to specific actors, are issues of social justice, not rights.

Despite its importance as a central and unresolved controversy, the empirical evidence behind the need for a relative standard has not been examined. What is the relationship between social and economic rights achievements and relative resource availability? Those who defend the concept merely assert in the abstract that realization is contingent on the availability of resources. Critics do not offer evidence to the contrary. They assume that even where resources in a country are limited, the shortfalls in rights realization must be due to an unwillingness on the part of the government to give priority to spending on schooling, health, and other sectors important for the fulfillment of social and economic rights. They offer no evidence on the scope or potential for improvement within the constraints of resources. Human rights research and practice have pursued these questions as abstract normative issues, not as empirical questions.

The CESCR has followed two strategies in developing social and economic rights monitoring. First, it has identified "minimum core" obligations and focused on identifying instances where a person's rights have been violated (Chapman 2007). Second, it has left state parties to set their own "benchmarks." In its very first General Comment, the

CESCR cautiously recommended setting national—rather than single global/universal—benchmarks, stating: "It may be useful for States to identify specific benchmarks or goals against which their performance in a given area can be assessed. Thus for example, it is generally agreed that it is important to set specific goals with respect to the reduction of infant mortality, the extent of vaccination of children, the intake of calories per person, the number of persons per health care provider, etc. In many of these cases, global benchmarks are of limited use, whereas national or other more specific benchmarks can provide an extremely valuable indication of progress" (1989, para. 6). This approach is further reinforced in *General Comment 14*, which invites states "to set appropriate national benchmarks in relation to each indicator" (U.N. CESCR 2000, paras. 57–58).

These approaches leave open the question of how the minimum core and national benchmarks should be set. While much work has been done by the CESCR on developing monitoring methods, as explained in chapter 2, the focus has been on developing indicators, and little attention has been paid to defining national benchmarks.

Closing the Escape Hatch—Setting Relative Benchmarks for Progressive Realization

Without understanding the empirical relationship between resources and pathways to achieving a society where no one is threatened with hunger, premature death, homelessness, and the absence of other social and economic rights, the concept of progressive realization to the maximum of available resources will forever be an undefined, open-ended standard subject to arbitrary interpretation. Human rights standard setting can turn to the literature of development economics, which is rich in studies of the empirical relationship between economic resources and attainments in health, education, and human development more broadly defined.[8] There is widespread consensus among economists that economic resources are a necessary but not a sufficient condition for human development. How effectively resources translate into improved human outcomes depends on how well government policies direct economic resources, create incentives, and foster patterns of growth that meet human priority needs, ensure equity in access to opportunities and distribution of benefits, and attend to the needs of the marginalized and vulnerable (see, for example, UNDP 1996, 2010; World Bank 2006).

These empirical findings imply that governments do indeed face resource constraints, but within those constraints, they are obligated to do their utmost to put in place the most effective policy measures possible for the realization of social and economic rights. In other words, a one-size-fits-all standard of immediate realization of socioeconomic rights does not make economic sense; relative standards or benchmarks need to be defined. Criticisms of applying global goals to countries serve to underscore the unfairness of a single one-size-fits-all target and the need for relative benchmarks that take account of different starting points and capacities. Economists have argued that the Millennium Development Goals are unrealistic targets for many countries (Clemens, Kenny, and Moss 2007), an unfair framework for assessing performance in Africa (Easterly 2009), and give false readings of country performance based on whether a target is achieved rather than the rate of progress toward reaching it (Fukuda-Parr, Greenstein, and Stewart 2013; Hailu and Tsukada 2011).[9]

The obligation of progressive realization therefore requires setting relative benchmarks. The SERF Index introduces a methodological innovation to set country-specific relative benchmarks, based on the empirical experience of countries. As explained in chapter 3, our methodology starts with a careful review of the empirical evidence available on different levels of well-being outcomes achieved over a twenty-five-year period by countries around the world. The resulting scatterplots (shown in Figures 4.1–4.4 in chapter 4) reveal that there is a remarkable range of outcome achievements at any given level of income. The benchmark obligation is to achieve the highest historical outcome—at the APF—in keeping with the normative content of international law. Two other articles (Cingranelli and Richards 2007; Kimenyi 2007) also took the empirical route and reviewed historical data relating rights enjoyment levels and levels of income. But they set benchmarks at the average achievement level, not the highest, which does not reflect the obligation to take all possible measures to fulfill rights.

Moreover, the shape of the APF indicates the point at which resources no longer pose a constraint. Although feasible rights fulfillment rises with income levels, at some level of income performance plateaus for most rights—meaning that increasingly higher incomes do not lead to better social and economic rights outcomes (shown on Table 4.5). Table 8.1 summarizes these plateau values for the eight core country indicators.

The empirical evaluation of resource constraints to rights fulfillment reveals four significant insights. First, resource constraints pose a serious challenge for countries at low levels of per capita income, particularly those in the World Bank's "low-income" category (2012 GNI per capita below $1,035).[10] All but three of the core country SERF Index indicators peak below $8,000 per capita income. In other words, resources are not a binding constraint after this point, and the principle of "progressive realization" is empirically a relatively low bar.

Second, resource constraints are generally not relevant for high-income OECD countries; their incomes are above the leveling-off point for most indicators, and none has an excuse for failing to ensure that all those under their jurisdiction achieve close to the maximum level, if not the maximum level, of rights enjoyment.

TABLE 8.1 Plateau Values for Eight Core Country Indicators

Right	Maximum Achievement Value	Income Level When Indicator Reaches Peak (2005 PPP$)
Food	98% not stunted	$7,806
Education	100% primary school completion	$1,076
	100% combined school enrollment rate	$25,112
Health	99.74% under-5 child survival rate	$6,350
	89.85% surviving to age 65	$26,450
	Contraceptive use	Asymptotic peak
Housing	100% rural population with access to improved water	$6,453
	100% population with access to improved sanitation	$3,970
Work	98% productive work providing income above $2.00/day	$3,824

Source: Table 4.5, this volume.

Third, at lower income levels there is a great deal of variation among countries with respect to rights outcomes. For example, while Sierra Leone's under-five survival rate was just seventy-three per hundred live births with an income of $661 in 2006, the survival rate was ninety-three per hundred in Eritrea with a similar income level at $610.

Fourth, resource constraints vary by right. For example, while full primary school completion can be achieved at a low income level of $1,076 per capita, 99.7 percent child survival to age five can only be achieved at $6,350, and survival to age sixty-five, at $26,450.

To conclude, these empirical findings demonstrate that although a lack of economic resources can impose an important constraint on countries' ability to ensure rights enjoyment, even in the face of limited resources, most countries can do a great deal more. These results reinforce the argument of many human rights advocates that most poor countries can do much more to achieve higher levels of social and economic rights enjoyment and that lack of resources is not a convincing explanation for the shortfalls in social and economic rights realization. The SERF Index provides evidence on the scope of improvement possible and is particularly helpful in evaluating how far these resource constraints go in explaining countries' low outcome levels and how much they can blame their lack of resources for falling short on ensuring full enjoyment of all rights.

Concluding Remarks

In a 2000 article, Philip Alston, a leading authority on social and economic rights, noted: "The International human rights regime is one of the most important positive legacies to emerge from the twentieth century. The principle of accountability is one of its indispensable characteristics. It is not surprising, then, that the greatest challenge confronting the international community in this domain at the beginning of the twenty-first century is to develop approaches that give substance and meaning to that principle. New initiatives are required at both national and international levels" (2000, 249). Our aim in developing the SERF Index is to respond to this challenge by developing a methodology that takes the obligation of progressive realization to the maximum of available resources seriously.

This has required a departure from some of the recent trends in developing indicators for human rights monitoring. We focus on positive obligations for progressive realization rather than on violations. Our unit of analysis is country performance in the aggregate with respect to its population or subgroups, not individual cases, and on the broad spectrum of substantive social and economic rights, rather than fragmented categories of rights and obligations. We do not create new data but, rather, rely on existing socioeconomic statistics. Finally, our approach is empirically driven and uses methods and concepts from development economics to give concrete substance to the abstract norms set out in international legal documents. The SERF Index fills a gap by providing a summary cross-country comparable quantitative measure of social and economic rights fulfillment that is rigorously based on international legal norms.

No statistical indicator can capture all the dimensions of progress in the realization of rights. Quantitative indicators complement qualitative evaluations, and the combination of different approaches makes possible a richer assessment of social and economic rights fulfillment.

Hunger, lack of education, premature death, dangerous unproductive work, and much more still blight the lives of billions. These are not just outrageous social conditions but a product of unjust social arrangements. Numbers illuminate the accountability of public authorities to act. No challenge facing the global community today is more pressing, more fundamental, or more existential for billions of people around the world than economic and social rights realization. Despite exponential increases in per capita incomes and astonishing growth rates in most countries over the past two centuries, too many people remain left out and left behind by these extraordinary leaps of technology, productivity, and opportunity. There is now a growing global consensus that the most essential measures of social performance and human well-being cannot be reduced to or reflected by our activity as mere producers and consumers. Social progress, at its most fundamental, means expanding the freedom for people to live full and meaningful lives. Economic and social rights, articulated and guaranteed by international law, are a core and inviolable aspect of human well-being and freedom. Our effort here with the SERF Index is to provide a new yardstick by which the performance of countries and peoples can be measured and judged—a yardstick that positions economic resources and growth as a necessary means for fulfilling social and economic rights, but not as ends in themselves, and that evaluates how well societies are doing in translating these resources into the social and economic rights outcomes that really matter for peoples' lives. With this new measure of performance, we can better hold ourselves accountable for realizing economic and social rights and expanding human freedom.

> Overcoming poverty is not a gesture of charity. It is an act of justice. It is the protection of a fundamental human right, the right to dignity and a decent life. While poverty persists, there is no true freedom.
>
> —Nelson Mandela, Johannesburg, July 2, 2005

APPENDIX

SERF Indicator Definitions and Data Sources

Indicator	Primary Source(s)[a]	Indicator Definition[b]
Resource Capacity		
Gross Domestic Product Per Capita (2005 PPP$)	World Bank World Development Indicators	GDP per capita based on purchasing power parity (PPP). PPP GDP is gross domestic product converted to international dollars using PPP rates. An international dollar has the same purchasing power over GDP as the U.S. dollar has in the United States. GDP at purchaser's prices is the sum of gross value added by all resident producers in the economy plus any product taxes and minus any subsidies not included in the value of the products. It is calculated without making deductions for depreciation of fabricated assets or for depletion and degradation of natural resources. Data are in constant 2005 international dollars.

(Continued)

SERF Indicator Definitions and Data Sources (Continued)

Indicator	Primary Source(s)[a]	Indicator Definition[b]
Right to Food		
Malnutrition Prevalence— Height for Age (% children under 5)	World Health Organization (WHO) Global Database on Child Growth and Malnutrition (http://apps .who.int/ghodata) and UNICEF (http://www .childinfo.org)	Prevalence of child malnutrition is the percentage of children under age 5 whose height for age (stunting) is more than two standard deviations below the median for the international reference population ages 0–59 months. For children up to 2 years old, height is measured by recumbent length. For older children, height is measured by stature while standing. The data use WHO's child growth standards released in 2006.
Low-Birth-Weight Babies	UNICEF, State of the World's Children, Childinfo, and Demographic and Health Surveys by Macro International	Low-birth-weight babies are newborns weighing less than 2,500 grams, with the measurement taken within the first hours of life, before significant postnatal weight loss has occurred.
Right to Education		
Primary School Completion Rate	U.N. Educational, Scientific, and Cultural Organization (UNESCO) Institute for Statistics	Primary completion rate is the percentage of students completing the last year of primary school. It is calculated by taking the total number of students in the last grade of primary school, minus the number of repeaters in that grade, divided by the total number of children of official graduation age. (Capped at 100%.)

Indicator	Primary Source(s)[a]	Indicator Definition[b]
Gross Combined School Enrollment Rate	UNESCO Institute for Statistics, extracted from http://stats.uis .unesco.org/unesco/ TableViewer/document .aspx?ReportId=143&IF_ Language=eng	Gross enrollment ratio. All levels combined (except pre-primary). All students. (Capped at 100%.)
Gross Secondary School Enrollment Rate	UNESCO Institute for Statistics, historical series, http://stats.uis. unesco.org/unesco/ TableViewer/document. aspx?ReportId=143&IF_ Language=eng	Gross enrollment ratio is the ratio of total enrollment, regardless of age, to the population of the age group that officially corresponds to the level of education shown. Secondary education completes the provision of basic education that began at the primary level, and aims at laying the foundations for lifelong learning and human development, by offering more subject- or skill-oriented instruction using more specialized teachers.
Average Math and Science Programme for International Student Assessment Score	Organisation for Economic Co-operation and Development Programme for International Student Assessment, extracted from http://pisacountry.acer .edu.au/	Average of country mean quality-of-learning outcome scores on mathematics and science subject tests.

Right to Health

Contraceptive Prevalence Rate (% women 15–49)	Household surveys, including Demographic and Health Surveys by Macro International and Multiple Indicator Cluster Surveys by UNICEF	Contraceptive prevalence rate is the percentage of women who are practicing, or whose sexual partners are practicing, any form of contraception. It is usually measured for married women ages 15–49 only.

(Continued)

SERF Indicator Definitions and Data Sources (Continued)

Indicator	Primary Source(s)[a]	Indicator Definition[b]
Survival to Age 65 (% cohort)	U.N. Population Division (UNPD)	Survival to age 65 refers to the percentage of a cohort of newborn infants that would survive to age 65 if subject to current age-specific mortality rates.
Life Expectancy at Birth	Derived from male and female life expectancy at birth. Male and female life expectancy sources: (1) UNPD, *World Population Prospects: The 2008 Revision* (2009) (advanced Excel tables); (2) Census reports and other statistical publications from national statistical offices; (3) Eurostat: Demographic Statistics; (4) Secretariat of the Pacific Community: Statistics and Demography Programme; and (5) U.S. Census Bureau: International Database	Life expectancy at birth indicates the number of years a newborn infant would live if prevailing patterns of mortality at the time of its birth were to stay the same throughout its life.
Child Mortality Rate	Inter-agency Group for Child Mortality Estimation (UNICEF, WHO, World Bank, UNPD, universities and research institutions)	Under-5 mortality rate is the probability per 1,000 that a newborn baby will die before reaching age 5, if subject to current age-specific mortality rates.

Indicator	Primary Source(s)[a]	Indicator Definition[b]
Right to Housing		
Improved Sanitation (% population with access)	WHO and UNICEF Joint Monitoring Programme, http://www .wssinfo.org/.	Access to improved sanitation facilities refers to the percentage of the population with at least adequate access to excreta disposal facilities that can effectively prevent human, animal, and insect contact with excreta. Improved facilities range from simple but protected pit latrines to flush toilets with a sewerage connection. To be effective, facilities must be correctly constructed and properly maintained.
Rural Improved Water (% rural population with access)	WHO and UNICEF Joint Monitoring Programme, http://www .wssinfo.org/.	Access to an improved water source refers to the percentage of the population with reasonable access to an adequate amount of water from an improved source, such as a household connection, public standpipe, borehole, protected well or spring, or rainwater collection. Unimproved sources include vendors, tanker trucks, and unprotected wells and springs. Reasonable access is defined as the availability of at least 20 liters a person a day from a source within one kilometer of the dwelling.

(Continued)

Indicator	Primary Source(s)[a]	Indicator Definition[b]
Improved Water (% population with access)	WHO and UNICEF Joint Monitoring Programme, U.N. Environment Programme (via Pacific Institute)	Access to an improved water source refers to the percentage of the population with reasonable access to an adequate amount of water from an improved source, such as a household connection, public standpipe, borehole, protected well or spring, or rainwater collection. Unimproved sources include vendors, tanker trucks, and unprotected wells and springs. Reasonable access is defined as the availability of at least 20 liters a person a day from a source within one kilometer of the dwelling.
Right to Work		
Poverty Head Count (<$2.00 per day)	World Bank Development Research Group. Data are based on primary household survey data obtained from government statistical agencies and World Bank country departments, http://iresearch.worldbank.org/PovcalNet/index.htm?3.	Population below $2.00 a day is the percentage of the population living on less than $2.00 a day at 2005 international prices.
Long-Term Unemployment Rate (% of unemployed)	International Labour Organization's Key Indicators of the Labour Market, http://www.ilo.org/empelm/what/WCMS_114240/lang--en/index.htm	Long-term unemployment refers to the number of people with continuous periods of unemployment extending for a year or longer, expressed as a percentage of the total unemployed.

Indicator	Primary Source(s)[a]	Indicator Definition[b]
Relative Poverty Rate	Luxembourg Income Study, extracted from its Key Figures on Poverty and Inequality online data tool, http://www.lisdatacenter.org/data-access/key-figures/	Percentage of population with less than 50% of the median income.

[a] Extracted from the World Bank's World Development Indicators online (http://data.worldbank.org/data-catalog/world-development-indicators) unless otherwise indicated.

[b] Definitions from website indicated.

Source: Fukuda-Parr, Lawson-Remer, and Randolph 2011, Table A.1. reproduced with permission.

NOTES

Chapter 1

1. Set in Victorian England, with its social context of widespread poverty, *A Christmas Carol* (Dickens 1843) relates the transformation of Ebenezer Scrooge from a bitter and miserly man to one who trusts in the common bonds of humanity and values of a dignified life.

2. The evidence for these patterns of growth is well documented in numerous references. See, for example, the annual U.N. Development Programme Human Development Reports that have highlighted the dislocative and exclusionary effects of growth since 1990, particularly the 1996 report. For references on experiences of the 1990s and 2000s, see *The Price of Inequality*, a study of the United States by Joseph Stiglitz (2012), or *An Uncertain Glory*, a study of India by Jean Dreze and Amartya Sen (2013).

3. Both Nussbaum and Sen have written extensively on capabilities and freedoms. Nussbaum provides an overview in her 2003 monograph *Creating Capabilities* (see 2011b), and Sen, in his 1999 volume *Development as Freedom*. For a useful survey of this literature and introduction to capabilities, see Robeyns's "The Capability Approach: A Theoretical Survey" (2005).

4. Capabilities are, according to the capability approach, the ends of well-being. Justice and development should be conceptualized in terms of people's capabilities to function—that is, their effective opportunities to undertake the actions and activities that they want to engage in and to be whom they want to be. These beings and doings, which Sen calls functionings, together constitute what makes a life valuable. Functionings include, for example, working, resting, being literate,

being healthy, and being part of a community. The distinction between achieved functionings and capabilities is between the realized and the effectively possible—in other words, between achievements, on the one hand, and freedoms or valuable options from which one can choose, on the other. What is ultimately important is that people have the freedoms or valuable opportunities (capabilities) to lead the kinds of lives they want to lead, to do what they want to do, and to be the person they want to be. Once they effectively have these substantive opportunities, they can choose those options that they value most. For example, every person should have the opportunity to be part of a community and to practice a religion; but if someone prefers to be a hermit or an atheist, he or she should also have this option.

5. The committee included experts in constitutional law from China, the United States, France, Russia, and Lebanon.

6. Sierra Leone's under-five mortality rates are among the highest in the world, registering 182 per 1,000 live births in 2012. The maternal mortality ratio is estimated at 890 per 100,000 live births.

7. "Standard threats" in Shue's terminology.

8. See Rosga and Satterthwaite 2009, 263–274, for a useful review of the historical background.

9. See, for example, Power 1997; Strathern 2000.

Chapter 2

* This chapter has benefited from the able research assistance of Madeleine Baer for the literature review.

1. The International Commission of Jurists, the Faculty of Law of the University of Limburg, and the Urban Morgan Institute for Human Rights, University of Cincinnati, convened a group of experts to provide further guidance on the nature and scope of the obligations of state parties to the ICESCR. The principles they unanimously agreed to are known as the *Limburg Principles* (United Nations 1987b).

2. They include *General Comment 4: The Right to Adequate Housing; General Comment 7: The Right to Adequate Housing, Forced Evictions; General Comment 12: The Right to Adequate Food; General Comment 13: The Right to Education; General Comment 14: The Right to Highest Attainable Standard of Health; General Comment 15: The Right to Water;* and *General Comment 19: The Right to Social Security.* See http://tbinternet.ohchr.org/_layouts/treatybodyexternal/TBSearch.aspx?Lang=en&TreatyID=9&DocTypeID=11, accessed February 13, 2014.

3. The International Commission of Jurists, the Urban Morgan Institute for Human Rights, and the Center for Human Rights of the Faculty of Law of Maastricht University convened a group of experts on the occasion of the tenth anniversary of the *Limburg Principles* to further elaborate those principles in light of subsequent jurisprudence. These guidelines were acknowledged by the United Nations (2000).

4. For overview of these debates, see Rosga and Satterthwaite 2009; Welling 2009. For papers that raise some key issues, see Green 2001; Raworth 2001.

5. While debates in the 1960s and 1970s emphasized the distinctiveness of economic, social, and cultural rights in incurring positive obligations and argued that this set them apart from civil and political rights, it has become increasingly recognized that these principles are just as relevant for civil and political rights. The realization of civil and political rights—freedom of speech, freedom of assembly, freedom from slavery, freedom from torture, and the right to a fair trial—cannot be achieved overnight by the stroke of a pen. For example, it takes resources and time to eliminate torture as much as it does to make schooling accessible universally. It requires training of the police force, just as training of teachers is necessary to provide education.

6. Treaty bodies are composed of experts and established by the Human Rights Council to monitor the implementation of treaties. States are obligated to report on their performance. See http://www.ohchr.org/EN/HRBodies/Pages/TreatyBodies.aspx. Special rapporteurs under "Special Procedures" are independent experts appointed by the Human Rights Council to advise on a thematic or country situation. See http://www.ohchr.org/en/HRBodies/SP/Pages/Welcomepage.aspx.

7. In 1988 the Organization of American States adopted the San Salvador protocol to set up a reporting system for peer monitoring and a working group to develop an indicators framework.

8. The U.K. Equality and Human Rights Commission developed an indicators framework for monitoring (Burchardt and Vizard 2011).

9. Riedel was a CESCR member from 2003 to 2010.

10. Hunt was special rapporteur for the right to the highest attainable standards of health from 2002 to 2008.

11. Definitions and data collection methods are defined nationally and not harmonized across countries.

12. Some, such as initiatives by Humana, Banks, Bollen, Gastil, and Lowenstein, among others, were not sustained, but others were institutionalized and continue to be published and maintained. Three composite indices comprising cross-national data sets on state performance are most widely used: the Political Terror Scale, the Cingranelli–Richards Index, and the Freedom House indices. These aggregate cross-country comparative data make possible comparative statistical analysis of trends and patterns in state behavior as well as causal relationships between human rights and other social variables (Landman 2004). From the 1980s, composite indices of civil and political rights fostered new research in political science and law on such questions as how much importance is given to human rights concerns in U.S. foreign policy, whether human rights violations are more or less likely to occur with economic prosperity (Cingranelli and Wright 1988), and whether ratification of human rights treaties affects state behavior (Claude and Jabine 1986; Hathaway 2002).

13. A network of NGOs—HURIDOCS—was created in 1979 to create a depository of data and advance and standardize methodologies and recording systems. Pioneered by Patrick Ball and others in El Salvador, many projects focused on developing evidence for human rights abuses by authoritarian regimes during civil wars of the 1990s and provided important evidence for peace and reconciliation processes in El Salvador, Bosnia, Guatemala, and elsewhere (Asher 2008).

14. One exception is the Toronto Initiative on Social and Economic Rights, an important initiative that uses qualitative rankings to create data on constitutional guarantees for social and economic rights.

Chapter 3

1. In the case of the SERF Index, there is no compelling reason to weight any right aspect more heavily than another when constructing the composite right index. The methodology can readily be adapted to weight some right aspects more heavily in contexts where it makes sense to do so.

2. Data extracted from World Bank 2013b.

3. Since the penalty formula is only applied when a country's resource capacity exceeds Yp, this "income ratio" will always exceed 1.0. This penalty formula uses the fact that multiples of a proportion diminish faster the smaller the proportion. The rescaled performance indicator is converted to a proportion, and the income ratio specifies the power function. Multiplying by 100 converts the proportion back to a percentage.

4. GDP is the value of output produced within a country's geographic boarders, while gross national income (GNI) excludes profit remittances of foreign-owned transnational corporations and includes remittances from a country's nationals. The difference in per capita GDP and GNI is not insubstantial for a few countries, but for most countries it is negligible. In our view, there is no clear advantage in selecting GNI over GDP as the indicator of a country's resource capacity, and there is a stronger historical precedence for using per capita GDP as a measure of a country's per capita national resource capacity. The decision to include GDP instead of GNI is explored in greater depth in chapter 7.

5. Much of official development assistance and foreign aid comes in the form of loans, rather than grants. Even though the loan must include at least a 25 percent concessional component to be considered development assistance, the actual concessional component of official development assistance and foreign aid differs among countries as well as over time. This makes comparisons across countries and over time suspect. Additionally, a given year's official development assistance and foreign aid value includes the net present value of any debt forgiven, yet only the current year's cost of servicing the debt forgiven is actually available to the country in that year (Organisation for Economic Co-operation and Development and Development Assistance Committee 2007). We do not include these flows in the construction of the International SERF Index.

6. We use data from 1990 to 2006, all data since 1990 that were available in 2008, the year the APFs were constructed. Beyond the need to ensure that the time frame encompasses the range of policy experience, the inclusion of data from multiple decades increases the sample size, thereby increasing the stability of the estimates.

7. Gleditsch et al. 2002; Uppsala Conflict Data Program/Peace Research Institute Oslo (UCDP/PRIO) *Armed Conflict Dataset Codebook: Version 4-2008* (UCDP/ PRIO 2008). The UCDP/PRIO database defines a major military conflict as a conflict in which there are at least one thousand battle-related deaths in a given year in the country concerned. Observations from those countries with a code of "2" in a given year on the variable "int" in the UCDP/PRIO *Armed Conflict Dataset Codebook: Version 4-2008* are excluded from the data used to estimate the frontier for the subsequent ten years. The ten-year standard rather than a shorter time period is used given the observed frequency with which civil conflicts, in particular, simmer below the level of a major conflict and then reerupt, thus likely compromising data reliability throughout the period.

8. The curves are fit using the curve-fitting routine in IBM's Statistical Package for the Social Sciences. With the measures taken to avoid measurement error, checks varying the specific observations included in the sample demonstrated that the estimated APFs were robust. As an alternative, data envelopment analysis or stochastic frontier production function estimation techniques could be used to estimate the frontiers. We rejected the first approach given its sensitivity to outliers. The second approach is less transparent, given its econometric sophistication, and additionally requires analysts to specify the functional form of the relationship in advance.

Chapter 4

* The contributions of Michelle Prairie, John Stewart, Patrick Guyer, and Louise Moreira Daniels to this chapter are gratefully acknowledged.

1. The General Comments of the CESCR include a separate comment, *General Comment 15*, on the right to water accessible "within, or in the immediate vicinity of each household, educational institution and workplace" (U.N. CESCR 2003, para. 12, c.i). This, in conjunction with *General Comment 4*, on the right to housing, which defines the right to housing to include ready access to facilities and infrastructure including safe drinking water (U.N. CESCR 1992, para. 8), links the right to water closely with the right to housing, and thus we include the right to water as an element of the right to housing.

2. It is also recognized in several other instruments under international law, notably the Rome Declaration on World Food Security adopted on November 13, 1996, at the World Food Summit.

3. Other international instruments further detail its content, including the World Declaration on Education for All (UNESCO 1994, Art. 1), the Vienna Declaration and Programme of Action (United Nations 1993, Part I, para. 33, and Part II, para.

80), and the Plan of Action for the United Nations Decade for Human Rights Education (United Nations 1996, para. 2).

4. Additionally, the Declaration on Social Progress and Development, Art. 10 (United Nations 1969); the Vancouver Declaration on Human Settlements, Sec. III.8 (Habitat 1976); the Istanbul Declaration on Human Settlements, paras. 8 and 9 (Habitat 1996); and the Declaration on the Right to Development, Art. 8.1 (United Nations 1986).

5. For example, it is affirmed in Part II, Art. 1, of the Revised European Social Charter (Council of Europe 1996), Art. 15 of the African Charter on Human and Peoples' Rights (Organization of African Unity 1982), and Art. 6 of the Additional Protocol to the American Convention on Human Rights in the Area of Economic, Social and Cultural Rights (Organization of American States 1988).

6. See, for example, Art. 9 of the Additional Protocol to the American Convention on Human Rights in the Area of Economic, Social and Cultural Rights (Organization of American States 1988) and Arts. 12, 13, and 14 of the European Social Charter (Council of Europe 1996).

7. The World Bank's World Development Indicators and other data sets compiled by international organizations do not restrict their indicators to those derived from socioeconomic and other administrative surveys but, rather, include indicators based on household perception and opinion surveys, expert judgment, and one-time surveys. As such, an indicator's inclusion in these data sets alone is not sufficient to pass our screen for consideration.

8. An alternative indicator that focuses on the nutritional status of the population as a whole is the proportion of the population below the minimum level of dietary energy consumption, the undernourishment rate. However, this indicator is available less frequently, and country coverage depends on supplementing survey data with estimates based on food balance sheets, the age and sex distribution of the population, and data on inequality in caloric consumption. The basic data underlying food balance sheets are often unreliable and frequently based on "expert judgment" rather than on survey or market data. Data on the quality of food production diverted from human consumption (e.g., used for animal feed, seed, etc.) are especially open to challenge. Beyond the issue of the accuracy of country food balance sheets, a major source of inaccuracy concerns the information on inequality in food consumption. Surveys providing the basis for this estimate are conducted infrequently, and a small difference in the inequality coefficient can make a substantial difference in the estimate of the undernourishment rate. In some countries data on inequality in food consumption are not available, and data from "similar" countries must be used to estimate the undernourishment rate.

9. A preferable indicator is the net combined school enrollment rate, but this would have further restricted the country coverage of the index. The secondary and tertiary school enrollment rates in combination were also considered, but country

coverage was considerably worse for the net secondary school enrollment rate, and the gross secondary school enrollment rate failed to discriminate well between upper-middle-income and high-income countries. The secondary school completion rate along with the number of college graduates (first level) out of one thousand were also considered, but again, country coverage was too limited. Thus the decision to use the gross combined school enrollment rate instead was driven by the realities of data limitations.

10. A number of low- and middle-income countries participate in alternative international testing programs such as the Progress in International Reading Literacy Study and the Trends in International Mathematics and Science Study (Institute of Education Sciences 2014), but coverage among low- and middle-income countries on any one program is still insufficiently wide.

11. The USDA Food Security Index is a direct indicator of food security encompassing the psychological dimensions (worry, social exclusion) as well as the quality and quantity dimensions. For a full description of the USDA Food Security Index and related information, see http://www.ers.usda.gov/topics/food-nutrition-assistance/food-security-in-the-us.aspx#.Up6MDuKoiul.

12. In the case of three of the indicators used to reflect rights fulfillment in high-income OECD countries—the percentage of unemployed not long-term unemployed, the percentage of those not relatively poor, and the percentage of normal-birth-weight babies—the Yp value is not directly observed because the frontier is flat over the entire relevant income range. In these cases, we set the Yp value at $16,000 (2005 PPP$), the per capita income-level breakpoint the World Bank uses to differentiate high-income countries from upper-middle-income countries. The value of the adjusted performance indicator is sensitive to the selected Yp value for countries failing to fulfill the right aspect concerned. As such, in these cases the Yp value we set somewhat overestimates the performance of high-income OECD countries on these right aspects since the penalty imposed is lower than it would be had the Yp value specified been lower. However, for those countries that are close to fulfilling the right aspect, the upward bias is only slight.

13. Full details on the construction of the International SERF Index Historical Trend Data Series can be found in Randolph and Guyer 2012.

Chapter 6

* The analysis in this chapter was undertaken with the capable assistance of Joshua Greenstein. His contribution is gratefully acknowledged.

1. Even among commentators reaching this conclusion, an emphasis on civil and political rights as primary to social and economic rights is still sometimes viewed as a "Western" bias, and a more communal approach in Africa is often still recommended (Agbakwa 2002; Rukooko 2010).

2. The democracy score takes into account three areas: competitive choice and openness of selection for the executive branch of government, constraints on the

executive branch, and competitiveness of political participation. The autocracy score takes into account all of the above as well as suppressions of and restrictions on political participation. It fails to take into account civil liberties such as freedom of speech or of the press and areas such as rule of law and corruption.

3. Spearman's rank correlation coefficient is a nonparametric measure of statistical dependence between two variables.

4. Voice and Accountability: Spearman's rank correlation coefficient of 0.22, significant at 5 percent; Rule of Law: Spearman's rank correlation coefficient of 0.25, also significant at 5 percent. Freedom House: Spearman's rank correlation coefficient of 0.22, significant at 5 percent.

5. CIRI assigns scores to countries for individual rights categories, as well as creating composite indices of these individual scores. The 2010 CIRI Empowerment Rights Index, an additive index encompassing rights to foreign and domestic movement, freedom of speech, freedom of assembly and association, workers' rights, electoral self-determination, and freedom of religion, ranges from 0 (no government respect for these seven rights) to 14 (full government respect for these seven rights). The CIRI Physical Integrity Index, which focuses on freedom from torture, extrajudicial killing, and political imprisonment, was also used for comparisons.

6. The only exception is a strong and significant correlation between the core SERF and the CIRI measure of women's economic rights. This result provides additional support for the relationship discussed in the section of this chapter concerning gender equality.

7. The Toronto Initiative for Economic and Social Rights database gives a quantitative score to developing countries based on the constitutional status of economic and social rights. For a variety of different rights categories, the dataset assigns countries to one of three categories:

   – The right is justiciable, the government can be taken to court for failing to fulfill the given right, or there is some other legal recourse available to citizens to ensure fulfillment of the right.
   – The right is aspirational, and it is enumerated as a constitutional right; but it is not binding, and citizens do not have legal recourse.
   – The right is not mentioned in the country's constitution.

8. Seven out of the ninety-nine countries in the sample did not ratify the ICESCR; every country in the sample ratified the CRC; and in the case of CEDAW, every country with a core SERF score, with the sole exception of Iran, has ratified.

9. Because the years in which these treaties were first adopted are different, the amount of variation for these measures is also different. The earliest adoption of the ICESCR was forty-three years ago; for the CRC, it was only twenty-one (all years calculated since 2011). Ratified in 2011 and not ratified both count as 0.

10. Social Watch is an international coalition of civil society organizations that, among other activities, engages in advocacy and monitoring work. As part of this work, Social Watch releases the GEI annually. The GEI calculates the gender gap for different indicators within the three dimensions: for education, school enrollment, and literacy; for economic equality, income gaps, and employment; and for empowerment, parliament membership, and attainment of certain professional or managerial positions. A value for the gender gap is computed for each area, where 0 indicates perfect inequality (e.g., no women are educated at all and all men are) and 100 indicates perfect equality. The GEI, in turn, is the simple average of the three dimensions. The GEI does not take into account level of achievement, only the difference in achievement between men and women.

11. The UNDP's GII is calculated using the following indicators: For reproductive health, the indicators used are adolescent fertility and maternal mortality; empowerment is measured by looking at parliamentary representation and by secondary education and higher attainment levels; and labor market is based on labor force participation rates. While the reproductive health variables only apply to women, for the other variables, indices for men and women are calculated and compared. A combination of these comparisons and the reproductive health index creates the GII.

12. The independent variables are public expenditure on health as a percentage of GDP (2009), HIV prevalence ages fifteen–forty-nine (2009), and rural population as a percentage of total population (2009), all from World Development Indicators. Two malaria indicators were used: malaria death rate per one hundred thousand (2008), also from World Development Indicators; and population at risk of fatal malaria, which estimates the percentage of the population at risk of contracting falciparum malaria, the most fatal species of the disease, in a country, from the Sachs Malaria DataSet. The malaria-related variables on their own produced the largest R-squared and seem to explain more of the SERF Right to Health Index by themselves than any other factor. In addition, the indicator for population at risk of malaria produced by far the largest coefficient—so large, in fact, that it suggests that this variable may be capturing other effects.

13. The analysis in this section was undertaken with the capable assistance of Patrick Guyer, Elizabeth Kaletski, and John Stewart. Their contributions are gratefully acknowledged.

Chapter 7

* The analysis in this chapter was undertaken with the capable assistance of Abid Khan, Elizabeth Kaletski, Michée Lachaud, Michelle Prairie, and John Stewart. We gratefully acknowledge their contributions.

1. A nonparametric method does not rely on assumptions that the data are drawn from a specific probability distribution or that the relationship between the variables takes a particular functional form (Sprent and Smeeton 2007).

2. In a statistical model, endogeneity is technically defined as the correlation between the error term and an independent variable in the model.

3. Life expectancy has a positive sign for non-OECD and a negative sign for OECD countries. This discrepancy likely reflects the fact that in OECD countries the baby boomer generation is now retiring and, due to the costs associated with retirement security, the net contribution to the economy of retirees is negative.

4. The choice of GDP per capita over GNI per capita influences the value of our index to the extent that the difference between GDP and GNI is large, such as in the case of countries with large positive net remittance flows that are not offset by profit remittances of an equal magnitude. To the extent that GNI per capita exceeds GDP per capita, a country's score on the SERF Index will tend to be biased upward. To the extent that GNI per capita is less than GDP per capita, a country's score on the SERF Index could be biased downward.

5. A more extensive discussion of the challenges posed and solutions used can be found in Randolph et al. 2009, 2012.

6. The aspects used include the under-five survival rate and the percentage of normal-birth-weight babies, in the case of the health index, and the percentage of population not relatively poor and the percentage not involuntarily part-time employed, in the case of the work index.

7. A substantially more extensive set of results by component right index and extending to a more refined classification scheme where feasible can be found in Randolph et al. 2009.

Chapter 8

1. The monitoring mechanisms comprise three main procedures. First, review by the CESCR, a body of independent experts appointed by member states at the United Nations; it monitors implementation of the International Covenant on Economic, Social and Cultural Rights by the states that are parties to the covenant. All state parties to the ICESCR must submit reports to the CESCR regularly, every five years, documenting performance regarding fulfillment of their rights obligations. The committee assesses each country's report and drafts concerns and recommendations directed to that country. Second, in a new procedure adopted in May 2013, independent individuals and groups who claim that their rights have been violated can submit complaints directly to the committee for consideration. Third, under special circumstances the committee can initiate inquiries regarding grave or systematic violations of rights obligations and in this context consider complaints between states.

2. Within the Americas, the Organization of American States is the foremost mechanism for monitoring and enforcing states' human rights commitments. Its Inter-American Commission on Human Rights, which works with the Inter-American Economic and Social Council and the Inter-American Court of Human Rights, monitors and enforces the economic and social rights obligations of member states. State parties to the "Protocol to the American Convention on Human Rights in the Area of Economic, Social, and Cultural Rights" submit

periodic reports detailing their performance in regard to their economic and social rights obligations. Specialized organs of the inter-American system can also submit reports to the Inter-American Economic and Social Council and the Inter-American Council for Education, Science, and Culture. For some rights, specifically those related to trade unions, social security, health, the environment, food, and education, impacted individuals alleging violations of state obligations can also submit individual petitions requesting an investigation to the Commission on Human Rights. The Inter-American Court of Human Rights applies and interprets the American Convention on Human Rights (Articles 61–64) through both a judicial and an advisory function. For the judicial function, cases can be submitted by the commission and by states that are parties to the convention, against states that recognize the court's jurisdiction. For the advisory function, the court can provide opinions regarding the interpretation and domestic application of human rights treaties, if requested by a member state.

3. The African Commission on Human and Peoples' Rights was created by the African Union to promote and protect the rights guaranteed under the African Charter on Human and Peoples' Rights—the main instrument on human rights in Africa. The charter specifically addresses several economic, social, and cultural rights, including the right to work under satisfactory conditions, the right to physical and mental health, the right to education, and the freedom to take part in community cultural life. The African Court on Human and People's Rights monitors and enforces economic, social, and cultural rights guarantees, with jurisdiction over all cases submitted concerning the interpretation and application of the charter. State parties are required to submit a report to the commission every two years regarding the measures taken to realize the rights and freedoms recognized under the charter. The court also receives and adjudicates complaints submitted by the commission, by states that agree to the optional protocol, and by African intergovernmental organizations.

4. In Europe, human rights guarantees are specified in the European Convention for the Protection of Human Rights and Fundamental Freedoms and in the European Social Charter. The convention secures civil and political rights and allows individual complaints to the European Court of Human Rights. The charter, which complements the convention by specifically guaranteeing social and economic human rights, including rights to housing, health, education, employment, legal and social protection, free movement of persons, and nondiscrimination, does not have a judicial mechanism. State parties to the charter are required to submit annual reports to demonstrate that laws and practices are in line with charter commitments. The European Committee of Social Rights then examines whether national laws and practices in member states conform to the charter and publishes yearly conclusions. If the committee finds that a member state is not acting in accordance with the charter, the committee recommends that the state change its practices and laws. Additionally, complaints of violations of the charter

can be made to the committee by the European Trade Union Confederation, the International Organisation of Employers, nongovernmental organizations with participative status in the committee, and employers' organizations and trade unions. The committee holds a public hearing on complaints, makes a decision on the merits of that specific complaint, and forwards its decision in the form of a report to the concerned parties.

5. For example, a civil society group submitted a shadow report for the 2013 CESCR review of Gabon (Global Initiative for Economic, Social and Cultural Rights 2013). But this report focused on the issue of women's access to land rather than the broad question of progressive realization.

6. For a useful summary of the state of knowledge on the causes of child mortality, see UNICEF's *Progress Report 2012* (2012).

7. The study was conducted as background analysis for the High-Level Task Force on the Implementation of the Right to Development to define operational criteria for implementation of the 1986 Declaration on the Right to Development. The declaration provides a useful framework for identifying state obligations for fostering social and economic rights. The core content of the right to development includes the promotion of comprehensive human development, adoption of equitable approaches to sharing the benefits of development, and distribution of the environmental, economic, and other burdens that can arise from development.

8. A very large body of empirical studies and theoretical literature on these relationships has been built up since the 1980s. For a recent review, see the U.N. Development Programme's *Human Development Report 2010* (2010).

9. When the Millennium Development Goals are applied without taking account of starting points or resource constraints, many low-income countries are labeled "off-track" in achieving the goals (World Bank 2013a), even though many of them are some of the best performers in making progress (Hailu and Tsukada 2011) and in meeting the obligations of progressive realization (Fukuda-Parr and Greenstein 2013).

10. GNI per capita (World Bank Atlas method) in 2012. Note that this is different from the income indicator used in the SERF Index methodology—GDP per capita in PPP$. The upper thresholds for income categories set by the World Bank for 2012 data (in GNI per capita, exchange rate, Atlas method) are $1,035 for low income, $4,085 for lower middle income, and $12,615 for upper middle income.

BIBLIOGRAPHY

Ablo, Emmanuel, and Ritva Reinikka. 1998. "Do Budgets Really Matter? Evidence from Public Spending on Education and Health in Uganda." World Bank Policy Research Working Paper No. 1926. Washington, D.C.: The World Bank.

Acemoglu, Daron, Simon Johnson, and James A. Robinson. 2001. "The Colonial Origins of Comparative Development: An Empirical Investigation." *American Economic Review* 91 (December 5): 1369–1401.

———. 2002. "Reversal of Fortune: Geography and Institutions in the Making of the Modern World Income Distribution." *Quarterly Journal of Economics* 117 (4): 1231–1294.

Acemoglu, Daron, Simon Johnson, James A. Robinson, and Pierre Yared. 2008. "Income and Democracy." *American Economic Review* 98 (3): 808–842.

———. 2009. "Reevaluating the Modernization Hypothesis." *Journal of Monetary Economics* 56 (8): 1043–1058.

Agarwal, Bina. 1997. " 'Bargaining' and Gender Relations: Within and Beyond the Household." *Feminist Economics* 3 (1): 1–51.

Agbakwa, Shedrack C. 2002. "Reclaiming Humanity: Economic, Social, and Cultural Rights as the Cornerstone of African Human Rights." *Yale Human Rights and Development Law Journal* 5: 177–216.

Aghion, P., and Howitt, P. 1998. "Capital Accumulation and Innovation as Complementary Factors in Long-Run Growth". *Journal of Economic Growth*, 3 (2): 111–130.

Aghion, P., E. Caroli, and C. Garcia-Penalosa. 1999. "Inequality and Economic Growth: The Perspective of the New Growth Theories." *Journal of Economic Literature* 37: 1615–1660.

Aixalá, José, and Gema Fabro. 2009. "Economic Freedom, Civil Liberties, Political Rights and Growth: A Causality Analysis." *Spanish Economic Review* 11: 165–178.

Alderman, H., P. A. Chiappori, L. Haddad, J. Hoddinott, and R. Kanbur. 1995. "Unitary versus Collective Models of the Household: Is It Time to Shift the Burden of Proof?" *World Bank Research Observer* 10: 1–19.

Almeida, Heitor, and Daniel Ferreira. 2002. "Democracy and the Variability of Economic Performance." *Economics and Politics* 14 (3): 225–257.

Alston, P. 2000. "Towards a Human Rights Accountability Index." *Journal of Human Development* 1 (2): 249–271.

Alston, Philip, and Gerard Quinn. 1987. "The Nature and Scope of States Parties' Obligations under the International Covenant on Economic, Social and Cultural Rights." *Human Rights Quarterly* 9 (2):156–229.

Amico, Peter, Christian Aran, and Carlos Avila. 2010. "HIV Spending as a Share of Total Health Expenditure: An Analysis of Regional Variation in a Multi-country Study." *PLoS ONE* 5 (9): e12997.

Anand, Sudhir, and Martin Ravallion. 1993. "Human Development in Poor Countries: On the Role of Private Incomes and Public Services." *Journal of Economic Perspectives* 7 (1): 133–150.

Anyanwu, John, and Andrew E. O. Erhijakpor. 2007. "Education Expenditures and School Enrolment in Africa: Illustrations from Nigeria and other SANE Countries," Working paper Series 227. Tunis-Belvedère, Tunisia: African Development Bank.

Aristotle. 350 BC. *Nicomachean Ethics*, bk. I. Internet Classics Archive, http://classics.mit.edu/.

Asher, Jana. 2008. "Introduction." In *Statistical Methods for Human Rights*, edited by Jana Asha, David Banks, and Fritz Scheuren, 3–36. New York: Springer.

Backman, Gunilla, Paul Hunt, Rajat Khosla, Camila Jaramillo-Strouss, Belachew Mekuria Fikre, Caroline Rumble, and David Pevalin. 2008. "Health Systems and the Right to Health: An Assessment of 194 Countries." *Lancet* 372 (9655): 2047–2085.

Balakrishnan, R., D. Elson, and R. Patel. 2011. *Rethinking Macroeconomic Strategies from a Human Rights Perspective (Why Macroeconomics for Human Rights II).* New York: Marymount Manhattan College.

Banik, Dan. 2010. "Support for Human Rights-Based Development: Reflections on the Malawian Experience." *International Journal of Human Rights* 14 (1): 34–50.

Barofsky, Jeremy, Claire Chase, Tobenna Anekwe, and Farshad Farzadfar. 2011. "The Economic Effects of Malaria Eradication: Evidence from an Intervention in Uganda." Program on the Global Demography of Aging, Working Paper No. 70. Harvard University, May. http://www.hsph.harvard.edu/pgda/working.htm.

Barro, Robert J. 1996. "Democracy and Growth." *Journal of Economic Growth* 1 (1): 1–27.

Barro, Robert J., and Jong-wha Lee. 1994. "Sources of Economic Growth." *Carnegie-Rochester Conference Series on Public Policy* 40 (1): 1–46.

Barsh, Russel Lawrence. 1993. "Measuring Human Rights: Problems of Methodology and Purpose." *Human Rights Quarterly* 15 (1): 87–121.

Bartram, Jamie. 2008. "Improving on Haves and Have-Nots." *Nature* 452 (7185), March 20: 283–284. PMID: 18354459.

Battese, G. E., and T. J. Coelli. 1992. "Frontier Production Functions, Technical Efficiency and Panel Data: With Application to Paddy Farmers in India." *Journal of Productivity Analysis* 3:153–169.

Beaman, Lori, Esther Duflo, Rohini Pande, and Petia Topalova. 2012. "Female Leadership Raises Aspirations and Educational Attainment for Girls: A Policy Experiment in India." *Science* 335: 582–586.

Behrman, Jere R. 1993. "The Economic Rationale for Investing in Nutrition in Developing Countries." *World Development* 21 (11), November: 1749–1771.

Behrman, Jere R., and Mark Rosenzweig. 2002. "Does Increasing Women's Schooling Raise the Schooling of the Next Generation?"*American Economic Review* 92 (1): 323–334.

Bertozzi, Stefano, Juan-Pablo Gutierrez, Marjorie Opuni, Neffi Walker, and Bernard Schwartlander. 2004. "Estimating Resource Needs for HIV/AIDS Health Care Services in Low-Income and Middle-Income Countries." *Health Policy* 69: 189–200.

Biehl, J., A. Petryna, A. Gestner, J. Amon, and P. Picon. 2009. "Judicialization of the Right to Health in Brazil." *Lancet* 373 (9682): 2182–2184.

Blecker, Robert A., and Stephanie Seguino. 2002. "Macroeconomic Effects of Reducing Gender Wage Inequality in an Export-Oriented, Semi-industrialized Economy." *Review of Development Economics* 6 (1), February: 3–19.

Bloom, David E., David Canning, and Jaypee Sevilla. 2004. "The Effect of Health on Economic Growth: A Production Function Approach." *World Development* 32 (1): 1–13.

Blyberg, A. 2009. "The Case of the Mislaid Allocation: Economic and Social Rights and Budget Work." *Sur: International Journal on Human Rights* 6 (11): 123–139.

Boix, Carles. 2001. "Democracy, Development, and the Public Sector." *American Journal of Political Science* 45 (1): 1–17.

Bollen, Kenneth A. 1986. "Political Rights and Political Liberties in Nations: An Evaluation of Human Rights Measures, 1950 to 1984." *Human Rights Quarterly* 8 (4): 567–591.

Borensztein, E., J. De Gregorio, and J.-W. Lee. 1998. "How Does Foreign Direct Investment Affect Economic Growth?"*Journal of International Economics* 45: 115–135.

Boyle, Elizabeth Heger, and Minzee Kim. 2009. "International Human Rights Law, Global Economic Reforms, and Child Survival and Development Rights Outcomes." *Law and Society Review* 43 (3): 455–490.

Brady, David. 2005. "The Welfare State and Relative Poverty in Rich Western Democracies, 1967–1997." *Social Forces* 83 (4): 1329–1364.

Breierova, Lucia, and Esther Duflo. 2003. "The Impact of Education on Fertility and Child Mortality: Do Fathers Really Matter Less than Mothers?" Working Paper No. 217. Paris: Organisation for Economic Co-operation and Development, Development Centre.

Brinks, D., and V. Gauri. 2012. "The Law's Majestic Equality? The Distributive Impact of Litigating Social and Economic Rights." Policy Research Working Papers. World Bank, http://elibrary.worldbank.org/doi/book/10.1596/1813-9450-5999.

Brown, David S., and Wendy Hunter. 2004. "Democracy and Human Capital Formation: Education Spending in Latin America, 1980–2007." *Comparative Political Studies* 37 (7): 842–864.

Burchardt, Tania, and Polly Vizard. 2011. "'Operationalizing' the Capability Approach as a Basis for Equality and Human Rights Monitoring in Twentieth Century Britain." *Journal of Human Development and Capabilities* 12 (1): 91–119.

Burnside, Craig, and David Dollar. 2000. "Aid, Policies, and Growth." *American Economic Review* 90 (4): 847–868.

———. 2004. "Aid, Policies, and Growth: Revisiting the Evidence." Working Paper 3251, March. Washington, DC: World Bank.

Caldwell, John C. 1986. "Routes to Low Mortality in Poor Countries." *Population and Development Review* 12 (2): 171–220.

———. 1994. "How Is Greater Maternal Education Translated into Lower Child Mortality?" *Health Transition Review* 4 (2): 224–229.

Carr Center for Human Rights. 2005. *Measurement and Human Rights: Tracking Progress, Assessing Impact.* Kennedy School of Government, Harvard University, Carr Center Project Report. Cambridge, Mass.: Carr Center for Human Rights. http://www.hks.harvard.edu/cchrp/mhr/publications/documents/.

Center for Economic and Social Rights. 2012. *The OPERA Framework: Assessing Compliance with the Obligations to Fulfill Economic and Social Rights.* http://www.cesr.org, accessed January 12, 2014.

Centre on Housing Rights and Evictions. 2009. *The Significance of Human Rights in MDG-Based Policy Making on Water and Sanitation: An Application to Kenya, South Africa, Ghana, Sri Lanka and Laos.* Geneva: COHRE.

Chapman, Audrey. 1996. "A 'Violations Approach' for Monitoring International Covenant on Economic, Social and Cultural Rights." *Human Rights Quarterly* 18 (1): 23–66.

———. 2007. "The Status of Efforts to Monitor Economic, Social, and Cultural Rights." In *Economic Rights: Conceptual, Measurement, and Policy Issues*, edited by Shareen Hertel and Lanse Minkler, 143–164. Cambridge: Cambridge University Press.

Charnes, Abraham, W. William Cooper, and Edwardo Rhode. 1978. "Measuring Efficiency of Decision-Making Units." *European Journal of Operational Research* 2: 429–444.

Cingranelli, David L., and David L. Richards. 2007. "Measuring Government Effort to Respect Economic and Social Human Rights: A Peer Benchmark." In *Economic Rights: Conceptual, Measurement, and Policy Issues*, edited by Shareen Hertel and Lanse Minkler, 214–232. Cambridge: Cambridge University Press.

Cingranelli, David L., and Kevin Wright. 1988. "Correlates of Due Process." In *Human Rights Theory and Measurement*, edited by David L. Cingranelli, 154–172. New York: St. Martin's Press.

"The Cingranelli–Richards (CIRI) Human Rights Data Set."2010. CIRI Human Rights Data Project, http://ciri.binghamton.edu/.

Chung, Haejoo, and Carlos Muntaner. 2007. "Welfare State Matters: A Typological Multilevel Analysis of Wealthy Countries." *Health Policy* 80: 328–339.

Claude, R., and T. Jabine. 1986. "Editors' Introduction.""Symposium on Statistical Issues in the Field of Human Rights," special issue. *Human Rights Quarterly* 8 (4): 551–566.

Clemens, M., C. Kenny, and T. Moss. 2007. "The Trouble with the MDGs: Confronting Expectations of Aid and Development Success." *World Development* 35 (5): 735–751.

Cobbah, Josiah A. M. 1987. "African Values and the Human Rights Debate: An African Perspective". *Human Rights Quarterly* 9.3 309–331.

Coleman, I., and T. Lawson-Remer. 2013. *Pathways to Freedom*. New York: Council on Foreign Relations.

Conley, Dalton, and Kristen W. Springer. 2001. "Welfare State and Infant Mortality." *American Journal of Sociology* 107 (3): 766–807.

Council of Europe. 1996. *European Social Charter*. Strasbourg: Council of Europe.

Davis, K., B. Kingsbury, and S. E. Merry. 2012. "Introduction: Global Governance by Indicators." In *Governance by Indicators*, edited by K. Davis, A. Fisher, B. Kingsbury, and S. E. Merry, 3–28. New York: Oxford University Press.

Deitchler, Megan, Terri Ballard, Anne Swindale, and Jennifer Coates. 2011. "Introducing a Simple Measure of Household Hunger for Cross-Cultural Use." FANTA 2 Technical Note No. 12, February. http://www.fantaproject.org/downloads/pdfs/TN12_HHS.pdf, accessed April 5, 2011.

Demombynes, Gabriel, and Sofia Karina Trommlerová. 2012. "What Has Driven the Decline of Infant Mortality in Kenya?" Policy Research Working Paper 6057. Washington, DC: World Bank. http://elibrary.worldbank.org/doi/pdf/10.1596/1813-9450-6057.

Deva, Surya. 2003. "Human Rights Violations by Multinational Corporations and International Law: Where from Here?" *Connecticut Journal of International Law* 19: 1–57.

Dickens, C. 1843. *A Christmas Carol*. London: Chapman and Hall.

Dixon, Simon, Scott McDonald, and Jennifer Roberts. 2002. "The Impact of HIV and AIDS on Africa's Economic Development." *BMJ: British Medical Journal* 324 (7331): 232–234.

Dollar, David. 1992. "Outward-Oriented Developing Economies Really Do Grow More Rapidly: Evidence from 95 LDCs, 1976–1985." *Economic Development and Cultural Change* 40 (3), April: 523–544.

Dollar, David, and Roberta Gati. 1999. "Gender Inequality, Income, and Growth: Are Good Times Good for Women?" Policy Research Report on Gender and Development, Working Paper Series. Washington, D.C.: World Bank Development Research Group/Poverty Reduction and Economic Management Network.

Domar, Evsey. 1946. "Capital Expansion, Rate of Growth, and Employment." *Econometrica* 14 (2): 137–147. JSTOR 1905364.

Donnelly, Jack. 2003. *Universal Human Rights in Theory and Practice*. Ithaka: Cornell University Press.

Drèze, Jean. 2003. "Democracy and the Right to Food." *Economic and Political Weekly* 39 (17): 1723–1731.

Dreze, J., and A. Sen. 2001. *Hunger and Public Action*. Oxford: Oxford University Press.

———. 2013. *An Uncertain Glory*.

Duvall, R, and M. Shamir. 1980. "Indicators from Errors: Cross-National Time-Series Measures of the Repressive Disposition of Governments." In *Indicator Systems for Economic, Political and Social Analysis*, edited by Charles Taylor. Cambridge, Mass: Oelgeschlager, Gunn & Hain.

Easterly, William. 2006. *The White Man's Burden*. New York: Penguin Books.

———. 2009. "How the Millennium Development Goals Are Unfair to Africa." *World Development* 37 (1): 26–35.

———. 2011. "Benevolent Autocrats." NBER Working Paper.

Easterly, William, and Ross Levine. 2003. "Tropics, Germs, and Crops: the Role of Endowments in Economic Development." *Journal of Monetary Economics* 50 (1), January: 3–39.

Engerman, Stanley L., and Kenneth L. Sokoloff. 1994. *Factor Endowments, Institutions, and Differential Paths of Growth among New World Economies: A View from Economic Historians of the United States*. Historical Paper No. 66. Cambridge, Mass.: National Bureau of Economic Research.

Fan, Shenggen, and Neetha Rao. 2003. *Public Spending in Developing Countries: Trends, Determination, and Impact*. EPTD Discussion Paper No. 99. Washington, D.C.: International Food Policy Research Institute.

Farr, W. Ken, Richard A. Lord, and J. Larry Wolfenbarger. 1998. "Economic Freedom, Political Freedom, and Economic Well-Being: A Causality Analysis." *Cato Journal* 18 (2): 247–262.

Felner, Eitan. 2009a. "Closing the 'Escape Hatch': A Toolkit to Monitor the Realization of Economic, Social and Cultural Rights." *Oxford Journal of Human Rights Practice* 1 (3): 402–435.

———. 2009b. "A New Frontier in Economic and Social Rights Advocacy? Using Quantitative Data for Human Rights Accountability." Center for Economic and Social Rights, http://www.cesr.org/downloads/A%20new%20frontier%20 in%20ESC%20advocacy.pdf.

Ferraz, Octavio Luiz Motta. 2011. "Harming the Poor through Social Rights Litigation: Lessons from Brazil." *Texas Law Review* 89: 1643–1668.

Filmer, Deon, and Lant Pritchett. 1997. *Child Mortality and Public Spending on Health: How Much Does Money Matter?* Washington, D.C.: World Bank.

Food and Agriculture Organization of the United Nations. 2004. *Voluntary Guidelines to Support the Realization of the Right to Food in the Context of National Food Security*. Rome: Food and Agriculture Organization of the United Nations.

Forbes, Kristen J. 2000. "A Reassessment of the Relationship between Inequality and Growth." *The American Economic Review* 90 (4): 869–887.

Foweraker, Joe, and Todd Landman. 1997. *Citizenship Rights and Social Movements: A Comparative and Statistical Analysis.* Oxford: Oxford University Press.

Freedom House. 2012. Political Rights Index. http://www.freedomhouse.org/report/freedom-world-aggregate-and-subcategory-scores#.VBtrhBbgXcw

———. 2013. *Freedom in the World 2013.* http://www.freedomhouse.org/report/freedom-world/freedom-world-2013#.U-6HToBdXhU.

Fukuda-Parr, S. 2011. "The Metrics of Human Rights: Complementarities of the Human Rights and Capabilities Approaches." *Journal of Human Development and Capabilities* 11 (1): 73–89.

Fukuda-Parr, S., and Joshua Greenstein. 2012. "Monitoring State Performance: South Africa's Scores on the Social and Economic Rights Fulfillment Index." *ESR Review: Economic and Social Rights in South Africa* 13 (2): 3–6.

———. 2013. "Monitoring MDGs: A Human Rights Critique and Alternative." In *The Millennium Development Goals and Human Rights: Past, Present and Future*, edited by M. Langford, A. Sumner, and A. Yamin, 439–460. New York: Cambridge University Press.

Fukuda-Parr, S., J. Greenstein, and D. Stewart. 2013. "How Should MDG Implementation Be Measured: Faster Progress or Achieving the Target?" *World Development* 41 (C): 19–30.

Fukuda-Parr, S., Terra Lawson-Remer, and Susan Randolph. 2011a. "The International SERF Index Data Set Version 2011.1." http://www.SERFindex.org/data/.

———. 2011b. "SERF Index Methodology: Version 2011.1, Technical Note." http://www.SERFindex.org/data/.

Fukuda-Parr, Sakiko, Susan Randolph, Patrick Guyer, Terra Lawson-Remer, and Louise Daniels. 2010. "Assessing State Compliance with Obligations to Fulfill Economic and Social Rights—A Methodology and Application to the States of Brazil." In *Bello Horizonte: Editora Forum*, edited by Flavia Piovesan and Ines Virginia Prado Soares, 425–462. Buenos Aires: Editoria Forum.

Gallup, John Luke, Andrew D. Mellinger, and Jeffrey D. Sachs. 2007. "Geography DataSets." Center for International Development, Harvard University, http://www.cid.harvard.edu/ciddata/geographydata.htm.

Gallup, John Luke, and Jeffrey D. Sachs. 2001. "The Economic Burden of Malaria." *American Journal of Tropical Medicine and Hygiene* 64 (1–2), January/February: 85–96.

Galor, Oded, and N. David Weil. 1996. "The Gender Gap, Fertility, and Growth." *American Economic Review* 86 (3): 374–387.

Gauri, Varun. 2011. "The Cost of Complying with Human Rights Treaties: The Convention on the Rights of the Child and Basic Immunization." *Review of International Organizations* 6: 33–56.

Gerring, John, Strom C. Thacker, and Rodrigo Alfaro. 2012. "Democracy and Human Development." *Journal of Politics* 74 (1): 1–17.

Gibney, M., L. Cornett, and R. Wood. 2008. http://www.politicalterrorscale.org, accessed July 9, 2013.

Gleditsch, Nils Petter, Peter Wallensteen, Mikael Eriksson, Margareta Sollenberg and Havard Strand. 2002. "Armed Conflict 1946–2001: A New Dataset." *Journal of Peace Studies* 39 (5): 615–637.

Glendon, Mary Ann. 2001. *A World Made New: Eleanor Roosevelt and the Universal Declaration of Human Rights*. New York: Random House.

———. 2004. "The Rule of Law in the Universal Declaration of Human Rights." *Northwestern Journal of International Human Rights* 2 (1), Spring: article 5.

Global Initiative for Economic, Social and Cultural Rights. 2013. *Shadow Report to the United Nations Committee on Economic, Social and Cultural Rights*. Office of the High Commissioner for Human Rights Treaty Bodies Sessions, http://tbinternet.ohchr.org_/layouts/treatybodiesexternal/.

Goodman, Ryan, and Derek Jinks. 2003. "Measuring the Effects of Human Rights Treaties." *European Journal of International Law* 14 (1): 588–621.

Government of Gabon. 2012. *Implementation of the Economic, Social and Cultural Rights: Initial Report Submitted by States Parties under Articles 16 and 17 of the Covenant on Economic, Social and Cultural Rights*. U.N. Economic and Social Council. New York: United Nations.

Green, Maria. 2001. "What We Talk about When We Talk about Indicators: Current Approaches to Human Rights Measurement." *Human Rights Quarterly* 23 (4): 1062–1097.

Greene, William H. 1993. "The Econometric Approach to Efficiency Analysis." In *The Measurement of Productive Efficiency*, edited by H. Fried, K. Lovell, and S. Schmidt, 68–119. Oxford: Oxford University Press.

———. 1999. "Frontier Production Functions." In *Handbook of Applied Econometrics 2*, edited by M. Hashem Pesaran and P. Schmidt, 81–166. Cambridge, Mass: Blackwell.

Grossman, Gene M., and Elhanan Helpman. 1991. "Trade, Knowledge Spillovers, and Growth." *European Economic Review* 35 (2–3), April: 517–526.

Grugel, Jean, and Enrique Peruzzotti. 2012. "The Domestic Politics of International Human Rights Law: Implementing the Convention on the Rights of the Child in Ecuador, Chile, and Argentina." *Human Rights Quarterly* 34 (1): 178–198.

Gupta, Sanjeev, Marijn Verhoeven, Erwin R. Tiongson. 2002. The effectiveness of government spending on education and health care in developing and transition economies. *European Journal of Political Economy* 18. 717–737.

HABITAT: United Nations Conference on Human Settlements. 1976. "The Vancouver Declaration On Human Settlement." Vancouver, Canada: United Nations Conference on Human Settlements.

———. 1996. "The Istanbul Declaration on Human Settlement." Istanbul, Turkey: United Nations Conference on Human Settlements.

Hailu, D., and R. Tsukada. 2011. "Achieving the Millennium Development Goals: A Measure of Progress." Working Paper 78, February 15. U.N. Development Programme International Policy Centre for Inclusive Growth.

Hansen, Kristian, Glyn Chapman, Inam Chitsike, Ossy Kasilo, and Gabriel Mwaluko. 2000. "The Cost of HIV/AIDS Care at Government Hospitals in Zimbabwe." *Health Policy and Planning* 15 (4): 432–440.

Haq, M. u. 1995. *Reflections on Human Development*. New York: Oxford University Press.

Hathaway, Oona A. 2002. "Do Human Rights Treaties Make a Difference?" *Yale Law Journal* 111 (8): 1935–2042.

———. 2007. "Why Do Countries Commit to Human Rights Treaties?" *Journal of Conflict Resolution* 51 (4): 588–621.

Heintz, J., R. Balakrishnan, and D. Elson. 2011. "Financial Regulation, Capabilities and Human Rights in the US Financial Crisis: The Case of Housing." *Journal of Human Development and Capabilities* 12 (1): 153–168.

Hertel, Shareen. 2006. "Why Bother? Measuring Economic Rights: The Research Agenda." *International Studies Perspectives* 7 (3): 215–230.

Hertel, Shareen. Forthcoming. "Hungry for Justice: Social Mobilization on the Right to Food in India." *Development and Change*.

Hertel, Shareen, and Susan Randolph. 2015. "The Challenge of Ensuring Food Security: Global Perspectives and Evidence from India." Chapter 8 in *Closing the Rights Gap: From Human Rights to Social Transformation*, edited by La Dawn Haglund and Robin Strykler. Oakland: University of California Press.

Hill, M. Anne, and Elizabeth M. King. 1995. "Women's Education and Economic Well-Being." *Feminist Economics* 1 (2): 21–46.

Hou, Xiaohui. 2011. "Women's Decision Making Power and Human Development: Evidence from Pakistan." World Bank Policy Research Working Paper 5830, October. Washington, D.C.: World Bank.

Howard, Rhoda. 1983. "The Full-Belly Thesis: Should Economic Rights Take Priority over Civil and Political Rights? Evidence from Sub-Saharan Africa." *Human Rights Quarterly* 5 (4): 467–490.

Human Rights Information and Documentation Systems, International. 2009. *Human Rights Council and International Criminal Court: The New Challenges for Human Rights Communications*. HURIDOCS Conference Report. Geneva: Human Rights Information and Documentation Systems, International, Secretariat.

Hunt, Paul. 2005. *Report of the Special Rapporteur on the Right of Everyone to the Enjoyment of the Highest Attainable Standard of Physical and Mental Health*. New York: United Nations.

Institute of Education Sciences. 2014. "International Activities Program." nces.ed.gov/surveys/international/faqs.asp, accessed August 9, 2014.

Inter-American Commission on Human Rights. 2008. *Guidelines for Preparation of Progress Indicators in the Area of Economic, Social and Cultural Rights*. Organization of American States.

International Labour Organization. 1944. "ILO Declaration of Philadelphia." Philadelphia: International Labour Conference, 26th Session.

International Labour Organization. 2014. Key Indicators of the Labour Market (KILM), Seventh Edition." http://ilo.org/empelm/pubs/WCMS_114060/langen/index.htm, accessed August 9, 2014.

Jones, Benjamin F., and Benjamin A. Olken. 2005. "Do Leaders Matter? National Leadership and Growth since World War II." *Quarterly Journal of Economics* 120 (3): 835–864.

Jung, Courtney. 2010. "Toronto Initiative for Economic and Social Rights Data Set." http://www.TIESR.org.

Karim, Syahirah Abdul, Terje A. Eikemo, and Claire Bambra. 2010. "Welfare State Regimes and Population Health: Integrating the East Asian Welfare States." *Health Policy* 94 (1): 45–53.

Kaufmann, Daniel, and Aart Kraay. 2002. "Growth without Governance." *Economia* 3 (1): 169–215.

Kaufmann, Daniel, Aart Kraay, and Massimo Mastruzzi. 2005. "Governance Matters IV: Governance Indicators for 1996–2004." World Bank Policy Research Working Paper Series 3630. Washington, D.C.: World Bank.

Kaufmann, Daniel, Aart Kraay, and Pablo Zoldo-Lobaton. 1999. "Governance Matters." Policy Research Working Paper 2196. Washington, D.C.: World Bank.

Keith, Linda Camp. 1999. "The United Nations International Covenant on Civil and Political Rights: Does It Make a Difference in Human Rights Behavior?" *Journal of Peace Research* 36 (1): 95–118.

Keith, L. C. 2011. *Political Repression: Courts and the Law*. Philadelphia: University of Pennsylvania Press.

Kenny, Charles, and Andy Sumner. 2011. "More Money or More Development: What Have the MDGs Achieved?" Working Paper 278. Washington, D.C.: Center for Global Development.

Kibwana, Kviuth. 1993. "Human Rights and/or Economic Development: Which Way Africa?" *Third World Legal Studies* 12: 43–57.

Kim, Ae-sook, Jr., and Edward T. Jennings. 2009. "Effects of US States' Social Welfare Systems on Population Health." *Policy Studies Journal* 37 (4): 745–767.

Kimenyi, Mwangi S. 2007. "Economic Rights, Human Development Effort, and Institutions." In *Economic Rights: Conceptual, Measurement, and Policy Issues*, edited by Shareen Hertel and Lanse Minkler, 182–213. Cambridge: Cambridge University Press.

Klasen, Stephan, and Francesca Lamanna. 2009. "The Impact of Gender Inequality in Education and Employment on Economic Growth: New Evidence for a Panel of Countries." *Feminist Economics* 15 (3): 91–132.

Knowles, Stephen, Paula K Lorgelly, and P. Dorian Owen. "Are educational gender gaps a brake on economic development? Some cross-country empirical evidence." *Oxford Economic Papers* 54 (2002): 118–149.

Koch, Josee. 2011. *The Food Security Policy Context in South Africa*. Country Study No. 21. Brasilia: International Policy Centre for Inclusive Growth.

Kramer, M. S. 1987. "Determinants of Low Birth Weight: Methodological Assessment and Meta-analysis." *Bulletin of the World Health Organization* 65 (5): 663–737.

Krueger, Alan B., and Mikael Lindahl. 2001. "Education for Growth: Why and for Whom?" National Bureau of Economic Research Working Paper No. 7591.

Kudamatsu, Massayuki. 2007. *Has Democratization Reduced Infant Mortality in Sub-Saharan Africa? Evidence from Micro Data.* Discussion Paper No. 685. Osaka: Institute of Social and Economic Research, Osaka University.

Kumbhakar, Subal, and C. A. Knox Lovell. 2000. *Stochastic Frontier Analysis.* New York: Cambridge University Press.

Kunnemann, R. 1995. "A Coherent Approach to Human Rights." *Human Rights Quarterly* 17 (2): 332–342.

Landman, Todd. 2004. "Measuring Human Rights, Practice and Policy." *Human Rights Quarterly* 26 (4): 906–931.

Landman, Todd, and Edzia Carvalho. 2010. *Measuring Human Rights.* London: Routledge.

Landman, Todd, David Kernohan, and Anita Gohdes. 2012. "Relativising Human Rights." *Journal of Human Rights* 11 (4): 460–485.

Langford, Malcolm. 2009. "Domestic Adjudication and Economic, Social and Cultural Rights: A Socio-legal Review." *Sur: International Journal on Human Rights* 6 (11): 91–121.

Langford, Malcolm, and Sakiko Fukuda-Parr. 2012. "The Turn to Metrics." *Norwegian Journal of Human Rights* 30 (3), November: 222–238.

Lawson-Remer, T. 2012. "Property Insecurity." *Brooklyn Journal of International Law* 38 (1), December 145–192.

Leckie, S. 1998. "Another Step towards Indivisibility: Identifying the Key Features of the Violations against Economic, Social and Cultural Rights." *Human Rights Quarterly* 20 (1): 81–94.

———. ed. 2003. *National Perspectives on Housing Rights.* Leiden: Brill/Njihoff.

Lee, Kwan Yew. 2001. "Culture is Destiny." In *Dealing with Human Rights: Asian and Western Views on the Value of Human Rights,* edited by Meijer. Bloomfield, Ct: Kumarian Press.

Levine, R., and D. Renelt. 1992. "A Sensitivity Analysis of Cross-Country Growth Regressions." *American Economic Review* 82 (September): 942–963.

Lindelow, Magnus. 2006. *Tracking Public Money in the Health Sector in Mozambique: Conceptual and Practical Challenges.* Washington, D.C.: World Bank, East Asia Human Development Unit.

Lipset, Seymour Martin. 1959. "Some Social Requisites of Democracy: Economic Development and Political Legitimacy." *American Political Science Review* 53 (1), March: 69–105.

Llewellyn, K. N. 1931. *The Bramble Bush.*

Luxembourg Income Study. 2009. "LIS Key Figures Online." http://www.lisproject.org/key-figures/key-figures.htm, accessed July 13, 2009.

Mahajan, M. 2012. "The Right to Health as Right to Treatment: Shifting Conceptions of Public Health." *Social Research* 4: 819–836.

Maine, D., and A. Yamin. 1999. "Maternal Mortality as a Human Rights Issue: Measuring Compliance with International Treaty Obligations." *Human Rights Quarterly* 21 (3): 563–607.

Malkani, L., and A. Vitali. 2010. "Where Every Pregnancy Is a Gamble." In *My Story, My Goal* blog. Knight Center for International Media, University of Miami, http://mdg.glocalstories.org/maternal.php#.

Mandela, N. 2005. "Africa Standing Tall Against Poverty." Speech delivered at Live 8, Johannesburg, July 2, 2005. Nelson Mandela Centre of Memory, http://db.nelsonmandela.org/speeches/pub_view.asp?pg=item&ItemID=NMS753&txtstr=Africa%20Standing%20Tall%20Against%20Poverty, accessed December 20, 2013.

Polity IV Project. no date. http://www.systemicpeace.org/polity/polity06.htm.

Mason, Andrew, ed. 2001. *Population Change and Economic Development in East Asia: Challenges Met, Opportunities Seized.* Stanford: Stanford University Press.

McKay, Andrew, and Ernest Aryeetey. 2004. "Operationalising Pro-Poor Growth." In *International Development.* London: World Bank. http://webarchive.nationalarchives.gov.uk/+/http://www.dfid.gov.uk.pubs/files/oppgghana.pdf, accessed November 7, 2009.

Merry, S. E. 2009. "Measuring the World: Indicators, Human Rights and Global Governance." *Current Anthropology* 52 (5): 83–95.

Merry, S. E., and S. B. Coutin. 2014. "Technologies of Trust in Anthropology of Conflict. AES/APLA Presidential Address, 2013." *American Ethnologist* 41 (1): 1–16.

Miller, Stephen M., and Mukti P. Upadhyay. 2000. "The Effects of Openness, Trade Orientation, and Human Capital on Total Factor Productivity." *Journal of Development Economics* 63 (2), December: 399–423.

Minkler, L. 2013. "Introduction: Why Economic and Social Rights?" In *The State of Economic and Social Human Rights: A Global Overview*, edited by L. Minkler, 1–20. Cambridge: Cambridge University Press.

Mohan, Giles and Holland, Jeremy (2001). "Human rights and development in Africa: moral intrusion or empowering opportunity?" *Review of African Political Economy* 28 (88): 177–196.

Nussbaum, M. 2000. *Women and Human Development: The Capabilities Approach.* Cambridge, MA: Cambridge University Press.

———. 2011a. "Capabilities, Entitlements, Rights: Supplementation and Critique." *Journal of Human Development and Capabilities* 12 (1): 23–37.

———. 2011b. *Creating Capabilities: The Human Development Approach.* Cambridge: Belknap Press of Harvard University Press.

O'Donoghue, K. 2010. "Free, Universal Health Care Rolls Out for Mothers and Children in Sierra Leone." UNICEF, http://www.unicef.org/infobycountry/sierraleone_55298.html.

Organisation for Economic Co-operation and Development and Development Assistance Committee. 2004. "Implementing the 2001 DAC Recommendations on Untying Official Development Assistance to Least Developed Countries: 2004 Progress Report." Paris: Organisation for Economic Co-operation and Development. http://www.oecd.org/dataoecd/15/22/35029066.pdf, accessed December 6, 2009.

———. 2007. OECD Data Glossary. Retrieved from http://www.oecd.org/statistics/

Organisation of African Unity. 1982. "African [Banjul] Charter on Human and Peoples' Rights" OAU Doc. CAB/LEG/67/3 rev. 5, 21 I.L.M. 58.Addis Ababa, Ethiopia: Organisation of African Unity.

Organisation of American States. 1988. "Additional Protocol to the American Convention on Human Rights in the Area of Economic, Social, and Cultural Rights: Protocol of San Salvador." San Salvador, El Salvador: Organisation of American States.

Perry, Guillermo E., Omar S. Arias, J. Humberto López, William F. Maloney, and Luis Servén. 2006. *Poverty Reduction and Growth: Virtuous and Vicious Circles.* Washington, D.C.: World Bank.

Persson, Torsten, and Guido Tabellini. 2006. "Democratic Capital: The Nexus of Political and Economic Change." NBER Working Paper No. 12175.

Porter, T. 1995. *Trust in Numbers: The Pursuit of Objectivity in Science and Public Life.* Princeton: Princeton University Press.

Pound, Roscoe. 1910. "Law in Books and Law in Action." *American Law Review* 44: 12–36.

Power, M. 1997. *The Audit Society: Rituals of Verification.* New York: Oxford University Press.

Przeworski, Adam, and Fernando Limongi. 1993. "Political Regimes and Economic Growth." *Journal of Economic Perspectives* 7 (3): 51–69.

———. 1997. "Modernization: Theories and Facts." *World Politics* 49 (2): 155–183.

Quinn, Dennis P., and John T. Woolley. 2001. "Democracy and National Economic Performance: The Preference for Stability." *American Journal of Political Science* 45 (3): 634–657.

Randolph, Susan, Sakiko Fukuda-Parr, and Terra Lawson-Remer. 2011. "Social and Economic Rights Fulfillment Index (SERF): A New Human Rights Approach." In *Social Watch, Social Watch Report 2012: The Right to a Future. Montevideo,* 52–58. Uruguay: Social Watch.

Randolph, Susan, and Patrick Guyer. 2012a. "International SERF Index Historical Trends: Technical Note, Version 2012.1." http://www.SERFindex.org/documentation.

———. 2012b. "Tracking the Historical Evolution of States' Compliance with their Economic and Social Rights Obligations of Result: Insights from the Historical SERF Index." *Nordic Journal of Human Rights* 30 (3): 297–324.

Randolph, Susan, Michelle Prairie, and John Stewart. 2009. "Economic Rights in the Land of Plenty: Monitoring State Fulfillment of Economic and Social Rights Obligations in the United States." Economic Rights Working Paper 12. Storrs: University of Connecticut, Human Rights Institute.

———. 2012. "Monitoring State Fulfillment of Economic and Social Rights Obligations in the United States." *Human Rights Review* 13: 139–165.

Randolph, Susan and Maria Green. 2013. "Bringing Theory into Practice: A new framework and proposed assessment criteria." Chapter 29 in *Realizing the Right to Development, Essays in Commemoration of 25 years of the United Nations Declaration on the Right to Development.* Geneva: OHCHR.

Ranis, G., Ramirez, A., Stewart, F. 2000. "Economic Growth and Human Development," *World Development* 28 (2): 197–219.

Ravallion, Martin, Shaohua Chen, and Prem Sangraula. 2008. "Dollar a Day Revisited." World Bank Policy Research Working Paper No. WPS 4620, May 1. Washington, D.C.: World Bank.

Raworth, Kate. 2001. "Measuring Human Rights." *Ethics in International Affairs* 15 (1): 111–131.

Richards, David, and K. Chad Clay. 2010. "Measuring Government Effort to Respect Economic, Social and Cultural Rights." Economic Rights Working Paper Series #13. Storrs: University of Connecticut, Human Rights Institute.

Riedel, Eibe. 2006. "The IBSA Procedure as a Tool of Human Rights Monitoring." http://virtualwww.rz.uni-mannheim.de/ionas/jura/riedel/inhalt/unterdoku-mente/downloads/ibsa/ibsa2/2_the_ibsa_procedure_as_a_tool_of_human_rights_monitoring_1_1.pdf, accessed August 9, 2014.

Right to Education Project. 2010. "Right to Education Project Indicators." November. http://www.right-to-education.org/node/948.

———. 2013. "Right to Education Indicators." http://www.right-to-education.org, accessed January 12, 2014.

Robertson, Robert E. 1994. "Measuring State Compliance with the Obligation to Devote the 'Maximum Available Resources' for Realizing Economic, Social and Cultural Rights." *Human Rights Quarterly* 16: 693–714.

Robeyns, I. 2005. "The Capability Approach: A Theoretical Survey." *Journal of Human Development* 6 (1): 93–117.

Rodrik, Dani, and Romain Wacziarg. 2005. "Do Democratic Transitions Produce Bad Economic Outcomes?"*American Economic Review* 95 (2): 50–55.

Romer, Paul M. 1990. "Endogenous Technological Change." *Journal of Political Economy* 98 (5), Pt. 2: "The Problem of Development: A Conference of the Institute for the Study of Free Enterprise Systems (October 1990)": S71–S102. http://www.jstor.org/discover/10.2307/2937632?uid=2129&uid=2&uid=70&uid=4&sid=21103337809917.

Rosga, Ann Janette, and Meg Satterthwaite. 2009. "The Trust in Indicators: Measuring Human Rights." *Berkeley Journal of International Law* 27 (2): 253–316.

Rukooko, A. Byaruhanga. 2010. "Poverty and Human Rights in Africa: Historical Dynamics and the Case for Economic and Social Rights." *International Journal of Human Rights* 14 (1): 13–33.

Sachs, J. D. 2003. "Institutions Don't Rule: Direct Effects of Geography on Economic Development." NBER Working Paper 9490. http://www.nber.org/papers/w9490.

Sala-i-Martin, X., G. Doppelhofer, and R. Miller. 2004. "Determinants of Long-Term Growth: A Bayesian Averaging of Classical Estimates (BACE) Approach." *American Economic Review* 94 (4): 813–835.

Salomon, M. 2007. *Global Responsibility for Human Rights: World Poverty and the Development of International Law*. Oxford: Oxford University Press.

Schultz, Theodore W. 1975. "The Value of the Ability to Deal with Disequilibria." *Journal of Economic Literature* 13 (3), September: 827–846.

Seguino, Stephanie. 2009. "The Global Economic Crisis, Its Gender Implications, and Policy Responses." Paper prepared for the "Gender Perspectives on the Financial Crisis Panel" at the Fifty-third Session of the Commission on the Status of Women, United Nations Headquarters, New York, New York.

Seguino, Stephanie, and Maria Sagario Floro. 2003. "Does Gender Have Any Effect on Aggregate Saving? An Empirical Analysis." *International Review of Applied Economics* 17 (2): 147–166.

Sen, Amartya. 1992. *Inequality Reexamined.* New York: Russel Sage; and Cambridge: Harvard University Press.

———. 1999. *Development as Freedom.* New York: Alfred A. Knopf, Anchor Books.

———. 2003a. "Capabilities, Lists and Public Reason: Continuing the Conversation." In *Amartya Sen's Work and Ideas: A Gender Perspective*, edited by B. Agarwal, J. Humphries, and I. Robeyns, 335–338. Abingdon, England: Routledge.

———. 2003b. "Development as Capability Expansion." In *Readings in Human Development*, edited by A S. Fukuda-Parr and A. Shiva Kumar, 3–16. New Delhi: Oxford University Press, India.

———. 2003c. "Foreword." In *Readings in Human Development*, edited by S. Fukuda-Parr and A. Shiva Kumar, vii–xiii. New Delhi: Oxford University Press, India.

———. 2004. "Elements of a Theory of Human Rights." *Philosophy and Public Affairs* 32 (4), Fall: 315.

Shue, H. 1980. *Basic Rights: Subsistence, Affluence and US Foreign Policy.* Princeton: Princeton University Press.

Sikkink, K. 2011. *The Justice Cascade: How Human Rights Prosecutions Are Changing World Politics.* New York: W.W. Norton.

Simmons, B. A. 2009. *Mobilizing Human Rights: International Law in Domestic Politics.* New York: Cambridge University Press.

Smith-Cannoy, H. 2012. *Insincere Commitments: Human Rights Treaties, Abusive States and Citizen Activism.* Washington, D.C.: Georgetown University Press (2012).

Social Watch. 2011. *Social Watch Report 2012: The Right to a Future.* Montevideo, Uruguay: Social Watch.

Sokoloff, Kenneth L., and Stanley L. Engerman. 2000. "History Lessons: Institutions, Factor Endowments, and Paths of Development in the New World." *Journal of Economic Perspectives* 14 (3): 217–232.

Solow, Robert M. 1956. "A Contribution to the Theory of Economic Growth." *Quarterly Journal of Economics* 70 (1): 65–94. DOI: 10.2307/1884513; JSTOR 1884513.

Solow, Robert M. 1957. "Technical Change and the Aggregate Production Function". *Review of Economics and Statistics* 39 (3): 312–320.

Spirer, Louise, and Herbert Spirer. 1993. *Data Analysis for Monitoring Human Rights.* Washington, D.C.: American Association for the Advancement of Science.

Sprent, Peter, and Nigel Smeeton. 2007. *Applied Non-parametric Statistical Methods*, 4th ed. Boca Raton: Chapman and Hall/CRC Press.

Stiglitz, Joseph E. 2004. "Capital Market Liberalization, Globalization, and the IMF." *Oxford Review of Economic Policy* 20 (1): 57–71.

———. 2011. *Rethinking Development Economics*. New York: Oxford University Press.

———. 2012. *The Price of Inequality: How Today's Divided Society Endangers Our Future*. New York: W.W. Norton.

Stiglitz, Joseph E., Amaytar Sen, and J. P. Fitoussi. 2010. *Mis-measuring Our Lives: Why GDP Doesn't Add Up*. New York: New Press.

Strathern, Marilyn, ed. 2000. Audit Cultures: Anthropological Studies in Accountability, Ethics and the Academy. London: Routledge.

Teklehaimanot, Awash, Gordon C. McCord, and Jeffrey D. Sachs. 2007. "Scaling Up Malaria Control in Africa: An Economic and Epidemiological Assessment." *American Journal of Tropical Medicine and Hygiene* 77 (6, Suppl.), December: 138–144.

Teorell. 2010. *Determinants of Democratization*. New York: Cambridge University Press.

Thomas, Duncan. 1990. "Intra-household Resource Allocation: An Inferential Approach." *Journal of Human Resources* 25 (4): 635–664.

Thomas, Duncan, Robert F. Schoeni, and John Strauss. 1996. "Parental Investments in Schooling: The Roles of Gender and Resources in Urban Brazil." Labor and Population Studies Working Paper Series. Los Angeles: RAND.

Tolhurst, Rachel, Y. P. Amekudzi, F. K. Nyonator, S. Bertel Squire, and S. Theobald. 2008. "He Will Ask Why the Child Gets Sick So Often: The Gendered Dynamics of Intra-household Bargaining over Healthcare for Children with Fever in the Volta Region of Ghana." *Social Science and Medicine* 66 (5): 1106–1117.

Tomasevski, Katarina. 2006. *The State of the Right to Education Worldwide: Free or Fee*. Global Report, Special Rapporteur on Education. Copenhagen: United Nations.

Turk, Danilo. 1990. *Realization of Economic, Social and Cultural Rights*. Progress Report by Special Rapporteur, Commission on Human Rights, United Nations Economic and Social Council. New York: United Nations.

U.N. Committee on Economic, Social and Cultural Rights. 1989. *General Comment 1: Reporting by States Parties*. Office of the High Commissioner for Human Rights.

———. 1990. *General Comment 3: The Nature of States Parties' Obligations* (Article 2, Para. 1 of the Covenant), (Fifth Session, 1990), U.N. Doc. E/1991/23, Annex III, p. 86 (1991). New York: Economic and Social Council, United Nations.

———. 1992. *General Comment 4: The Right to Adequate Housing (Article 11 (1) of the Covenant)*. New York: Economic and Social Council, United Nations.

———. 1998a. *General Comment No. 7: The Right to Adequate Housing (Article 11 (1) of the Covenant): Forced Evictions*. New York: Economic and Social Council, United Nations.

———. 1998b. *General Comment 9: The Domestic Application of the Covenant*. E/C. 12/1998/24. New York: Economic and Social Council, United Nations.

————. 1999a. *General Comment 11: Plans of Action for Primary Education (Article 14)*. E/C.12/1999/4. New York: Economic and Social Council, United Nations.

————. 1999b. *General Comment 12: The Right to Adequate Food (Article 11)*. New York: Economic and Social Council, United Nations.

————. 1999c. *General comment 13: The Right to Education (Article 13)*. New York: Economic and Social Council, United Nations.

————. 2000. *General Comment 14: The Right to the Highest Attainable Standard of Health*. E/C.12/2000/4. New York: Economic and Social Council, United Nations.

————. 2003. *General Comment 15: The Right to Water*. E/C.12/2002/11. New York: Economic and Social Council, United Nations.

————. 2005. *General Comment 18: The Right to Work* (Article 6). E/C.12/C/18/. New York: Economic and Social Council, United Nations.

————. 2008. *General Comment 19: The Right to Social Security (Article 9)*. New York: Economic and Social Council.

————. 2009. *General Comment 20: Non-discrimination in Economic, Social and Cultural Rights* (Article 2, para. 2). E/C.12/GC/20. New York: Economic and Social Council, United Nations.

U.N. Committee on the Elimination of Discrimination against Women. 1989. *General Recommendation 9: 1989 Statistical Data*. New York: United Nations.

————. 1991. *General Recommendation 17: Measurement and Quantification of the Unremunerated Domestic Activities of Women and Their Recognition in the GNP*. New York: United Nations.

————. 1992. *General Recommendation 19: Violence against Women*. New York: United Nations.

————. 1997. *General Recommendation 23: Women in Political and Public Life*. New York: United Nations.

U.N. Development Programme. 1996. *Human Development Report 1996: Growth for Human Development*. New York: Oxford University Press.

————. 2000. *Human Development Report 2000: Human Rights and Human Development*. New York: Oxford University Press.

————. 2002. *Human Development Report 2002: Deepening Democracy in a Fragmented World*. New York: Oxford University Press.

————. 2010. *Human Development Report 2010: The Real Wealth of Nations: Pathways to Human Development*. London: Palgrave Macmillan.

————. 2011. *Human Development Report 2011: Sustainability and Equity*. New York: U.N. Development Programme.

UNESCO, 1994. "World Declaration on Education for All." http://unesdoc.unesco.org/images/0012/001275/127583e.pdf

U.N. Committee on the Rights of the Child. 2003. General Comment 1. New York: United Nations.

U.N. Educational, Scientific and Cultural Organization (UNESCO) 1994. World Declaration on Education for All. http://images/0012/001275/127583e.pdf

U.N. Educational, Scientific and Cultural Organization Institute for Statistics. 2014. "Glossary." http://www.uis.unesco.org/Pages/Glossary.aspx.

UNICEF (U.N. Children's Fund). 2012. *Progress Report 2012—Committing to Child Survival: A Promise Renewed.* New York: UNICEF.

————. 2013a. "At a Glance: Sierra Leone." UNICEF, http://www.unicef.org/infobycountry/sierraleone_statistics.html.

————. 2013b. "At a Glance: United States of America." UNICEF, http://www.unicef.org/infobycountry/usa_statistics.html.

United Nations. 1945. "Charter of the United Nations." New York: United Nations.

————. 1948. "Universal Declaration of Human Rights." New York: United Nations.

————. 1965. "International Convention on the Elimination of All Forms of Racial Discrimination." New York: United Nations.

————. 1966a. "International Covenant on Civil and Political Rights." New York: United Nations.

————. 1966b. "International Covenant on Economic, Social and Cultural Rights." New York: United Nations.

————. 1969. "Declaration on Social Progress and Development." U.N. doc. A/7630. New York: United Nations.

————. 1979. "Convention on the Elimination of All Forms of Discrimination against Women." New York: United Nations.

————. 1986. "Declaration on the Right to Development." A/RES/41/128. New York: United Nations.

————. 1987a. "International Covenant on Economic, Social and Cultural Rights." New York: United Nations.

————. 1987b. *The Limburg Principles on the Implementation of the International Covenant on Economic, Social and Cultural Rights.* E/CN.4/1987/17. New York: United Nations.

————. 1989. "Convention on the Rights of the Child." New York: United Nations.

————. 1990. "International Convention on the Protection of the Rights of All Migrant Workers and Members of Their Families." New York: United Nations.

————. 1993. *Report of the Seminar on Appropriate Indicators to Measure Achievements in the Progressive Realization of Economic, Social and Cultural Rights.* A/CONF.157/PC/73. New York: United Nations.

————. 1993. *Vienna Declaration and Program of Action.* Vienna: United Nations.

————. 1996. "Plan of Action for the UN Decade for Human Rights Education, 1995–2004." U.N. doc. A/51/506/Add.1

————. 2000. *The Maastricht Guidelines on Violations of Economic, Social and Cultural Rights.* E/C.12/2000/13. Maastricht: United Nations.

————. 2006. Convention on the Rights of Persons with Disabilities. A/RES/61/106. New York: United Nations.

————. 2013. "The Millennium Development Goals Report, 2013: Addendum." New York: United Nations.

United Nations University World Institute for Development Economics Research. 2008. "UNU-WIDER World Income Inequality Database, Version 2.0c, May 2008." http://wider.unu.edu/research/Database/.

U.N. Office of the High Commissioner for Human Rights. 2006. *Report on Indicators for Monitoring Compliance with International Human Rights Instruments.* HRI/MC/2006/7. New York: United Nations.

———. 2008a. *Claiming the MDGs: A Human Rights Approach.* New York: United Nations.

———. 2008b. *Report on Indicators for Promoting and Monitoring the Implementation of Human Rights.* HRI/MC/2008/3. New York: United Nations.

———. 2012. *Human Rights Indicators: A Guide to Measurement and Implementation.* HR/PUB/12/5. New York: Office of the High Commissioner for Human Rights, United Nations.

———. 2013a. "Committee on Economic, Social and Cultural Rights Considers Report of Gabon." November 19. United Nations Human Rights, http://www.ohchr.org/en/NewsEvents/Pages/DisplayNews.aspx?NewsID=14008&LangID=E, accessed December 18, 2013.

———. 2013b. "Special Rapporteur on Extreme Poverty and Human Rights." United Nations Human Rights, http://www.ohchr.org/EN/Issues/Poverty/Pages/SRExtremePovertyIndex.aspx, accessed December 20, 2013.

U.N. Population Division. 2009. *World Population Prospects: The 2008 Revision.* New York: U.N. Department of Economic and Social Affairs.

Uppsala Conflict Data Program and the International Peace Research Institute, Oslo. 2008. UCDP/PRIO *Armed Conflict Dataset Codebook: Version 4-2008.* Accessed August 9, 2014 from http://www.prio.org/Global/upload/CSCW/Data/UCDP/2008/Codebook.pdf.

Vandenbussche, J., P. Aghion, and C. Meghir. 2006. "Growth, Distance to Frontier and Composition of Human Capital." *Journal of Economic Growth* 11 (2): 97–127.

Vidar, Margret. 2006. *State Recognition of the Right to Food at the National Level.* Research Paper No. 2006/16. Helsinki: United Nations University World Institute for Development Economics Research.

Vizard, P., S. Fukuda-Parr, and D. Elson. 2011. "Capabilities and Rights: An Interdisciplinary Conversation." *Journal of Human Development* 12 (1): 1–22.

Weil, David N. 2007. "Accounting for the Effect of Health on Economic Growth." *Quarterly Journal of Economics* 122 (3): 1265–1306.

Welling, Judith V. 2009. "International Indicators and Economic, Social and Cultural Rights." *Human Rights Quarterly* 30: 933–958.

World Bank. 2006. *World Development Report 2006: Equity and Development.* Washington, D.C.: World Bank.

———. 2010. *Worldwide Governance Indicators.* http://info.worldbank.org/governance/wgi/index.aspx#home

———. 2012. *World Development Indicators 2012.* Washington, D.C.: World Bank. http://data.worldbank.org/data-catalog/world-development-indicators.

———. 2013a. *Global Monitoring Report 2013.* Washington, D.C.: World Bank.

World Bank. 2013b. *World Development Indicators 2013.* http://databank.world-bank.org/data, accessed August 13, 2013.

———. 2013c. *Worldwide Governance Indicators 2013.* World Data Bank. http://info.worldbank.org/governance/wgi/index.aspx#home, accessed December 19, 2013.

World Bank and African Development Bank. 2010. *Joint Country Assistance Strategy for the Republic of Sierra Leone.* Washington, D.C.: World Bank.

World Health Organization. 2006. *Promoting Optimal Fetal Development: Report of a Technical Consultation.* Geneva: World Health Organization.

———. 2013. "Feto-maternal Nutrition and Low Birth Weight." World Justice Project Rule of Law Index, http://www.who.int/nutrition/topics/geto_maternal/en/, accessed June 24, 2013.

Wozniak, Gregory D. 1984. "The Adoption of Interrelated Innovations: A Human Capital Approach." *Review of Economics and Statistics* 66: 70–79.

———. 1987. "Human Capital, Information, and the Early Adoption of New Technology." *Journal of Human Resources* 22: 101–112.

Yamin, Alicia Ely, and Siri Gloppen. 2011. *Litigating Health Rights.* Harvard University Press ed. Cambridge: Human Rights Program, Harvard Law School.

Yamin, Alicia Ely, and Deborah P. Maine. 1999. "Maternal Mortality as a Human Rights Issue: Measuring Compliance with International Treaty Obligations." *Human Rights Quarterly* 21 (3): 563–607.

Youde, Jeremy. 2010. *Biopolitical Surveillance and Public Health in International Politics.* New York: Palgrave Macmillan.

ABOUT THE AUTHORS

Sakiko Fukuda-Parr is Professor of International Affairs at the New School. She is a development economist who has published widely on a range of topics, and is best known for her work as director of the UNDP Human Development Reports 1995-2004. Her current research focuses on: economic policies and the right to food; the political economy of global goals; and the use of quantitative methods in economic and social rights. She is Vice Chair of the UN Committee on Development Policy and serves on the board of the Centre for Economic and Social Rights, the International Association for Feminist Economics. Her recent publications include: *Human Rights and the Capabilities Approach, an Interdisciplinary Dialogue,* (coedited with Diane Elson and Polly Vizard), Routledge, London, 2012; *A Handbook on Human Development* (with A.K. Shivakumar), 3rd edition, Oxford University Press, New Delhi, 2010; and *The Gene Revolution: GM Crops and Unequal Development,* Earthscan, 2006.

Terra Lawson-Remer is Assistant Professor of International Affairs & Economics at The New School, and Non-Resident Fellow in Global Economy & Development at the Brookings Institution. Her work addresses opportunity and exclusion in the global economy. In this vein she examines poverty and inequality, property rights, natural resources and extractive industries, international economic law, the political economy of democratic transitions, grassroots accountability, social and economic rights, economic development, and rule of law and informal social norms. She has written numerous articles and books on these issues, and conducted research in Latin America, Asia, and the South Pacific. Long a committed civic leader, Dr. Lawson-Remer previously worked as Senior Advisor in the U.S. Department of Treasury during the first Obama administration. Long a committed civic leader, Terra has also worked as an organizer, action coordinator, fundraiser, and strategist for a number of grassroots environmental and social justice organizations.

Susan Randolph is Associate Professor of Economics at the University of Connecticut. Her research focuses on a broad range of issues in development economics, including poverty, inequality, food security, and economic and social rights, at both the country and regional levels and has been published in numerous refereed multidisciplinary as well as economic journals. One stream of her work has emphasized measurement while other streams have emphasized development policy. Her work on marginal malnutrition and food security has focused on Mexico, Senegal, and India, while her other work on development policy has been focused cross-nationally as well as on Malaysia, Sudan, Bangladesh, Mexico, Egypt, Nepal, and Indonesia.